# Online Society in China

I0009070

This book discusses the rich and varied culture of China's online society, and its impact on offline China. It argues that the Internet in China is a separate 'space' in which individuals and institutions emerge and interact. While offline and online spaces are connected and influence each other, the Chinese internet is more than merely a technological or media extension of offline Chinese society. Instead of following existing studies by locating online China in offline society, this book discusses the carnival of the Chinese Internet on its own terms.

Examining the complex relationship between government officials and the people using the Internet in China, this book demonstrates that culture is highly influential in how technology is used. Discussing a wide range of different activities, this book examines what Chinese people actually *do* on the Internet, and how their actions can be interpreted within the online society they are creating.

**David Kurt Herold** is a Lecturer for Sociology in the Department for Applied Social Sciences (APSS) at the Hong Kong Polytechnic University.

**Peter Marolt** is a Research Fellow at the Asia Research Institute, National University of Singapore.

# Media, Culture and Social Change in Asia

Series Editor: Stephanie Hemelryk Donald
*RMIT University, Melbourne*

Editorial Board:
Devleena Ghosh, *University of Technology, Sydney*
Yingjie Guo, *University of Technology, Sydney*
K.P. Jayasankar, *Unit for Media and Communications, Tata Institute of Social Sciences, Bombay*
Vera Mackie, *University of Melbourne*
Anjali Monteiro, *Unit for Media and Communications, Tata Institute of Social Sciences, Bombay*
Laikwan Pang, *Chinese University of Hong Kong*
Gary Rawnsley, *University of Leeds*
Ming-Yeh T. Rawnsley, *University of Leeds*
Adrian Vickers, *University of Sydney*
Jing Wang, *MIT*

The aim of this series is to publish original, high-quality work by both new and established scholars in the West and the East, on all aspects of media, culture and social change in Asia.

# Online Society in China

Creating, celebrating, and instrumentalising the online carnival

**Edited by David Kurt Herold
and Peter Marolt**

LONDON AND NEW YORK

This edition published 2011
by Routledge
2 Park Square, Milton Park, Abingdon, Oxon, OX14 4RN

Simultaneously published in the USA and Canada
by Routledge
711 Third Avenue, New York, NY 10017

*Routledge is an imprint of the Taylor & Francis Group, an informa business*
First issued in paperback 2013

© 2011 David Kurt Herold and Peter Marolt for selection and editorial
material. Individual chapters, the contributors.

The right of the editors to be identified as the authors of the editorial
material, and of the authors for their individual chapters, has been asserted
in accordance with sections 77 and 78 of the Copyright, Designs and
Patents Act 1988.

All rights reserved. No part of this book may be reprinted or reproduced
or utilised in any form or by any electronic, mechanical, or other means,
now known or hereafter invented, including photocopying and recording,
or in any information storage or retrieval system, without permission in
writing from the publishers.

*British Library Cataloguing in Publication Data*
A catalogue record for this book is available from the British Library

*Library of Congress Cataloging-in-Publication Data*
Online society in China : creating, celebrating, and instrumentalising the
online carnival / edited by David Kurt Herold and Peter Marolt.
    p. cm. -- (Media, culture and social change in Asia)
    Includes bibliographical references and index.
    1. Internet--Social aspects--China. I. Herold, David Kurt.
    II. Marolt, Peter.
    HN740.Z9I56789 2011                                303.48'33--dc22
    2010039442

ISBN: 978-0-415-56539-4 (hbk)
ISBN: 978-0-415-83822-1 (pbk)
ISBN: 978-0-203-82851-9 (ebk)
Typeset in Times New Roman by Bookcraft Ltd, Stroud, Gloucestershire

# Contents

# Contributors

**Peng Hwa Ang** is Professor at the Wee Kim Wee School of Communication and Information, Nanyang Technological University (NTU), Singapore, where he is Director of the Singapore Internet Research Centre. A former journalist and a qualified lawyer, his research covers legal and policy issues in the media in such areas as copyright, media self-regulation and free speech and censorship. His 2005 book, *Ordering Chaos: Regulating the Internet* (Thomson), argues that the Internet can be, is being and should be regulated.

**Xiaoyan Chen** received her PhD from NTU's Wee Kim Wee School of Communication and Information in 2007, where she did her dissertation on defamation in China. She is now Assistant Professor at the School of Communication and Journalism, Xiamen University, China. Her research interests are in Chinese media law and policy.

**Chung-tai Cheng** received his PhD from the Sociology Department of Peking University in 2010. He has researched and published on the normative implications of ICT uses in China, especially in relation to self-identification and social relationships among Chinese workers. His presentation 'Imagined performativity: the great virtue of cyberspace in contemporary Chinese workers' social lives' won the Best Presentation Award at the COST Action 298 conference: The Good, the Bad, and the Challenging. He has also published several journal articles and book chapters, mainly focused on the social and cultural impacts of ICTs.

**Rodney Wai-chi Chu** is Assistant Professor in the Department of Applied Social Sciences, The Hong Kong Polytechnic University. He obtained his PhD at the University of Queensland, Australia. His research focuses on the socio-cultural impact of ICTs on contemporary Chinese society, with particular reference to the use of mobile telephony and the Internet. He led a team in a large-scale nation-wide survey on mobile phone use in China. His publications include 'Mobile phones and new migrant workers in a South China village' and 'The dynamics of cyber China: the characteristics of Chinese ICT use'. He also co-guest edited two special issues on Chinese mobile phones for the *Journal of Knowledge, Technology and Policy*.

**Kenneth Farrall** is a post-doctoral Research Fellow in the philosophy and politics of computing, digital media and information systems at New York University's Department of Media, Culture and Communication. Ken received his PhD in Communication from the University of Pennsylvania in 2009. His dissertation, 'Suspect until proven guilty, a problematization of state dossier systems via two case studies: the United States and China', examines the factors driving the expansion of and resistance to national ID and personal record systems. Prior to receiving his PhD, Ken worked for six years in China's Internet industry, chronicled in part in the 2000 Harvard business case, 'VirtualChina.com: the building of a virtual community'.

**David Kurt Herold** taught and researched in China for over nine years, before joining the Hong Kong Polytechnic University in 2007 as Lecturer for Sociology. His research is focused on the use of ICTs by humans. In particular, he studies the Chinese Internet, encounters between Chinese and non-Chinese online, the impact of the Internet on offline society and online education. His recent publications include 'Cultural Politics and Political Culture of Web 2.0 in Asia' (2009); 'Mediating Media Studies – Stimulating Critical Awareness in a Virtual Environment' (2010); 'Imperfect Use? ICT Provisions and Human Decisions' (2010).

**Hongmei Li** is Assistant Professor of International Communication at Georgia State University. She was a George Gerbner Postdoctoral Fellow at the Annenberg School for Communication, University of Pennsylvania in 2008–2010. She obtained her PhD from the Annenberg School for Communication, University of Southern California. Her research interests centre on advertising and consumer culture, nation branding, nationalism, cultural identity, globalization, gender and sexuality, and the Internet in Chinese society. She has published in *Critical Studies in Media Communication*, *Public Relations Review* and the *International Journal of Communication*.

**Silvia Lindtner** is a PhD candidate in the Department of Informatics at University of California, Irvine. Her research interests generally concern media studies and China studies, anthropology, science and technology studies and social informatics. Her main research focuses on the role digital media play for youth and young professionals in urban China and the ways in which they position themselves in relation to political, social and economic shifts. Silvia's background is in new media design and in her work she draws on her knowledge both of design practice and qualitative research, in particular of ethnography. Her work is published across various disciplines and she regularly engages with scholars from diverse backgrounds to inform her interdisciplinary work, e.g. at venues such as the annual meeting of the Society for Social Studies of Science, the Annual Conference on Computer Supported Cooperative Work and the Conference on Digital Media and Learning.

**Peter Marolt** is a Research Fellow at the Asia Research Institute, National University of Singapore. His research interests include cultural-political and urban geographies, and studies pertaining to social activism, the Internet and

Asia. In particular, he strives to understand the relationship between our virtual and physical worlds, and related multidirectional processes of social development. He is currently working on a monograph on China's blogosphere; his newest project investigates environmental activisms in 'cyburban' Asia and how individual and shared aspirations and values influence what 'political action' means in our Global Information Age.

**Marcella Szablewicz** is a doctoral candidate in the Department of Language, Literature and Communication at Rensselaer Polytechnic Institute. She first began researching Internet gaming and Internet café culture in 2004, while completing an MA in China Studies at Duke University. From 2009 to 2010 Marcella conducted ethnographic research in Shanghai as a US Fulbright Fellow and a Foreign Visiting Scholar at the Shanghai Academy of Social Sciences. Marcella's dissertation will explore the various ways that Internet gaming is imagined in urban China, both how young Chinese perceive the importance of games in their social lives and how gaming is portrayed in government and media discourse.

**Matteo Tarantino** is a Lecturer in New Media at the Catholic University of the Sacred Heart of Milan. His research interests focus on the nexus of culture and ICTs, especially in non-Western contexts.

**Nicolai Volland** received his PhD from the University of Heidelberg, Germany and he is currently Assistant Professor of Chinese Studies at the National University of Singapore. His research interests include print culture, media and the Internet in contemporary China. His articles have appeared in the journals *Modern China*, *Twentieth-Century China* and *Modern Chinese Literature and Culture*, among others.

**Xiying Wang** is an Assistant Professor in the School of Social Development and Public Policy at the Beijing Normal University. Her research and teaching interests include Chinese women's studies, gender politics and human sexuality, qualitative research methods, violence against women, HIV/AIDS and public health, and post-disaster community development.

**Weihua Wu** is Associate Professor of Media Studies in the School of Television and Journalism at the Communication University of China. His research and teaching interests include cultural studies, new media, visual sociology, civil society and crisis communication.

# Introduction

## Noise, spectacle, politics: carnival in Chinese cyberspace

*David Kurt Herold*

The Internet in China was developed at about the same time as the Internet in Europe and America, but its structures and set-up were quite different. During the late 1980s and early 1990s, academic institutions in China began to set up intranets on their campuses that were later connected to each other, with help from European and North American universities. The networks were continuously expanded and updated, and in 1994 they were linked to the emerging World Wide Web through a dedicated line between China and the USA. Over the next two years, additional connections to the Internet were created, linking China with Japan, Southeast Asia and Russia, and the central government issued regulations to structure the Chinese Internet (China Internet Network Information Centre [CNNIC], 2010 – also below).

Four organizations were created by the central government to provide Internet access in China, and although initially these networks only provided access to the Internet for academic institutions, this was soon changed to allow commercial access to the Internet. In early 1997, private access was granted to ordinary citizens for the first time, but only through the existing networks. The central government decided to keep ownership and control over the access routes to the Internet, and to allow private enterprises and individuals only the rental of bandwidth from government-owned entities, which set the stage for the development of online China as a very different space from the non-Chinese Internet.

### Internet with Chinese characteristics

State or state-controlled entities own the physical backbone of the Internet in China and privately held companies can rent bandwidth only from them, which is a marked difference to the situation in other countries, where multiple private Internet Service Providers run their own networks in competition to each other under the legislated oversight of their respective governments. This difference means that the central government in China has a much stronger position than governments elsewhere. It starts from a position of control over and ownership of Chinese cyberspace. The government does not have to gain control over the Internet, instead it has to explicitly or implicitly allow everything that happens on the Internet in China. While American and European governments have to legislate themselves the power to control the Internet, this is the default position for the Chinese government, and therefore constitutes one of the defining features of online China. The Internet, and by extension online China, are 'government allowed'.

The freedom Chinese people enjoy on the Internet and the rich and varied online culture that has developed in China as a result of this freedom are ultimately granted to them by the central government or its agencies, and are not an expression of the Chinese government's inability to control the Internet, as suggested by, for example, Hays (2010), MacKinnon (2010, March 23), or Pan (2006, February 19). The Chinese government seems willing to allow Chinese Internet users quite a lot of leeway, but – if it so chooses – it does have the ability to curtail or even deny the Internet to its citizens, as it demonstrated very effectively in 2009.

After riots by the Muslim Uighurs during the summer of 2009, the Chinese central government first shut down the entire Internet in Xinjiang province, in Northwest China, and later allowed people to access a very limited version of the Internet, before restoring 'normal' access in May 2010 (Heacock, 2009, July 6; Lewis, 2010, May 14; Mudie, 2010, March 23; Summers, 2009, December 6). Chinese authorities had the technological capability to stop residents of one of China's provinces from accessing the Internet. It had the capability and the power over private companies providing online services in China to create a 'mini' Internet for the citizens of that province, and it had the political will to use them.

Despite the level of control the central government can exercise over the Chinese Internet, though, it appears as if it is willing to allow some freedom on the Internet as long as matters do not get out of hand. When pushed to do so, the central government will shut down parts of the Chinese Internet, be they online blogs, forums, or more recently, pornographic websites running on servers inside China. Extreme levels of control are, however, only rarely employed by the Chinese authorities and usually only in cases where an intervention is part of a larger political campaign or crackdown on specific issues.

The control of the Chinese government over the Internet in China has also led to a second main characteristic of online China, i.e. its quasi-separation from the rest of the World Wide Web. The aim of the 'normal' control exercised by the Chinese government over the Internet in China seems to be the creation of obstacles and hassles for Internet users, rather than a complete cutting-off of undesirable Internet access. This aim is achieved through four strategies and their disciplining effect on Chinese citizens accessing the Internet from within China. They are the 'Great Firewall of China' (GFW), ISP-enforced blacklisting of specific words or phrases, the coercion of multi-national technology corporations and real-world access controls (Fallows, 2008). These strategies have to be seen as a mixture between boundary markers and obstacles for Internet users, and serve to draw up guidelines for acceptable and unacceptable behaviour by Chinese Internet users, as well as to make the accessing of undesirable information more difficult.

The GFW exists as a multi-faceted and ever-changing system of both national as well as local rules, combined with technical limitations caused by the set-up of the Internet infrastructure. Access to websites outside China can vary widely between different cities and changes from time to time. One constant in the GFW is the relatively slow access and loading speed of websites located on servers outside China as compared to websites inside China. Only a small number of cables connect China to the outside world, which creates a technological bottleneck that makes frequent visits to websites outside China unattractive. While not cutting off Chinese people's access to international websites, this slowdown of the Internet on sites outside China deters casual Chinese Internet users not willing to suffer the lack of speed and frequent time-outs.

The limited number of access points to the Chinese Internet also makes the blocking of specific websites or domains easier to set up, by equipping each access point with scripts to block all web pages from the servers of, for example, http://news.bbc.co.uk/, while allowing users to continue browsing http://www.bbc.co.uk/. Such scripting allows for temporary restrictions, local variations and bans on specific sites, e.g., for a ban of CNN, Reuters, BBC and other international news sites during the annual meetings of the National People's Congress.

ISP-enforced blacklisting of specific words is another form of control government departments at all levels can exercise in China. If a Chinese netizen, for instance, tries to access sites with the terms 'Falun Gong' or 'Tian An Men Massacre' on them, the connection between the Internet user's computer and the server with the offensive content is interrupted. Experienced users can circumvent these blocks via Internet proxies or VPN connections, but the method is highly effective against the large numbers of China's casual Internet users.

The combination of being able to target specific servers and to blacklist specific terms or phrases has the additional benefit for the Chinese government of allowing them to put pressure on multi-national technology corporations to co-opt them in their efforts to police the Internet. Multi-national technology corporations, for example, Yahoo!, Google, Microsoft, Cisco, etc. have found it easier and more economically viable to work with Chinese authorities instead of trying to ignore their demands while still doing business in and with China. Even though, for example, Google transferred some of its business from China to Hong Kong in 2010 in a highly publicized and largely misrepresented move, this did not stop its collaboration with Chinese government departments in most of its Chinese offerings (see, for example, Dsouza, 2010, March 2; Furuya & Yamakawa, 2010, July 23; Helft & Wines, 2010, March 23; MacManus, 2010, February 24; Ward, 2010, March 24).

A final method of control uses 'real-world' access controls focusing on individual computer users, rather than addressing the content of websites. According to Chinese laws and regulations, all Internet users in China have to register before being able to access the Internet. Before Internet lines are installed in a home, the main user has to register for the service with his/her national ID card or passport. Internet cafés are legally required to register for business permits and to record personal details for all users. The measures are less than effective, though, as they are only rarely enforced by the authorities unless the central government pushes for their enforcement during a high-profile national campaign. Outside of such campaigns, controls are very lax, as local law enforcement does not prioritize the supervision of Internet cafés and it is not in the interests of the owners to carefully register all of their customers, resulting in tangible proof of their taxable income.

In combination, these four measures of control ensure that the Chinese Internet and its users remain largely separated from the World Wide Web, or as Sherman

So put it: *'China is not on the Internet, it's basically an intranet'* (Fong, 2009). While it is possible to access the non-Chinese Internet from China and vice versa, the lack of speed, occasional time-outs and blocked sites make such access unattractive enough for most Chinese Internet users not to bother trying. A website hosted on servers inside China will load much faster than one hosted outside China, and it will be in Chinese as opposed to English, Spanish, French, German, etc. As a result, online China remains apart, separated from the rest of the world, and has developed many idiosyncrasies not found elsewhere, as the chapters in this volume demonstrate.

Two final characteristics of online China that are worth mentioning here are the relative youth of its users, and the general 'wildness' encountered on many websites in China's cyberspace. While the latter is the topic of a number of chapters in this volume and has also already been discussed in the academic literature (e.g. Golub & Lingley, 2008), the relative youth of China's netizens (Inter-*net* + cit-*izens*) is often ignored by studies of the Chinese Internet, despite its influence on the ways in which the Internet is used and perceived in China.

According to the latest report by CNNIC (2010: 19), over 60% of all Internet users in China are under the age of 30, while the average age of frequent Internet users in, for example, the USA is 42 (European Travel Commission, 2010). A recent survey in the south of China, in Guangdong province, 'found 80 percent of the 1,000 primary and high school students polled started surfing the Internet before they turned 10' (China Daily, 2010, July 8). These young Internet users have different preferences than the more mature users outside China. They go online during their leisure time, as '[t]here's nowhere else to go' and 'say they are excited about the Web [...] because it gives them a wide variety of social and entertainment options' (Barboza, 2010). '[F]or the vast majority of Chinese, Internet means play, not work' (Fong, 2009), both in the form of online games and in the attitude many young Chinese have towards computers in general and the Internet in particular.

Young Chinese see the Internet as 'fun' or a 'game' (Barboza, 2007), and they assume that their online behaviour will not have any consequences for their offline lives and therefore engage in far more risky actions online than many of their peers in other countries:

> [F]or Chinese youth the virtual world provides a venue for expressing autonomy that is not available to them in the real world. In the virtual world, Chinese youth can do as they choose without concern about the impact of their behavior on others.
>
> (Jackson et al., 2008: 285)

The wildness and youth of Chinese Internet users, combined with online China's separation from the non-Chinese Internet, have produced the online space that can be accessed in China today, with the added 'spice' of a largely passive, but powerful and at times strict, (state) owner. The marked differences between the Chinese and the non-Chinese Internet, as exemplified by these four characteristics, raise questions of how online China can or should be conceptualized or studied, and whether approaches to the study of the non-Chinese Internet are applicable in the Chinese context. In the next section, several approaches to the study of the Chinese Internet will be discussed with a view to these differences, before an outline is presented of a more general conceptualization of the Chinese Internet as a uniquely Chinese online space, separate from but connected to offline China.

## The Chinese Internet in academic studies

### *Control and resistance*

Many academic studies of the Internet in China attempt to locate online China within discourses of control and resistance, arguing that the Internet is providing Chinese citizens with new ways of resisting government attempts to control their lives. It is argued that anonymous netizens are employing the anonymity and the communicative reach of the Internet to evade government surveillance and censorship.

The power of the Internet lies in its use as a new platform for dissent against the state by its citizens (Chase & Mulvenon, 2002), and the relationship between government and netizens is portrayed as a constantly evolving 'game' between control and resistance, or as 'contention' (Yang, G., 2008, 2009). In this game, the government attempts to increase its control over the Internet, while netizens employ ever new tools to escape from government control. This evasion of government surveillance is in turn the starting point for netizens to access or disseminate 'true' information about China and the world outside the control of the government's propaganda machine (MacKinnon, 2007).

The information netizens manage to obtain on the 'free' Internet can then be distributed to other netizens, so as to create rudimentary associations of savvy Internet users, with the goal of eventually winning over others and of organizing a grassroots resistance movement against the Chinese state (Tai, 2004). Using these new forms of associations based solely on the Internet, Chinese netizens are empowered to challenge the Communist Party's hegemonic rule over the provision of information, as well as the construction of personal identities (Giese, 2006; Goldsmith & Wu, 2006).

Similarly, the Internet is seen as a tool allowing for new forms of interaction for use by established political actors in Chinese society. Researchers have studied how some Communist Party officials have employed their technological knowledge to promote political reforms (Lagerkvist, 2005), both within the Party and without. Others have focused on how different government institutions are using the Internet to improve their interaction with and responsiveness to ordinary citizens (Hartford, 2005).

While some of the studies in this area can be interpreted as supportive of a dichotomy between the 'evil' Chinese government, and the 'good' netizens, especially those that attempt to produce an overview over the Chinese Internet in general (e.g. Hachigian, 2001; Kluver, 2005), most offer a far more nuanced picture in their discussions of the many different groupings and individuals expressing their opinions online (Damm & Thomas, 2006; Shie, 2004).

Nevertheless, a strong tendency survives in this group of studies to see the Internet and online China as tools of resistance that relatively powerless Chinese individuals can employ against the hegemonic rule of the Communist Party in China. Government officials are portrayed as belonging to ossified institutions, fighting to stay relevant and desperate to control the emerging new arenas for public discussion.

## A tool for interaction and organization

A second strand of discourses on the Internet in China focuses less on the polit-ical implication of the Internet, and more on the ways in which social organi-zations and movements are attempting to employ new forms of technology to reach wider audiences. Civic associations are using the Internet to increase their reach at a lower cost than previously possible, and are therefore becoming more visible (Yang, G., 2007). Similarly, non-profit organizations are using the new technology to broaden their public appeal and to make their causes known to more people (Yang, B., 2008), so as to increase the numbers of people involved in collective action (Zheng & Wu, 2005).

Aside from formal institutions and associations, the Internet in China is providing ordinary citizens with the means to voice their feelings and to gather large groups of people both online and offline for, e.g., expressions of nationalistic sentiments for China without the organized support of either governmental or non-governmental institutions (Wu, 2007). Out of such unsupported activities of large numbers of netizens, new forms of organization are emerging that alter the way Chinese citizens interact with each other and with their government – both online and offline (Yang, G., 2003a). While previously, many of China's poorer citizens depended on government provision, new studies are showing that even less advantaged segments of the population are employing ICTs in general, and the Internet in particular, to interact with each other to network and to increase their own mobility, and therefore employability (Cartier, Castells, & Qiu, 2005).

In addition to the social concerns of groups of Chinese citizens, the Internet has also become both an expression of and a way to share Chinese culture. Individuals and groups are using the Internet to meet others interested in or identifying with Chinese culture, even beyond China's borders (Yang, G., 2003b). The Chinese Internet itself and online China have taken on some of the characteristics of Chinese culture, and netizens have developed Chinese forms of online interactions (Chu, 2008; also his chapter in this volume) and of attitudes towards the relationship between online and offline China, and an individual's responsibilities in both (Weber & Jia, 2007).

The Internet is changing the ways in which Chinese people interact with each other, but the process is not just one way. Just as Chinese society and culture are influenced by the introduction of the affordances of Internet technology, so is the Internet, and in particular online China, influenced by Chinese society and culture (Herold, 2009) so as to create an Internet 'with Chinese characteristics', to borrow an official phrase. The changes brought about by this mutual influence can be seen in Chinese society, as well as in the differences between online China and the non-Chinese Internet.

## A driver of progress and development

A third group of academic researchers is interested in the impact the introduction of the Internet has had on China's development and its less developed areas. In such studies, the Internet is often presented as an instrument to speed up the development of China. Some studies, and even official government documents in China, suggest that the Internet may be a way for China to leapfrog European and American advances and to become a developed country without going through the stages of industrialization and post-industrialization.

By applying technological diffusion theories to the introduction of the Internet in China, researchers are looking at the introduction of a new technology into Chinese society and are interested in establishing the patterns of technological diffusion for China through detailed investigations of the availability of the Internet across China (Foster, 2001). Detailed studies of specific communities of less-developed Chinese are meant to demonstrate the effects that the introduction of the Internet has on the economic development of, for example, rural areas in China (Zhao, 2008; 2009), while others investigate how differences in the exposure to technology are causing disruptions in Chinese society between those who can afford or have been given access to the Internet and those who do not have access to the new technology (Damm, 2007).

In general, these developmental discourses are all based around the assumption that the introduction of the Internet into Chinese society is good and will have a positive effect both on individual Chinese citizens and on Chinese society. A lack of uptake of the affordances the new technology offers is interpreted as a 'problem' or a 'lack of understanding' of the possibilities the Internet grants its users.

> Developmental discourses on the introduction, discovery, or diffusion of new technology emphasize the affordances new technologies offer and their impact on the lives of users of new technologies. While neither linear nor deterministic, such discourses still convey the idea that new technologies are responsible for improvements to the lives of their users [...].
>
> (Herold, 2010)

## New media

A final set of studies approaches the Chinese Internet from a media studies perspective and seeks to understand the Internet as a new form of (interactive) media. Research here focuses on new forms of entertainment that the Internet makes possible, and how this affects Chinese society as a whole. Some of these studies focus on how the Internet as media in China differs from in the non-Chinese world (Lagerkvist, 2008), and what the ideologies are that drive such 'Ideotainment' in online China. This is often combined with comparisons between Chinese and non-Chinese Internet users and their cultural differences (Li & Kirkup, 2007).

Other media researchers study the differences and the interplay between different types of media in China and their effect on the general public (Zhou &

Moy, 2007), or the forms of media consumption and access to Internet content, and how this is regulated in different parts of China (Sun, 2003). Such studies are done with the intention of eliciting the contexts into which the Internet is embedded within offline China, and how the embedding is regulated by the state, and are therefore aimed at defining the 'place' *online* China has within *offline* China.

Discussions of the Internet as a new form of media in China are not always positive, though. Many studies on the Chinese Internet have attempted to define and document what has come to be known as 'Internet addiction' (Cao & Su, 2006). Within China media discourses tend to emphasize the dangers of the Internet, particularly for young people. The danger of the Internet is seen in its highly addictive nature, which is capable of corrupting young Chinese (Cha, 2007, February 22; China Daily, 2010, February 3; Fryer, 2010, January 23; Griffiths, 2005, October 10; Macartney, 2008, November 11; Stewart, 2010, January 13; Tian, 2010, January 4). The actual contents of Internet sites, for example pornographic images, subversive political messages, etc. are seen as an additional danger, but the emphasis is mostly on teenagers spending too much time online and neglecting their offline obligations to family, school and society, which again aims to 'anchor' online China within established discourses on offline China.

## Beyond the offline world: the Internet as space

### *Shortcomings of offline-centred approaches*

Confronted with the wealth of existing research on the Internet in China, it is easy to lose sight of what is *not* being studied. A closer look reveals, though, that the discourses outlined above attempt to *locate* the Internet within offline society. None of them studies *online* China as such, instead they offer studies of a new development of *offline* China from a variety of perspectives, which is less than helpful if the goal is to understand what is happening *in* online China, as opposed to studying what is happening *with* or *to* online China.

After the 'discovery' of America by Europeans, studies of the impact of this discovery on European societies and cultures were very appropriate and valuable. Such studies cannot, however, contribute to an understanding of the societies and cultures of America then or now, for which the people actually *in* America have to be studied without reference to their ancestral roots, unless this is necessary in a specific research context. While *in some contexts* a reference to, for example, an individual's ancestral roots in Kenya or in Switzerland might be relevant, their impact on *many other contexts* is negligible – especially when compared to his current *role* as President of the USA.

In a similar manner the insistence on an offline *anchoring* of online events is often not very helpful in understanding interactions, inter-human networks, forum discussions, blogs, etc. Many people do not project their offline identity onto their online actions, and instead attempt to hide their offline identity behind online forms of anonymity – especially in China (see Farrall & Herold in this volume). To use just one example, young people get addicted to online games not merely because of their perceived joyless *offline* lives, but because they like the games, they like the company of their fellow gamers, they can play, chat, interact, etc. while online (Lindtner and Szablewicz, this volume).

The rich and varied events in online China are not examples of the introduction of a new technology, nor are (primarily) known 'social actors' involved (even Chinese officials are only involved peripherally), nor can they be described fully as production or consumption of a new form of media. To explain, for example, a forum discussion in Chinese cyberspace requires a different frame of reference that does not rely on tracking down the real-life personas of Internet users, nor does it require offline comments by known social actors. In other words, understanding online China involves listening to the voices of Chinese netizens *online* and (often) without attempting to track individual Internet users down *offline* to verify their online statements. Online China itself constitutes an independent space for entertainment, political, social, etc. discourse, or simply for meeting others. Through the interaction between online and offline China, Chinese society reinvents itself, expressing and negotiating viewpoints that are often at odds with 'official' presentations of the status quo.

Such a vantage point yields insight into a range of issues emerging in the ways individual Chinese are reconfiguring their own identities and their perceptions of China, Chinese culture, 'others', etc. It redirects attention from an emphasis on the structural changes offline China is undergoing as a result of the introduction of the Internet to 'the people on the Internet': to individual everyday life agency, as well as to the concrete expressions and processes that operate through, and in turn configure, the Chinese Internet. A closer look at the embedding of the multiplicity of diverse phenomena occurring in online China is crucial for a better understanding of the multi-faceted relationship between information technology and societal transformation in online and offline China. As Tom Boellstorff argues:

> To demand that [...] research always incorporate [...] the actual world for 'context' presumes that virtual worlds are not themselves contexts; it renders [...] inaccessible the fact that most residents of virtual worlds do not meet their fellow residents offline.
> Studying a virtual world in its own terms does not mean ignoring the myriad ways that ideas from the actual world impinge upon it; it means examining those interchanges as they manifest in the virtual world, for that is how residents experience them when they are inworld.
> (Boellstorff, 2008: 61 and 64)

By going beyond existing fields of research and established literatures, this edited collection wants to contribute to a better theoretical understanding of online China's networked society and of how China's online and offline societies interact with and influence each other. To achieve this aim, it becomes crucial to engage with the fascinating and often-reported on yet under-theorized phenomena in China's cyberspace, and to see the Internet as more than merely a 'tool' used in offline society, but rather as its own 'space' linked to and interacting with offline China.

## Studying the Internet as space

### *Habermas and the Internet as public sphere*

One theoretician, whose works seem ideal for a discussion of the Internet as a separate space, is the German philosopher, sociologist, etc. Jürgen Habermas. His writings on the concept of the 'public sphere' provide an intriguing starting point for the study of the Internet, as in his view 'the public sphere represents a space in which questions can be raised and negotiated publicly, freed from the constraints of tradition and power' (Freundlieb, Hudson, & Rundell, 2004: 7). This theoretical construct seems tailor-made for discussions of the Internet, and has been used widely in studies of online phenomena (e.g. Castells, 2008; Dahlberg, 2001; Gerhards & Schäfer, 2010; Gimmler, 2001; Papacharissi, 2002).

In his own writings, Habermas argues that the 'core of the public sphere comprises communicative networks amplified by a cultural complex' in which 'a public of citizens of the state' can 'participate in the social integration mediated by public opinion' (1987: 319). This integration of public opinion is supposed to lead to the legitimization (Habermas uses 'legitimation') of the state through its citizens (1976; 2006). The continuous rational deliberations of independent individual citizens are seen as leading to the acceptance of shared sets of basic rules for society and the shaping and expression of public wishes for the government of the state (1987: 81).

> Habermas' work is fuelled by a single motivating idea that has permeated all of his work – the public and non-violent force of the better argument. Habermas' insistence on the validity of norms that are argued out, indicates a commitment to philosophies of right articulated in universalistic terms, as against substantialist or contextualist ones which are oriented to images of the social good.
>
> (Freundlieb, Hudson, & Rundell, 2004: 3)

The citizens of the state rely on this 'sphere of public discourses in which the individual both loses herself and creates her individuality' (Ginev, 2004: 78) to adapt their own identity and their relationships with other citizens to the needs of the collective. The adaptation does not represent a subjugation to a higher power, though, as ideological domination is not possible in the public sphere, where a hegemony exists of the 'self-created order of civil society's pluralist public sphere' (Ginev, 2004: 103).

An application of this concept of the 'public sphere' to the Internet seems tantalizingly easy, but is nevertheless highly problematic. The Internet is rarely a space for the rational exchange of points of view, nor is the Internet free from either tradition or power. The Habermasian public sphere is tied to the idea of the nation-state, i.e. each nation-state has one public sphere, in which all of its citizens participate equally. Within this space, debating citizens produce the basis for the legitimacy of nation-states, which is not easily achievable online, given both the international character of the Internet's set-up and the tendency towards ghettoization and splintering displayed by many of its users.

Habermas himself argues against an interpretation of the Internet as a public sphere, warning against the online 'fragmentation of large but politically focussed mass audiences into a huge number of isolated issue publics', especially 'within established national public spheres' (Habermas, 2006: 423). In countries with authoritarian regimes, he argues, the Internet can only be understood as a highly specialized form of public sphere that 'can undermine the censorship of authoritarian regimes that try to control and repress public opinion' (ibid.).

In studies of online China, researchers have used but found it difficult to employ the concept of the public sphere, and have mostly tried to 'make it fit' by altering the definition of the public sphere to include government authorities and by re-introducing notions of unequal power between different actors in the public sphere (e.g. Lagerkvist, 2006; Yang, B., 2010; Yang & Calhoun, 2007). This has made it possible to use Habermas' legitimation of governments through the public sphere as one of the main arguments supporting an interpretation of online China as a public sphere, but the fit is still far from perfect.

The (Chinese) Internet cannot be described as a space for rational and detached deliberations, nor can it be seen as an egalitarian tool for the equal expression of opinions by all the citizens of a state. Instead of a *polyphony* of voices creating rational bases for the legitimization and the running of the state according to the wishes of its citizens, the (Chinese) Internet is filled with a *cacophony* of conflicting opinions, irrelevant or emotional outbursts, images stretching from the beautiful to the grotesque and beyond, etc. While the notion of the Habermasian 'public sphere' is therefore intriguing and attractive, its application to interpretations of the (Chinese) Internet produces less than desirable results.

## Bakhtin and the online carnival

In contrast to the very rational public sphere proposed by Habermas and his followers, the Russian philosopher and literature researcher Mikhail Bakhtin argues for a less rational and more chaotic and emotional space as the locus for 'free' public interactions. In his studies of the works of Rabelais, of Dostoevsky, and of novels in general, Bakhtin describes the multiplicity of voices in a novel by using the concept of the wild and even grotesque *carnival* of the renaissance or medieval times. This Bakhtinian notion of the *carnival* and its relationship to 'real' life offers many points of comparison to descriptions of the (Chinese) Internet which could serve as apt metaphors and framing devices for a study of online China and its relationship to offline society.

A carnival is an event in which rules of propriety are laid aside, in an area and a time set apart from the constraints of 'normality' by general consensus (Bakhtin, 1984b: 10). It allows people to escape from their normal lives to enjoy themselves, but also to be informed about distant places, people and cultures, or to be shocked, titillated, amused, etc. A carnival is loud, with many people expressing themselves about multiple topics they often know little about. It can get out of hand and begin to impact on 'normal' life, at which point the authorities tend to act (Bakhtin, 1984a: 127–130). As may be obvious, a substitution of 'offline' for 'normal', and 'online' for 'carnival' in this paragraph already describes the (Chinese) Internet very well.

> It could be said (with certain reservations, of course) that a person of the Middle Ages lived, as it were, *two lives:* one was the *official* life, mono-lithically serious and gloomy, subjugated to a strict hierarchical order, full of terror, dogmatism, reverence, and piety; the other was the *life of the carnival square*, free and unrestricted, full of ambivalent laughter.
>
> (Bakhtin, 1984a: 129)

According to Bakhtin, the 'life of the carnival' was the antithesis to 'normal' life, and functioned as both an escape valve and a challenge to 'normal' life for people in Europe during the Middle Ages and the Renaissance (Bakhtin, 1984b: 8f). The carnival 'space' was clearly demarcated and accessible to all, as 'by its very idea carnival belongs to the whole people, it is universal, everyone must participate in its familiar contact' (Bakhtin, 1984a: 128). *Within* the carnival, rules were suspended, *outside* it, normality ruled. As the chapters in this volume show, online China allows netizens a far greater degree of freedom than offline China, and although online events at times influence offline society, Chinese authorities appear to be more lenient towards online provocation, but react very fast to offline challenges (see, for example, the chapter by Herold in this volume).

> Carnival is a pageant without footlights and without a division into perform-ers and spectators. In carnival everyone is an active participant, everyone communes in the carnival act. Carnival is not contemplated and, strictly speaking, not even performed; its participants *live* in it, they live by its laws as long as those laws are in effect; that is, they live a *carnivalistic life.*
>
> (Bakhtin, 1984a: 122)

The Chinese Internet has remarkably few 'heroes' or outstanding 'performers', given its size. The lists for the most-often searched-for people on China's top search engine, Baidu (http://top.baidu.com/buzz/renwu.html), demonstrate how rare it is for a Chinese netizen to become 'a performer' online. The numbers of netizens who have become famous, for example, Muzi Mei, Furong Jiejie, Backdorm Boys, Hu Ge, Han Han, etc. are surprisingly small, compared to China's 400 million plus Internet users who spend an average of almost 19 hours per week online (CNNIC, 2010), indicating that online China is less about performances and more about participation, or 'living' online.

The Bakhtinian carnival challenges 'normal' life in multiple ways, aiming its provocations both at 'normal' power hierarchies (Bakhtin, 1984a: 127) and at the rigidity and 'fixedness' of life in 'normal' society. It – just like the (Chinese) Internet, allows people to rebel against 'normal' (offline) life, using the 'serio-comical' tools of laughter, parodies, grotesque images, etc. (Bakhtin, 1981: 21–23; 1984b: 11–32).

> Every event, every phenomenon, everything, every object of artistic repre-sentation loses its completedness, its hopelessly finished quality and its

immutability that had been so essential to it in the world.

(Bakhtin, 1981: 30)

In his discussion of Dostoevsky, Bakhtin provides a long list of all the features of 'normal' life that are suspended during the carnival (Bakhtin, 1984a: 122–124; see also Beasley-Murray, 2007: 11–14; Brandist, 2002: 137–154), and the different chapters in this volume demonstrate that similar suspensions occur in online China. There are, first of all, the laws, regulations and power structures of 'normal' (offline) life, which no longer apply during the carnival (online), including all reverence rendered to those with a higher social status. This suspension of hierarchies, according to Bakhtin, and observable online, also applies to inequalities on the grounds of age or gender – thanks to the anonymity of the carnival (mask) or the Internet, and as, for example, Hongmei Li shows in her chapter, leads to

> *profanation*: carnivalistic blasphemies, a whole system of carnivalistic debasings and bringings down to earth, carnivalistic obscenities linked with the reproductive power of the earth and the body, carnivalistic parodies on sacred texts and sayings, etc.

(Bakhtin, 1984a: 123)

Bakhtin also argues that the suspension of hierarchies results in freer attitudes towards relationships, as interpersonal distances are erased and new relationships are formed that exist only during the carnival (online) and do not carry over to 'normal' life. The 'virtuality' of the carnival or of online China allows people who would not interact in their 'normal' lives to meet and to build relationships within this virtual world, based solely on their perception of 'the other' during the carnival (online).

> All *distance* between people is suspended, and a special carnival category goes into effect: *free and familiar contact among people*. [...] People who in life are separated by impenetrable hierarchical barriers enter into free familiar contact on the carnival square. [...] Carnival is the place for working out, in a concretely sensuous, half-real and half-play-acted form, a *new mode of inter-relationship between individuals*, counterposed to the all-powerful socio-hierarchical relationships of noncarnival life.

(Bakhtin, 1984a: 123)

Any metaphor can be stretched too far, and it is dangerous to attempt to over-interpret research data to make it fit one over-arching 'grand narrative'. However, the use of the Bakhtinian notion of the carnival to describe online China and its relationship to offline society and politics appears very apt and provides a good starting point for research of the Internet in general. It allows researchers to treat cyberspace as a 'place' similar and connected to, but different and separate from, the offline world. The (Chinese) Internet can be studied on its own merits, without attempting to situate online events in specific offline contexts, which have proved inadequate to explain the characteristics and interactions on the Chinese Internet.

The authors of this volume are presenting the results of their research studies within this framework, that is, as discussions of Chinese Internet structures, interactions, personalities, etc. without attempting to 'explain' them as new technological expressions of offline China's structures, interactions, personalities, etc. They discuss online China on its own merits and, in doing so, demonstrate the validity of comparing online China to Bakhtin's carnival.

The chapters in Part I focus on descriptions of the set-up and limits of online China, i.e. its 'setting' within and connection to offline China. In the first chapter, Rodney Chu and Chung-Tai Cheng argue that online China's cultural roots in Chinese traditional thinking have to be taken seriously, and that the Chinese Internet cannot be interpreted using approaches and frameworks developed in 'Western' contexts. The authors of the second chapter, Xiaoyan Chen and Peng Hwa Ang, provide an overview of the laws and regulations that define and limit the Internet within the Chinese state. Peter Marolt uses his chapter to argue that studies of the Chinese Internet that force their descriptions to fit into dichotomies of state vs. people, censorship vs. resistance, etc. are missing the point. As he shows, the Chinese Internet is a far more varied space in which individual netizens act not primarily to resist the Chinese state, but rather to avoid its influence on their own personal lives and activities. While resistance may be an implied consequence of their actions, it is not their primary focus, nor should it be the main topic of academic discourses.

Part II picks up Peter Marolt's idea of the complexity and variety of Chinese cyberspace and illustrates it with case studies of some of the interactions between netizens that have produced and are still constantly changing online China. Hongmei Li is the author of the first chapter in Part II and discusses the many ways in which Chinese netizens are amusing themselves with online parodies, jokes, scatological humour, grotesque presentations, etc. and how their amusement challenges the 'serious' rule of the party-state and its officials. Silvia Lindtner and Marcella Szablewicz present the result of many years of in-depth studies and fieldwork and offer an overview over the differentiation of online gamers in China into myriad sub-groups divided by background, gaming choices, financial status, etc. They demonstrate, though, that they can ignore their differences if their activities are threatened or curtailed by an outside agency, e.g. the Chinese government in general or regulatory bodies in particular, providing evidence for the notion that Chinese Internet users are not primarily interested in resisting the government, but will do so if the government interferes with their interests. Weihua Wu and Xiying Wang outline how notions of gender and identity have become categories for experimentation online, and how netizens are exploring new ways of expressing their gender identities through a reflection of the possibilities that online games in particular are offering their users. The different gender configurations possible online and the different marriage permutations they enable Internet users to engage in provide a fertile ground for the development of new attitudes towards gender among China's younger people.

Part III shifts the focus from a discussion of the variety of phenomena visible online to studies of the uses made of online China by Chinese netizens. David Kurt Herold presents his research on the ways in which Chinese netizens are using online 'manhunts', or 'Human Flesh Search Engines' (Renrou Sousuo = RRSS) to identify and punish people *offline* for perceived misdeeds, and how Chinese government officials have begun to engage with such RRSS, condoning and at times encouraging their use, even against other government officials. Matteo Tarantino discusses the online and offline interactions in a Linux user group whose members include both Chinese and non-Chinese. His research illustrates the different approaches of Chinese and non-Chinese to 'free' software, to the Linux user movement and to the idea of Open Source Software in general, and demonstrates that cultural backgrounds and differences in expectations frame most of the online and offline interactions between members. Kenneth Farrall and David Kurt Herold discuss how the approach to the Internet and to online identities by Chinese netizens is producing new forms of online anonymities that are different from the anonymity sought by non-Chinese Internet users. They demonstrate that the construction of online identities is often not tied to an Internet user's offline persona in China, and that this makes the linking of individual *online* users to their *offline* identities, by the state in particular, difficult but not impossible. This disjuncture between online and offline identity has had measurable effects on online interactions on the Chinese Internet. Last, but not least, Nicolai Volland discusses how Chinese people interested in the preservation of the courtyard houses (*hutongs*) of old Beijing are employing the Internet to discuss their aims and goals, to plan for offline events supporting preservation and to publicize their concerns with a wider audience. He presents a fascinating insight into the ways in which online discussions are used by the people congregating at the 'Old Beijing' website (*Lao Beijing Wang*) to clarify their goals, debate different approaches to conservation and discuss the balancing of the needs of a modern capital and its traditional neighbourhoods with their traditional architecture.

The common thread running through all of the chapters, or maybe the underlying basic observation of all the authors, is that online China is a wild and relatively unregulated space, allowing Chinese people to enjoy freedoms they do not have offline – despite the censorship, the restrictions, the government ownership of cyber-China, etc. It might not now, nor ever, be the Habermasian public sphere leading China towards a European or American-style democracy that some have tried to describe, but it empowers ordinary Chinese citizens in its own, carnivalesque ways that, ironically, can be far more democratic (people-rule) than any representative democracy (see, for example, Wang & Hong, 2010; or the chapter by Herold in this volume).

Carnival is [...] sensing the world as one great communal performance [...], liberating one from fear, bringing the world maximally close to a person and bringing one person maximally close to another [...], with its joy at change and its joyful relativity, is opposed to that one-sided and gloomy official seriousness which is dogmatic and hostile to evolution and change, which seeks to absolutize a given condition of existence or a given social order. From precisely that sort of seriousness did the carnival sense of the world liberate man.

(Bakhtin, 1984a: 160)

# References

Bakhtin, M. (1981). Epic and novel: Toward a methodology for the study of the novel. In C. Emerson & M. Holquist (Eds.), *The Dialogic Imagination* (pp. 3–40). Austin: University of Texas Press.

Bakhtin, M. (1984a). *Problems of Dostoevsky's poetics.* Minneapolis and London: University of Minnesota Press.

Bakhtin, M. (1984b). *Rabelais and his world.* Bloomington: Indiana University Press.

Barboza, D. (2007, February 5). Internet Boom in China Is Built on Virtual Fun – New York Times. *The New York Times.* Retrieved April 27, 2010, from http://www.nytimes.com/2007/02/05/world/asia/05virtual.html?_r=2&th=&oref=slogin&emc=th&pagewanted=print

Barboza, D. (2010, April 18). Entertainment trumps politics on Chinese web sites. *New York Times.* Retrieved July 24, 2010, from http://www.nytimes.com/2010/04/19/technology/19chinaweb.html?_r=1

Beasley-Murray, T. (2007). *Mikhail Bakhtin and Walter Benjamin: Experience and form.* Houndmills and New York: Palgrave Macmillan.

Boellstorff, T. (2008). *Coming of age in second life: An anthropologist explores the virtually human.* Princeton: Princeton University Press.

Brandist, C. (2002). *The Bakhtin circle: Philosophy, culture and politics.* London and Sterling, VA: Pluto Press.

Cao, F., & Su, L. (2006). Internet addiction among Chinese adolescents: Prevalence and psychological features. *Child: Care, Health and Development, 33*(3), 275–281.

Cartier, C., Castells, M., & Qiu, J. L. (2005). The information have-less: Inequality, mobility, and translocal networks in Chinese cities. *Studies in Comparative International Development (SCID), 40*(2), 9–34.

Castells, M. (2008). The new public sphere: Global civil society, communication networks, and global governance. *The Annals of the American Academy of Political and Social Science, 616*(1), 78–93.

Cha, A. E. (2007, February 22). In China, stern treatment for young Internet 'addicts'. *The Washington Post.* Retrieved April 26, 2010, from http://www.washingtonpost.com/wp-dyn/content/article/2007/02/21/AR2007022102094.html

Chase, M., & Mulvenon, J. C. (2002). *You've got dissent!: Chinese dissident use of the Internet and Beijing's counter-strategies.* Santa Monica, CA: Rand Corporation.

China Daily. (2010, February 3). Young Internet addicts on the rise. *China.org.cn.* Retrieved April 26, 2010, from http://www.china.org.cn/china/2010–02/03/content_19360107.htm

China Daily. (2010, July 8). In Internet age, age no bar for surfers. *Xinhuanet.* Retrieved July 24, 2010, from http://news.xinhuanet.com/english2010/china/2010–07/08/c_13389620.htm

Chu, W.-C. R. (2008). The dynamics of cyber China: The characteristics of Chinese ICT use. *Knowledge, Technology, and Policy, 21*(1), 29–35.

CNNIC. (2010). *The 25th Statistical Survey Report on the Internet Development in China.* Beijing: China Internet Network Information Center (CNNIC).

Dahlberg, L. (2001). The Internet and democratic discourse: Exploring the prospects of online deliberative forums extending the public sphere. *Information, Communication & Society, 4*(4), 615–633.

Damm, J. (2007). The Internet and the fragmentation of Chinese society. *Critical Asian Studies, 39*(2), 273–294.

Damm, J., & Thomas, S. (Eds.). (2006). *Chinese cyberspaces: Technological changes and political effects.* Abingdon and New York: Routledge.

Dsouza, K. (2010, March 2). Google still censors China search results. *Techie Buzz*. Retrieved April 27, 2010, from http://techie-buzz.com/tech-news/google-still-censoring-china-search-results.html

European Travel Commission. (2010, July 12). Demographics. *New Media Trendwatch*. Retrieved July 23, 2010, from http://www.newmediatrendwatch.com/markets-by-country/17-usa/123-demographics

Fallows, J. (2008). The connection has been reset. *The Atlantic*. Retrieved August 1, 2010, from http://www.theatlantic.com/magazine/archive/2008/03/-ldquo-the-connection-has-been-reset-rdquo/6650/

Fong, C. (2009, October 1). 'Sea turtles' powering China's Internet growth. *CNN*. Retrieved July 24, 2010, from http://edition.cnn.com/2009/TECH/09/30/digitalbiz.redwired/index.html#cnnSTCText

Foster, W. A. (2001). *The diffusion of the Internet in China*. Tucson: University of Arizona.

Freundlieb, D., Hudson, W., & Rundell, J. (2004). Reasoning, language and intersubjectivity. In D. Freundlieb, W. Hudson, & J. Rundell (Eds.), *Critical theory after Habermas* (pp. 1–34). Leiden and Boston: Brill.

Fryer, W. (2010, January 23). Beatings, electric shock and death for Internet addicted Chinese youth. *Moving at the Speed of Creativity*. Retrieved April 26, 2010, from http://www.speedofcreativity.org/2010/01/23/beatings-electric-shock-and-death-for-internet-addicted-chinese-youth/

Furuya, K., & Yamakawa, I. (2010, July 23). Google needs China, as China needs Google. *The Asahi Shimbun*. Retrieved July 23, 2010, from http://www.asahi.com/english/TKY201007220507.html

Gerhards, J., & Schäfer, M. S. (2010). Is the Internet a better public sphere? Comparing old and new media in the USA and Germany. *New Media & Society, 12*(1), 143–160.

Giese, K. (2006). *Challenging party hegemony: Identity work in China's emerging virreal places*. Hamburg: German Overseas Institute.

Gimmler, A. (2001). Deliberative democracy, the public sphere and the Internet. *Philosophy & Social Criticism, 27*(4), 21–39.

Ginev, D. (2004). The pluralistic public sphere from an ontological point of view. In D. Freundlieb, W. Hudson, & J. Rundell (Eds.), *Critical theory after Habermas* (pp. 77–103). Leiden and Boston: Brill.

Goldsmith, J., & Wu, T. (2006). *Who controls the Internet? Illusions of a borderless world*. Oxford, New York: Oxford University Press.

Golub, A., & Lingley, K. (2008). Just like the Qing empire: Internet addiction, MMOGs, and moral crisis in contemporary China. *Games and Culture, 3*(1), 59–75.

Griffiths, D. (2005, October 10). Treating China's online addicts. *BBC News*. Retrieved April 26, 2010, from http://news.bbc.co.uk/2/hi/4327258.stm

Habermas, J. (1976). *Legitimation crisis* (T. McCarthy, Trans.). London: Heinemann.

Habermas, J. (1987). *The theory of communicative action* (T. McCarthy, Trans. *Vol. 2: Lifeworld and system: A critique of functionalist reason*). Boston: Beacon Press.

Habermas, J. (2006). Political communication in media society: Does democracy still enjoy an epistemic dimension? The impact of normative theory on empirical research. *Communication Theory, 16,* 411–426.

Hachigian, N. (2001). China's cyber-strategy. *Foreign Affairs, 80*(2), 118–133.

Hartford, K. (2005). Dear Mayor: Online communications with local governments in Hangzhou and Nanjing. *China Information, 19*(2), 217.

Hays, J. (2010). Government control of the Internet in China. *China: Facts and details*. Retrieved April 27, 2010, from http://factsanddetails.com/china.php?itemid=232&catid=7&subcatid=43

Heacock, R. (2009, July 6). China shuts down Internet in Xinjiang region after riots. *OpenNet Initiative*. Retrieved April 27, 2010, from http://opennet.net/blog/2009/07/china-shuts-down-Internet-xinjiang-region-after-riots

Helft, M., & Wines, M. (2010, March 23). After China move, Google faces the fallout. *New York Times*. Retrieved April 27, 2010, from http://www.nytimes.com/2010/03/24/technology/24google.html

Herold, D. K. (2009). Cultural politics and political culture of Web 2.0 in Asia. *Knowledge, Technology, and Policy, 22*(2), 89–94.

Herold, D. K. (2010). Imperfect use? ICT provisions and human decisions: An introduction to the special issue on ICT adoption and user choices. *The Information Society, 26*(4), 243–246.

Jackson, L. A., Zhao, Y., Qiu, W., Kolenic III, A., Fitzgerald, H. E., Harold, R., & Von Eye, A. (2008). Cultural differences in morality in the real and virtual worlds: A comparison of Chinese and US youth. *CyberPsychology & Behavior, 11*(3), 279–286.

Kluver, R. (2005). US and Chinese policy expectations of the Internet. *China Information, 19*(2), 299–324.

Lagerkvist, J. (2005). The techno-cadre's dream: Administrative reform by electronic governance in China today? *China Information, 19*(2), 189.

Lagerkvist, J. (2006). *The Internet in China: Unlocking and containing the public sphere.* Lund University, Lund.

Lagerkvist, J. (2008). Internet ideotainment in the PRC: National responses to cultural globalization. *Journal of Contemporary China, 17*(54), 121–140.

Lewis, C. (2010, May 14). Internet connection (finally) restored in Xinjiang. *Shanghaiist*. Retrieved July 22, 2010, from http://shanghaiist.com/2010/05/14/xinjiang_Internet_restoredthis_time.php

Li, N., & Kirkup, G. (2007). Gender and cultural differences in Internet use: A study of China and the UK. *Computers & Education, 48*(2), 301–317.

Macartney, J. (2008, November 11). Internet addiction made an official disorder in China – Times Online. *The Times*. Retrieved April 26, 2010, from http://www.timesonline.co.uk/tol/news/world/asia/article5125324.ece

MacKinnon, R. (2007). Flatter world and thicker walls? Blogs, censorship and civic discourse in China. *Public Choice, 134*(1–2), 31–46.

MacKinnon, R. (2010, March 23). China, the Internet and Google: Congressional testimony. *RConversation*. Retrieved April 27, 2010, from http://rconversation.blogs.com/rconversation/2010/03/china-the-Internet-and-google.html

MacManus, R. (2010, February 24). Despite tough talk, Google still censoring in China. *Read Write Web*. Retrieved April 27, 2010, from http://www.readwriteweb.com/archives/google_still_censoring_in_china.php

Mudie, L. (2010, March 23). Xinjiang Internet 'still limited'. *Radio Free Asia*. Retrieved April 27, 2010, from http://www.rfa.org/english/news/uyghur/gfw-03232010113848.html

Pan, P. P. (2006, February 19). The click that broke a government's grip. *Washington Post*. Retrieved April 27, 2010, from http://www.washingtonpost.com/wp-dyn/content/article/2006/02/18/AR2006021801389.html

Papacharissi, Z. (2002). The virtual sphere: The Internet as a public sphere. *New Media & Society, 4*(1), 9–27.

Shie, T. R. (2004). The tangled web: does the Internet offer promise or peril for the Chinese Communist Party? *Journal of Contemporary China, 13*(40), 523–540.

Stewart, C. S. (2010, January 13). Obsessed with the Internet: A tale from China. *Wired Magazine*. Retrieved April 26, 2010, from http://www.wired.com/magazine/2010/01/ff_internetaddiction/

Summers, J. (2009, December 6). The truth about Xinjiang's Internet situation. *Xinjiang: Far West China*. Retrieved April 27, 2010, from http://www.farwestchina.com/2009/12/truth-about-xinjiangs-Internet.html

Sun, H. L. (2003). *Internet policy and use: A field study of Internet cafes in China*. Unpublished PhD, Florida State University, Tallahassee.

Tai, Z. (2004). *Civil society and Internet revolutions in China*. University of Minnesota, Duluth.

Tian, L. (2010, January 4). Is the Internet re@lly a danger to children? *China Daily*. Retrieved April 26, 2010, from http://www.chinadaily.com.cn/china/2010–01/04/content_9257677.htm

Wang, S. S., & Hong, J. (2010). Discourse behind the forbidden realm: Internet surveillance and its implications on China's blogosphere. *Telematics and Informatics, 27*(1), 67–78.

Ward, J. (2010, March 24). The world from Berlin: Google's move to Hong Kong 'a face-saving capitulation'. *Der Spiegel*. Retrieved April 27, 2010, from http://www.spiegel.de/international/world/0,1518,685452,00.html

Weber, I., & Jia, L. (2007). Internet and self-regulation in China: The cultural logic of controlled commodification. *Media, Culture & Society, 29*(5), 772–789.

Wu, X. (2007). *Chinese cyber nationalism – evolution, characteristics, and implications*. Lanham, Boulder, New York, Toronto, Plymouth: Lexington Books.

Yang, B. (2008). NPOs in China: Some issues concerning Internet communication. *Knowledge, Technology & Policy, 21*(1), 37–42.

Yang, B. (2010). Social spaces and new media: Some reflections on the modernization process in China. *Procedia Social and Behavioural Sciences, 2*, 6941–6947.

Yang, G. (2003a). The co-evolution of the Internet and civil society in China. *Asian Survey, 43*(3), 405–422.

Yang, G. (2003b). The Internet and the rise of a transnational Chinese cultural sphere. *Media, Culture and Society, 25*(4), 469–490.

Yang, G. (2007). How do Chinese civic associations respond to the Internet? Findings from a survey. *China Quarterly, 189*(March), 122–143.

Yang, G. (2008). Contention in cyberspace. In K. J. O'Brien (Ed.), *Popular protest in China* (pp. 126–143). Cambridge, MA: Harvard University Press.

Yang, G. (2009). *The power of the Internet in China: Citizen activism online*. New York: Columbia University Press.

Yang, G., & Calhoun, C. (2007). Media, civil society, and the rise of a green public sphere in China. *China Information, 21*(2), 211–236.

Zhao, J. (2008). ICT4D: Internet adoption and usage among rural users in China. *Knowledge, Technology, and Policy, 21*(1), 9–18.

Zhao, J. (2009). ICTs for achieving Millennium Development Goals: Experiences of connecting rural China to the Internet. *Knowledge, Technology, and Policy, 22*(2), 133–143.

Zheng, Y., & Wu, G. (2005). Information technology, public space, and collective action in China. *Comparative Political Studies, 38*(5), 507–536.

Zhou, Y., & Moy, P. (2007). Parsing framing processes: The interplay between online public opinion and media coverage. *Journal of Communication, 57*(1), 79–98.

# Part I

# Creating the carnival

Netizens and the state

# 1 Cultural convulsions

## Examining the Chineseness of cyber China

*Rodney Wai-chi Chu and Chung-tai Cheng*

## Introduction

This chapter wants to argue for a better capture of the dynamics of cyber China, and for an acknowledgment of her cultural-historical roots. In discussions of cyber China, two discourses have been dominant, the first being the 'liberation discourse', which associates technological advancement with the development of civil society. The second, the 'control discourse', discusses how successful the Communist party state has been in taking advantage of its economic success to protect its vested interest. In this chapter, though, we maintain that a fair understanding of the development of cyber China requires an appreciation of her unique historical, political and cultural contexts. China has been 'riding a double juggernaut' (the introduction of modern capitalism and of cyberization at almost the same time), but the modernization of the country has been accompanied by a new 'rule by morality', and China's culture and her worldview are shaping interpersonal relationships and people's understanding of civil society – which should be taken into account in an analysis of cyber China.

After a brief look at the current state of analysis of the development of cyber China, we discuss a series of studies on the meaning of modernization, technology and civil society from a Chinese perspective. The section outlines how the historical-cultural logic of Chinese society affects the governance of China's rulers as well as the behavioural patterns of the people in cyber China, thus challenging Western assumptions about cyber practices in China. By using the cases of the Green Dam Youth Escort Online Filtering Software (hereafter referred to as 'Green Dam') affair and the subsequent '2009 Declaration of the Anonymous Netizens' (hereafter referred to as 'The Declaration'), we want to argue that it is misleading to see these events as an illustration of emerging civic power in China, as this ignores the contradictory views expressed about both cases in Chinese cyberspace. Instead of presenting clear-cut divisions between people for or against the Green Dam or The Declaration, we want to emphasize the cultural threads underlying online responses, with the goal of a clearer articulation of what is happening in Chinese cyberspace. We hope that this chapter will contribute to an understanding of the uniqueness of cyber China, grown out of her history and culture.

**The current state of analysis**

The history of ICTs in China is very short, but her ICT market has expanded at a phenomenal rate. According to the 24th Statistical Report issued by the China Internet Network Information Centre (CNNIC) on July 16, 2009, 338 million people were accessing the Internet, allowing China formally to overtake the United States as the country with the largest numbers of Internet users (CNNIC, 2009). Less than one year later, Xinhua News Agency, citing data from the State Council Information Office, stated that the number of Internet users had reached 400 million, indicating an 18% increase (Agence France Presse, 2010). Based on these figures, increasing numbers of scholars believe that ever more Chinese people are taking advantage of the Internet to express and discuss their own views on social matters, which in turn contributes to the Internet becoming a public sphere which will enhance and promote democracy in China (Buchstein, 1997; Dittmer & Liu, 2006; Froomkin, 2003; Wu, 2007; Yang, 2009b; Zheng, 2008). Phrases such as 'online activism' (Yang, 2009a), 'cyber rights' (Godwin, 2003), or 'liberation discourse' (Damm, 2009: 83–85) are employed in a liberal democratic sense, thus associating technological advancement in China with the emergence and development of a civil society. The argument made is that the Chinese government, in its pursuit of economic and social progress, is forced to accept a compromise of its control over the Internet, otherwise China's economic reforms and its Opening-Up policy would be obstructed and fail (Harwit & Clark, 2001).

Some, however, argue that the Internet will not bring revolutionary change to China, as the central government has implemented the most powerful, sophisticated, and far-reaching filtering system on the Chinese Internet to curtail the circulation of information that could threaten the stability of the country (Chase & Mulvenon, 2002). This seems to be supported by China's growing unwillingness to compromise on her opinions, based on her rapid economic growth, which, in the view of the Chinese government (and the Chinese people), proves that China is strong enough to guarantee a 'controlled change', or to allow a 'controlled discourse' (Damm, 2009: 86–87), both online and offline. A good illustration of these beliefs is the high-profile contest between Google and Chinese authorities during the first half of 2010 about Google's obligation to censor search results on its Chinese website. Google announced its intention to quit China at the beginning of the year, and since March 2010 has redirected users of its search engine to its (uncensored) Hong Kong site as a show of its determination not to submit to Chinese censorship demands. By the end of June 2010, though, Google had resubmitted an application for the renewal of its license to provide online content in China (Efrati & Batson, 2010), implying its willingness to obey Chinese laws. Google's u-turn surely embarrassed its supporters (Ai, 2010) but, comparing US debts with the huge (and affluent) Chinese market, Western multi-nationals queuing up for their share of that market know better than anyone that China is holding all the trumps these days (Garten, 2010).

Additionally, it is argued that the degree of censorship in cyber China is not new at all. Zhao points out that China's military-led techno-nationalism has had a profound impact on her 'digital revolution' from the beginning of and throughout the post-Mao era (Zhao, 2007: 96). The development of ICTs is seen as instrumental in the state's modernization of its military and surveillance capabilities, and against this backdrop the paradoxical nature of China's digital revolution becomes more easily understandable: on the one hand, ICTs have been widely promoted, if unevenly diffused, among the population; on the other hand, state control over content of and access to ICTs has always been a focus of the Chinese state (ibid.: 92). To some extent this echoes the portrayal of Chinese media reforms as having gone through stop-go cycles since the 1980s (Chan & Qiu, 2002: 33–34), based on the pattern of reform and retrenchment rooted in the fear of the Chinese Communist Party leadership that freedom in related areas (from conventional press freedom to freedom of expression online) will pose a threat to its political power. Such an interpretation provides an internal logic to the series of state acts starting with the 'anti-spiritual pollution campaign' from October 1983 to February 1984 and the 'anti-liberalization campaign' from January to May 1987, as they can be interpreted as attempts by the conservative wing of the Chinese Communist Party to open the economy but not the polity (see Zhao, 2009: 183–96).

In a recent attempt to escape this political sociology perspective of the Internet, Chu (forthcoming) tries to introduce a wider perspective into the study of cyber China by arguing that China has been 'riding a double juggernaut'. Put simply, China's reform era has coincided with a period of rapid technological innovations globally, and has therefore experienced socio-cultural and techno-economic upheavals of such a magnitude that all Chinese people throughout China have been affected by them. Providing a strong sense of coincidence, both developments began in the early 1990s. In 1992, Deng Xiaoping went on his famous southern tour of China, travelling to Guangzhou, Shenzhen, and Shanghai between mid January and late February, which has generally been regarded as his way of reasserting control over China's economic policy after the crackdowns in June 1989. The tour was instrumental in deepening the Chinese reforms of the telecommunications sector, while during the same time period the global cyber era began, with the historic move towards a World Wide Web. Around the world, the pace of development of the Internet and of Web culture has been staggering. The World Wide Web first became publicly available in 1991, followed by the introduction in 1993 of the Mosaic Web browser, which evolved into the Netscape Navigator during the following year. In 1997 a new form of web environment – the blog – emerged and allowed private individuals to express themselves on the Internet, which has since become ubiquitous. In the context of this chapter, we merely want to point out that, in an unintended convergence of circumstances, China – because of her determination to join the rest of the world – stumbled into revolutionary changes to the social experience of 'the West', and had to cope with industrialization and cyberization at the same time.

There is nothing in the history of Western countries that compares to China's experience as such, as their development progressed in a more linear fashion. One very good example of this difference is the introduction of the telephone, which can serve as a benchmark of the process of industrialization. In the West, there was a gradual process of development from the use of fixed telephones to mobile phones, and sociological enquiry also moved from studying the implications on human lives of fixed telephones to the study of mobile phones. In China, however, the mobile phone is often the first phone experienced by a person, as there was limited state investment in landlines across the country before the 1990s, resulting in private phone lines being too costly and time-consuming to connect. As a result the 'fixed phone experience' is not the 'normal experience in the modern era' for many Chinese people (He, 1997: 68–78; Yan & Pitt, 2002: 13–19; Yu & Tng, 2003: 187).

The density of the Chinese experience of modernity – learning to live with modern capitalism and rapid cyberization at the same time – while moving from a closed society (under totalitarian rule) to a more open one within a very short period of time, is reason enough to expect the Chinese experience to be unique. Added to this are China's long and unbroken cultural heritage and traditions, which form the backdrop for China's development, and that we turn to now in more detail.

## The Chinese cultural realm

Borge Bakken (2000a) discussed the main problem of Chinese society in dealing with disorder on the path to modernization: China's insistence on the maintenance of an 'exemplary society', which refers to an education- and discipline-oriented society in which 'human quality' and model behaviour are moulded and promoted. Bakken emphasized the influence of the cultural realm on the form of a social change. He contended that Chinese modernization seemed to follow deeply rooted patterns of controlled change aimed at taming and directing the path as well as the pace of the road to modernization. In the Chinese context, 'human quality' is regarded as a force for realizing a modern society of perfect order, or for the creation of a harmonious modernity, based on roots in and memories of the past (Bakken 2000a: 1). In this process, tradition and modernization are interlinked through a system of social controls in which 'tradition' is seen as serving transforming purposes and 'modernization' can mean stability and order (ibid.: 4–5). An apt metaphor for their relationship is to put brakes on a runaway engine, to control the path and pace of the juggernaut of modernity. Concepts such as 'social engineering' (*shehui gongcheng*), 'moral construction' (*daode jianshe*), or 'two civilizations – material and spiritual' (*wuzhi wenming* and *jingshen wenming*) that are frequently mentioned in official statements and that are popular among political and technocratic elites in China are never empty slogans (ibid.: 50–54), but reflect a striving for a 'rule by morality' in the course of the ride to capitalism. The aim is to produce 'a rational social equilibrium' (*heli de shehui pingheng*) – although it is another matter whether such a goal is achievable or not. However, such a moral rule, Bakken argues, is deeply embedded in Chinese culture, where the classical values of 'self cultivation, family regulation, ordering of the state, and bringing tranquillity and order under heaven' (*xiu shen, qi jia, zhi guo, ping tian xia*) are expressed in the Confucian classic *Great Learning* (*Daxue*), and form the founding principle for creating both an ideal individual personality and a perfect society (ibid.: 42).

This cultural framework can be traced, for example, in a study of elections or 'voting' in the Chinese context (Bakken, 2000b). The Chinese cultural background as outlined above represents a normative basis, with a focus on problems of governance and of democratization within the setting of sustaining social integration and community well-being. Though the meaning of community varies considerably from family, to clan, to nation, it represents the centre of Chinese society, which does not emphasize treating individuals on equal terms, but rather focuses on the relationships between people as the basic unit of society. The belief that good society will develop through the upholding of morality and strict standards based on objective norms rather than subjective decisions leads to a preference for evaluation (*ping*) rather than election (*xuan*). Consequently, Bakken argues, the Chinese are sceptical about elections and representative democracy in particular, and place immense importance on the evaluation of all aspects of everyday life in general (ibid.: 110–11).

Yu (1984) argues that, unlike Western thought with its emphasis on rationality, Chinese thought has a very this-worldly practical focus, while it is through articulation from within, what is known as 'immanent transcendence' (*neizai chaoyue*), that one may come to terms with one's destiny, or the Mandate of Heaven (*tian ming*) (Yu, 1984: 23–25). This cultural orientation favours the development of 'technical skills' (*jishu*) rather than of 'science' (*kexue*), the former emphasizing practical wisdom, while the latter focuses on finding truth, which had significant consequences during China's development from the mid 19th century onwards. Her turbulent modern history had brought about the burning desire among many to 'save the nation' (*jiuguo*), and many activists not only overlooked that there were different levels of westernization (e.g. technological, legal, etc.), but mistakenly equated westernization with modernization (Yu, 1984: 19). During the height of the May Fourth Movement, the Chinese intelligentsia called for Renaissance and Enlightenment in China, symbolized by their outspoken support for 'Mr Democracy' (*de xiansheng*) and 'Mr Science' (*cai xiansheng*). However, this constituted merely a mechanical transplantation and a distorted and partial understanding of the causes of democracy and science in the Western world (ibid.: 44). Yu contended that the eagerness to adopt 'Western science' since the May-fourth movement has limited itself to its 'technical' (*jishu*) instead of its 'scientific' (*keyin*) aspects, and the impact of this misunderstanding can still be seen today in the emphasis on technology (*keji*) rather than science (*kexue*), which is vividly exemplified by the four modernization theses of the Chinese Communist Party that are still in place as national doctrines (ibid.: 70–71).

We can construct a clear logical flow between the historical fact that China was responsible for many technological advances (such as the four great inventions), and the fact that these sophisticated technological skills did not evolve into a coherent system of scientific knowledge (Law & Chu, 2008: 3–4), the reasons for which can be traced back to the cultural orientation of Chinese society which forms the basis of Chinese learning. The May Fourth period was characterized by a spirit of emancipation and modernization that was hardly aware of its distorted and partial capture of the Western experience, as it was too focused on its own problems. The attention on technical details instead of on the spirit of scientific exploration further distanced the Chinese soul-searching exercise from a critical reflection on Western human nature. Consequently, Chinese learning – then and now – focuses on techniques and there is little reflection on the relationship between technological progress and the scientific (Western) mind-set or culture that sustains such development.

Chinese attempts to develop using Western models are further complicated by the different perceptions of the relationships between one person and the next, and between an individual person and society in Western and in Chinese culture. Xiao-tung Fei depicted the difference between the two societies more than half a century ago (Fei 1992 [which is the English version of *Xiangtu Zhungguo*, written in 1947]). To him, individuals in the West have established their societies by applying an 'organizational mode of association' (*tuantigeju*) rooted in the Christian tradition. People in China, however, organize their society by adopting a 'differentiated mode of association' (*chaxugeju*) based on Confucian ethics. In Fei's view, the far-reaching impact of Christianity in the West is reflected in the parameters for personal relationships in social life, i.e. justice, impartiality, and love. All people are equal to one another, and an individual is a soul-bearing self, a unique entity who is permanently and intrinsically linked to no human, but only to God. Fei argued that notions of the protection of individual rights, of the respect of personal autonomy, and of the mutual recognition of one's social boundaries are inherent in the moral system of the Western mode of organization, while social relationships among Chinese have a very different basis.

Confucianism talks about this-worldly concerns. To achieve the highest goal of Confucianism, harmony (*he*), one should act in a proper way, employing courtesy (*li*). The cardinal relationships (*lun*) become the central tenet of Confucian ideas, which stresses the importance of differentiation or distinction (*bei*) within hierarchical relationships. The maturity of a person raised in Chinese culture is measured by one's ability to know how to push or extend out (*tui*), like ripples spreading out from the centre of the splash made when a stone is thrown into water. This metaphor of Fei captures the essence of Chinese patterns of interaction in the form of *chaxu*: the self, embedded in social relationships and emotionally tied to personal obligations as defined by those relationships, acts with the required *li* according to the relationships. The underlying philosophy is that a person is *not treated as* a person per se (that is, *not* as an equal individual), but *only according to* the relationship of that person with oneself.

The Confucian scholar Shu-ming Liang (1987[1949]) concluded that the chief characteristic of Chinese society is that it is ethics based (*lunli benwei*), which means that the focus of the social system of China is on the specific nature of the relationship between interacting individuals. Francis Hsu coined the term 'situation-centred' nature of Chinese culture to compare it with the 'individual-centred' nature of the West (Hsu 1981[1953]). The preferred outcome of an interaction does not depend on individual desires in itself, but on who is involved and/or affected by the situation – the desire of the self in initiating an act or a decision is less important. This is the essence of the 'relational being' described by Ambrose King: the life of the traditional Chinese is largely determined by a person's concrete obligations toward concrete people in the form of affection (*qing*), righteousness (*yi*), differentiation (*bie*), order (*xu*), and sincerity (*cheng*) (King, 1985: 63–66). Interpersonal relationships have to be evaluated, and the evaluation in turn sets the ethical standards one has to follow in dealing with other people. As a result, in relationships with others, *particularism* (that is, treating people differently) instead of *universalism* (that is, treating people equally) becomes the norm, which is another sharp distinction between the Chinese and the West.

Against this backdrop, Thomas Metzger's discussion of the differences in the concept of civil society between China and the West is more easily understood (Metzger, 1994, 1998). After a detailed review of discussions on civil society in the Western tradition, Metzger concluded that 'civil society' refers to an un-utopian, bottom-up political order in which ordinary, economically oriented citizens fallibly organize themselves to monitor an incorrigible state, so as to protect the freedom of the three (intellectual, political and economic) market-places against state intervention or against those claiming to have a better under-standing of the public good than other citizens have (Metzger, 1998: 10–11). The 'civility' of the civil society has two aspects – individual autonomy, and equality between individuals – which is the normative basis of the Western liberal tradition. The underlying assumption here is that the general population should share norms that would facilitate cordial, trustful relations between fellow citizens – even if they are strangers to one another. This assumption, however, is not appropriate for Chinese culture, which favours the development of exclusive ties of solidarity between those who know each other well or are close to each other, as compared to 'strangers' (Metzger, 1994: 277). This echoes the logic of *chaxugeju* and *lunli benwei* as outlined above, as, for a relational being, relationships become meaningless if one does not differentiate between those one knows and those one does not.

When applied to the relationship between the state and civil society, Confucian thinkers would argue that the road to better government does not consist of increasing the freedom from state control enjoyed by morally degenerate social strata, but by raising the moral level of both the state and society (Metzger, 1994: 299). Metzger is arguing that the Chinese do have a civil society, but that it follows different principles. The roots of civil society in Chinese tradition are in the realm of thoughts, and Confucian intellectuals, seeing themselves as a moral community, believe it is their duty to articulate the true needs of the people, as they are the group who know the 'divine route' (*tian dao*) and the 'divine principle' (*tian li*) (ibid.: 285, 299). This intellectual tradition, pre-eminent until the late Qing period, was occupied with the agenda of creating a world based on benevolence (*ren*), which shaped the vision of democracy that developed in China at the turn of the 20th century – democratization would take selfishness out of governance, and the enlightened elite would raise the moral level of the benighted souls (of ordinary people) by transforming them (ibid.: 301). Thus, the agents of political improvement in China are not thought to be ordinary, economically oriented citizens fallibly organizing themselves to monitor an incorrigible state, but saintly super-citizens ready to guide society from a top-down position in accordance with the state, in what amounts to the opposite of the Western version of what a civil society should be (Metzger, 1998: 9–10).

In research of the Chinese Internet many of the above differences between Chinese culture and Western culture have produced similar differences in the interpretation of events in cyber China. In her numbers of Internet and mobile phone users nationwide, China ranks first in the world and has to be understood as having entered the cyber age. Cyberization, though, has too easily been associated with liberalization, or the democratization of a place. What this chapter wants to explore is the role played by Chinese culture in this global process, and the historical-cultural logic of Chinese society, including its effects on the governance models used by China's rulers and on the behavioural patterns of Chinese people entering the cyber age. The purpose of our next section is to present as a case study the dramatic announcements of, first, the launch and later, the postponement of the 'Green Dam' by the Chinese government in June 2009, to examine the cultural threads embedded in this cyber event. This case was chosen because the official statements present a showcase illustration of the 'rule by morality', while 'The Declaration' in response to this policy appeared to be a display of ordinary citizens' muscle and power as an expression of emerging civic power, and yet, the responses to 'The Declaration' also reflect the mixed feelings of many Chinese about such a Western-style statement of defiance.

## The Green Dam Youth Escort

On 8 June 2009, China's Ministry of Industry and Information Technology (MIIT) announced that all computer manufacturers would be required to install the 'Green Dam' filtering software on machines sold in China starting from 1 July onwards, including those imported from abroad, for the purpose of protecting the psychological health of the young from pollution through pornography and violence. As one analyst argued (MacKinnon, 2009), the 'Green Dam' affair is representative of a growing movement globally, as parents and family-support organizations are increasingly pressuring governments 'to do something' in the face of all the perceived threats to children abounding on the Internet. Human rights advocates and Internet users in China, however, have remained very critical. A good summary of the views expressed on the Chinese Internet against the 'Green Dam' launch can be found in Fauna (2009): that the software was just a thinly veiled attempt by the government to expand censorship. After a dramatic series of events, on 30 June 2009 Xinhua News Agency announced the government's decision to delay the requirement for installation. The formal reason given was that the government was listening to the advice of computer manufacturers who had claimed that it would take time to prepare for this move, but it cannot explain, however, why the 'Green Dam' has been put on hold indefinitely (Fang, 2009).

Guobin Yang (Yang, 2009a) maintains, in an article posted on the Columbia University Press Blog, that the whole incident reflects a degree of bluntness by the party-state in its efforts to exercise control over the Internet, but that – echoing another of his publications (Yang, 2009b) – the online protest and eventual success of Chinese netizens illustrates the maturity of online activism, which is powerful enough to seriously undermine efforts to control the Chinese Internet. Firstly, the social uses of the Internet in China have fostered a discussion in the public sphere, have changed the structure of the organization of society by incorporating the online community, and have introduced new elements capable of igniting social protest (Yang, 2003a). Secondly, the development of the Internet and of civil society is somewhat co-evolutionary, indicating that the urge for public discussion, the dynamics of social organizations, and an active social movement will also contribute to the diffusion of the Internet in China (Yang, 2003b).

Perhaps the best illustration of the awakening power of Chinese netizens is, as Li Datong contends in his analysis (Li, 2009), the *direct challenge* against China's rulers, illustrated by the 'The Declaration' posted all across cyber China's websites, the full text of which is quoted below:

To the Internet censors of China,

We are the Anonymous Netizens. We have seen your moves on the Internet. You have deprived your netizens of the freedom of speech. You have come to see technology as your mortal enemy. You have clouded and distorted the truth in collaboration with Party mouthpieces. You have hired commentators to create the 'public opinion' you wanted to see. All these are etched into our collective memory. More recently, you forced the installation of Green Dam on the entire population and smothered Google with vicious slander. It is now clear as day: what you want is the complete control and censorship of the Internet. We hereby declare that we, the Anonymous Netizens, are going to launch our attack worldwide on your censorship system starting on July 1st, 2009.

For the freedom of the Internet, for the advancement of Internetization, and for our rights, we are going to acquaint your censorship machine with systematic sabotage and show you just how weak the claws of your censorship really are. We are going to mark you as the First Enemy of the Internet. This is not a single battle; it is but the beginning of a war. Play with your artificial public opinion to your heart's content, for you will soon be submerged in the sea of warring netizens. Your archaic means of propaganda, your epithets borrowed straight from the Cultural Revolution era, your utter ignorance of the Internet itself – these are the tolls of your death bell. You cannot evade us, for we are everywhere. Violence of the state cannot save you – for every one of us that falls, another ten rises. We are familiar with your intrigues. You label some of us as the 'vicious few' and dismiss the rest of us as unknowing accomplices; that way you can divide and rule. Go ahead and do that. In fact, we encourage you to do that; the more accustomed you are to viewing your netizens this way, the deeper your self-deception.

You are trying in vain to halt the wheels of history. Even with your technocratic reinforcements, you will not understand the Internet in the foreseeable future. We congratulate you on your adherence to your Cultural-Revolution style conspiracy theories in your dealings with dissent; for we too get nostalgic at times. We toast to your attempts to erect a Great Wall among your netizens, for such epic folly adds spice to any historical narrative. Still, there's something we feel obliged to tell you.

NOBODY wants to topple your regime. We take no interest whatsoever in your archaic view of state power and your stale ideological teachings.

You do not understand how your grand narrative dissipated in the face of Internetization. You do not understand why appealing to statism and national- ism no longer works. You cannot break free from your own ignorance of the Internet. Your regime is not our enemy. We are not affiliated in any way with any country or organization, and we are not waging this war on any country or organization, not even on you. YOU are waging this war on yourself. YOU are digging your own grave through corruption and antagonization. We are not interested in you, destined for the sewage of history. You cannot stop the Internetization of the human race. In fact, we won't bat an eyelid even if you decide to sever the transpacific information cables in order to obtain the total control you wanted. The harder you try to roll back history, the more you strain the already taut strings, and the more destructive their final release. You are accelerating your own fall. The sun of tomorrow does not shine on those who are fearing tomorrow itself.

We are the Anonymous Netizens. We are the sum of the world's entire online population. We are coordinated. We are dominant. We are innumer- able. For every one of us that falls, another ten joins. We are omnipresent. We are omnipotent. We are unstoppable. We have no weaknesses. We utilize every weakness. We are the humanity under every mask. We are the mirrors of conscience. We are created equal. We are born free. We are an army. We do not forgive. We do not forget.

Liberty leads the Internet. We're coming.

(Tan, 2009)

Although 'The Declaration' does not mention the announcement of launching the 'Green Dam' directly, reports from, for example, Deutsche Welle (Miao, 2009), or the Boxun News Web (Asian Weekly, 2009) have argued for the asso- ciation of these two incidents. Simply put, the 'Green Dam' announcement trig- gered the protests of dissidents on the Internet and their desire to provoke the authorities. A few days before the planned launch of the Green Dam, performing artist Ai Weiwei, a well-known dissident figure in the eyes of Western audiences, called for an Internet boycott on 1 July, asking people to refrain from all online activities so as to demonstrate the netizens' power (Yu & Graham-Harrison, 2009). Another Internet dissident, Bei Feng (North Wind), popularized the slogan '*fan luba, qi fanqiang*' (protest against the Green Dam, climb over the firewall together), proposing that each participant who used the TOR software to channel past Chinese Internet controls should teach five other people to '*fanqiang*' so as to protest against this new, severe gate-keeping policy (Miao, 2009).

The tone of 'The Declaration' is extremely provocative, and highly confronta- tional in the Chinese context. This could be understood as evidence for the asso- ciation of cyberization with openness, democratization, etc. – even in the case of China. It could even be argued that this declaration shows a maturing civil society in China and demonstrates the 'power of the powerless'. Such an interpretation is not without its problems, though, as there this group of 'anonymous citizens' has never been identified, neither the number of people behind the declaration, nor who their 'we' actually represents. Additionally, it remains unclear what this declaration *has contributed* to the backing down of the Chinese government over the launch of the 'Green Dam' software, given the questions about effectiveness of the software in doing its filtering work, the accusations of software piracy against the 'Green Dam' itself, and the negative feedback from business circles and in the international media, all of which have to be regarded as contributing factors to the government's decision to stop the implementation of the 'Green Dam' policy. According to a report from New Tang Dynasty Television (2010), the American software company CyberSitter has formally sued the Chinese government and several software companies in China involved in the development and distribution of the 'Green Dam' software for copyright violations and asked for an award of US\$2.2 billion.

A celebration of the 'Green Dam' affair from a liberal democratic point of view should therefore be treated with caution, as this might be wishful thinking rather than sound judgement. Furthermore, while the 'Green Dam' does not have to be installed on all new PCs sold in China anymore, as envisaged by the original regulation, a version of the regulation has been implemented in educational institutions, i.e. primary schools, secondary schools, and universities have installed the 'Green Dam' on many of their computers (Kirchner & Li, 2009).

Beyond the status of 'Green Dam' installations in China in general, though, an even more complicated picture emerges out of the many negative responses to 'The Declaration' on the Chinese Internet, which contradicts the supposed striving for liberated, open spaces that Western political correctness predicted for the Internet. While a quantitative analysis of the comments for or against 'The Declaration' is impossible, given the still-existing and powerful filtering and cleaning-up activities of the Chinese state apparatus on this sensitive issue, a closer look at some of the online voices can still provide us with several insights into the lines of argument in cyber China. The following responses from netizens A to M, collected on various Internet forums, show that consideration should be given to Chinese culture when assessing the online behaviour of Chinese netizens, and that an interpretation of the 'Green Dam' affair using Western political ideas might be missing the mark.

NETIZEN A: Who wrote this article? I am represented again, without my consent though. Would you please deduct me out from your statement of 'we are the sum of the world's entire online population' and 'we are coordinated'?

NETIZEN B: After reading his article, I have the feeling that our government should manage and control the Internet.

NETIZEN C: The one who wrote this article should examine and compare what kind of strategies for managing the Internet are being adopted among different countries, and then list them out for our government to make reference to.

As a follow-up to Netizen C, Netizen J continues the dialogue:

NETIZEN J: Ordinary people would not care much in detail. So many people just want to find a way to express personal feelings. As for what one is accusing, and what should be blamed, this is not the main point, as complaining per se is cool. To discuss with emotional crowds [noted: Netizen J is referring to the writer of the Declaration] is pointless, and in fact they are more willing to be fooled. Freedom, democracy, equality, peace ... these are all magic words, but how many people do really comprehend their meaning?

NETIZEN D: I hereby openly challenge the author of this declaration. Please don't count me in as one of the so-called yours, although I have already been a netizen for more than ten years.

NETIZEN E: If you want to make a declaration, you must have well-grounded points. It is pointless to just scold your country and your government, we should base our views on facts and issues in proposing solutions; although implementation is another problem.

NETIZEN F: Can this article be regarded as a declaration? Only those with concrete suggestions are contributing, this kind of emotional high-sounding loud cry is far from being a declaration.

NETIZEN G: Although I feel bad with this government policy, but if you look around and see how large China is, the number of races grouped under this country, it is sometimes reasonable to be harsh. Stability is what this country needs most; harmony may be bad for somebody, but we just cannot use our own moral yardstick to compare with all the people.

NETIZEN H: My view is that the government is not effective enough for many people, but from a macro stand, such a move is reasonable. Does/do the writer(s) of this declaration know how many people in China are still illiterate or under-educated? The first-hand information they obtain from the Internet may instruct their behaviour from then onwards. So many websites are talking bullshit, but so long as media is assumed to be true, people may also believe that it is true on the whole, such as the case of the June 4 Incident. Lots of contents on the Internet are without grounds, but just nobody would introduce the event in itself.

NETIZEN I: Had the Chinese not adopted such a high-handed style of management, China would have been split up, and the country would have been separated a long time ago. Just see what is happening to North Korea, and you know it is such a blessing that we can feel full after each meal.

(OGRM BBS, 2009)

NETIZEN K: Although the Internet is a free zone and the Green Dam is certainly putting restrictions on the freedom of netizens, only those freedoms that are protected by legal and humanitarian stands are true freedoms. The current suggestion from the government is for the sake of using the Internet in a better and safer manner, and I think most of the netizens would acknowledge this act. Violence and pornography are doing great harm to youngsters. I am not trying to be morally sound, indeed lots of youth crimes are caused by such contacts at the start. The ability for self-constraint of a person is limited, and a prolonged contact with such media will easily cause one to lose a sensible and right attitude towards life.

NETIZEN L: If you want to have a normal and healthy life, would you let your family members or loved ones become obsessed with pornography and violent websites? Would you allow them to visit these websites frequently? ... The influence is unobtrusive and imperceptible, and in the long run, they will change. Do you know why there are so many divorce cases? It is because of extramarital relations. This is the reason. To conclude, if the government wants to forbid freedom of speech on the Internet, I will strongly disagree. But if it aims to shut down those unhealthy websites, I will support it wholeheartedly.

(Fenghua de lian, 2009)

NETIZEN M: One World, One Ideology

The declaration believes that, when faced with the irreversible trend of the Internetization of the human race, grand narratives must dissipate, especially conservative ideologies within authoritarian regimes; and the more the ruling try to obstruct the wheel of history, the more destructive the outcome [...] This declaration is definitely the best text during our times to show what is meant by historical determinism, and it has succeeded in adopting the most important feature of the Communist Manifesto: the declarer is representing a new era, while teasing and downplaying the old system and its protectors. [...] If we claim that we need to make a radical stand to confront a strong oppressive system, we can easily fall prey to extreme ideas – using historical deterministic anarchic Internetization-ism to replace historical deterministic Marxism. This is just old wine in a new bottle, and far from the kind of new epoch the human race is supposedly stepping into, as claimed by the declaration. In fact, to use a discourse of a 'historical trend' to prove the unstoppable nature of an event is itself the trendiest trick used to form another grand narrative. [...] An inspired free society should be a gentle and progressive one, without historical essentialism acting as its basis. An iron fist cannot bring about peace, why should we believe that two fists at loggerheads can bring about peace?

(Han, 2009)

Netizen B clearly states the paradox underlying these debates: 'The Declaration' is itself proof of the free and anarchistic nature of cyber society and of the need for constraints on cyber practices. Two reasons are given by the other netizens for the need to constrain statements like 'The Declaration' online. In the context of how to present a reasonable argument, Netizens C and E complain about the lack of constructive ideas in 'The Declaration', while Netizen F even objects that this post does not qualify to be called a declaration. In addition, there is some support for the installation of the 'Green Dam' among the netizens. Netizens G, H and I argue for the installation of the software to protect the stability of the country and its cultural harmony.

Netizens K and L quote social concerns about both crime and divorce rates in their arguments for the 'Green Dam', but reveal deeper concerns as well. K argues that 'freedom' must be defined within a specific context, while L maintains that one must differentiate between two types of control and restrictions: the one against the 'freedom of expression', which is objectionable, the other against the 'freedom of accessing any website', which should be supported. This differentiation by the netizens is interesting, as it recognizes the importance of the 'freedom of expression', while arguing that the context of this freedom has to be assessed as well. As discussed earlier, the Chinese netizens introduce a moral dimension into this political debate. Netizens A and D merely protest that 'The Declaration' does not have the right to represent them, although they are also Internet users themselves, and Netizen J queries whether the person(s) behind 'The Declaration' is/are just being blinded by the good-sounding concepts 'freedom' and 'democracy' without actually understanding them. Netizen M, in article form, provides an even higher-level response, accusing 'The Declaration' of being nothing but a repetition of what it pretends to oppose, that it uses a violent tone and threats of violence to overthrow what it calls an oppressive system.

Guobin Yang has a point when he claims that the social uses of the Internet in China have fostered public discussion – for better or worse, the appearance of 'The Declaration' and the responses to it are examples showing the active and dynamic side of Chinese cyberspace. However, to use a Habermasian perspective and equate such public discussions as a 'public domain' against state control (Yang, 2003a), constitutes merely the projection onto China of the same 'civil society' the West has developed, which is what Metzger tried to caution us against in his work. The arguments in the statements quoted above, i.e. the accusation against 'The Declaration' of not being constructive, the query of its provocative and uncompromising nature, the claim of its insensitivity to the stages of China's national development, should be understood in the context of Chinese culture – as discussed earlier – as a striving for harmony, and as a belief in the importance of achieving a rational social equilibrium – even at the price of sacrificing self-interest for the public good. If we assume that these are genuine expressions of the views of Chinese netizens, we can argue that these statements give legitimacy to China's rulers, who can expect to be held responsible for the maintenance of a 'good society'. The 'checks and balances' of the West, which provide a bottom-up protection for the people against state manipulation, are not to be found in the paragraphs quoted above. The dislike expressed for an over-emphasis on such concepts as 'democracy' or 'freedom' then becomes understandable, as the overall emphasis is on sustaining social integration and community well-being. Democracy and freedom are rejected in their narrowly defined individual focus, while the core concern is how to raise the moral level of Chinese society. In this setting, the 'Green Dam', as a programme of social engineering, is merely another attempt to 'rule by morality' – this in a cyber package.

If the creation of moral individuals and a harmonious society are understood as traditional Chinese endeavours, then, to pursue these goals, state officials have the responsibility to lead and guide society from above, and this guidance is expected by the ruled. This cultural orientation has to be taken into account when assessing events in the Chinese context, including Chinese cyberspace. The cultural threads discussed in the previous section are reproduced and reassembled in different online dialogues. It is immaterial to argue – as 'The Declaration' does – that comments against freedom and democracy are 'created' public opinion by commentators paid for by the Chinese government. One could just as well argue that 'The Declaration' is nothing but an American or Western plot to stir up cyber discontent, or even to cause social unrest. We cannot judge what we cannot see, but what we can see, we can interpret. Within these limits, and only within them, we can conclude that the cases of the 'Green Dam' and 'The Declaration' demonstrate how the normative force of Chinese culture applies even in cyberspace.

## Concluding remarks

The Internet is never just a technological product – it always has a socio-cultural dimension. While the activist side of cyber China has to be acknowledged, the existence of a public online communication platform does not necessarily imply the creation of a democratic atmosphere, nor should the presence of online activism, for example, the publication of the Charter 08, be balanced against nationalistic Internet vigilantism at other times. In particular, in the case of China, our framework for the study of ICTs should not only depict the relation between a social self and a communication technology, but also capture the relationship *between* social actors *through* communication tools. As social actors, Chinese ICT users are embedded in a particular socio-political environment and cultural tradition. While the use of ICTs affects the manifested level of their lives, at a deeper level, the social actors have a role to play in the construction and changing of meanings. This might be an aspect that even an authoritarian government cannot take full control of.

## Note

The research for this chapter has been supported by research funding from the Department of Applied Social Sciences, The Hong Kong Polytechnic University, under the project name 'Cyber China on the move: A socio-cultural capture' [A-PH-72].

## References

Agence France Presse. (2010, May 1). China's online population passes 400 million: State media. *Google News*. Retrieved July 10, 2010, from http://www.google.com/hostednews/afp/article/ALeqM5jXip8Th7BJWL6PE9cdKbvw9bPNaQ
Ai, W. (2010, February 10). Google gives us hope. *Wall Street Journal*. Retrieved July 10, 2010, from http://online.wsj.com/article/SB10001424052748703630404575054331237346618.html?mod=WSJ_latestheadlines
Asian Weekly. (2009, July 2). Niming wangmin xuanyan xiang wangluo shencha xuanzhan: Zhongguo dangju rangbu zanhuan tuixing Luba. *Boxun News Web*. Retrieved July 12, 2010, from http://www.peacehall.com/news/gb/china/2009/07/200907022120.shtml
Bakken, B. (2000a). *The exemplary society: Human improvement, social control and the dangers of modernity in China*. Oxford: Oxford University Press.
Bakken, B. (2000b). Principled and unprincipled democracy: The Chinese approach to evaluation and election. In H. Antlov & T. W. Ngo (Eds.), *The cultural construction of politics in Asia* (pp. 107–130). Richmond, Surrey: Curzon Press.
Buchstein, H. (1997). Bytes that bite: The Internet and deliberative democracy. *Constellations, 4*(2), 248–263.

Chan, J. M., & Qiu, J. (2002). China: Media liberalization under authoritarianism. In M. E. Price, B. Rozumilowicz, & S. G. Verhulst (Eds.), *Media reform: Democratizing the media, democratizing the state* (pp. 27–46). London and New York: Routledge.

Chase, M., & Mulvenon, J. (2002). You've got dissent! Chinese dissident use of the Internet and Beijing's counter-strategies. Santa Monica, CA: RAND.

Chu, R. W. C. (forthcoming). Riding the double juggernaut: Depicting the Chinese mobile communication context. In R. W. C. Chu, L. Fortunati, & S. Yang (Eds.), *Mobile communication and Greater China.*

CNNIC. (2009, July 28). CNNIC publishes 24th Statistical Report on Internet Development in China. *CNNIC.* Retrieved July 10, 2010, from http://www.cnnic.net.cn/html/Dir/2009/07/28/5644.htm

Damm, J. (2009). The Internet and the fragmentation of Chinese society. In R. Murphy & V. L. Fong (Eds.), *Media, identity, and struggle in 21st century China* (pp. 83–95). London: Routledge.

Dittmer, L., & Liu, G. (2006). *China's deep reform: Domestic politics in transition.* Lanham, MD: Rowman & Littlefield.

Efrati, A., & Batson, A. (2010, June 29). Google tries new China approach. *Wall Street Journal.* Retrieved July 10, 2010, from http://online.wsj.com/article/SB100014240527 4870410390457533613325402 6128.html

Fang, Y. (2009, June 30). China postpones mandatory installation of controversial filtering software. *Xinhua News Agency.* Retrieved July 10, 2010, from http://news.xinhuanet.com/english/2009–06/30/content_11628335.htm

Fauna. (2009, June 11). Chinese netizen reactions to 'Green Dam Youth Escort'. *Chinasmack.* Retrieved July 10, 2010, from http://www.chinasmack.com/2009/stories/chinese-netizen-reactions-to-green-dam-youth-escort.html

Fei, X. (1992). *From the soil: The foundations of Chinese society.* Berkeley and Los Angeles: University of California Press.

Fenghua de lian. (2009). Guanyu niming wangmin xuanyan yiji Luba. *Zouguo de lu.* Retrieved July 12, 2010, from http://user.qzone.qq.com/260047729/blog/1246158371

Froomkin, A. M. (2003). Habermas@ discourse.net: Toward a critical theory of cyber-space. *Harvard Law Review, 116,* 749–873.

Garten, F. (2010, January 25). Chipping away. *South China Morning Post,* p. A15,

Godwin, M. (2003). Cyber rights: Defending free speech in the digital age. Cambridge, MA: MIT Press.

Han, Q. (2009, June 25). Tongyi ge shijie, tongyi ge yishixingtai. *Wuwu zhi zhen.* Retrieved July 12, 2010, from http://blog.hanqian.net/2009/06/blog-post_24.html

Harwit, E., & Clark, D. (2001). Shaping the Internet in China. Evolution of political control over network infrastructure and content. *Asian Survey, 41*(3), 377–408.

He, Z. (1997). A history of telecommunication in China: Development and policy implications. In P. S. N. Lee (Ed.), *Telecommunications and development in China* (pp. 55–88). Cresskill, NJ: Hampton Press.

Hsu, F. L. K. (1981). *Americans and Chinese: Passage to differences* (3rd ed.). Honolulu: University of Hawaii Press.

King, A. Y. C. (1985). The individual and group in Confucianism: A relational perspective. In D. Munro (Ed.), *Individualism and holism: Studies in Confucian and Taoist values* (pp. 57–70). Ann Arbor, MI: Center for Chinese Studies, University of Michigan.

Kirchner, R., & Li, Y. (2009, July 1). Luba bei tuichi shi gongmin shehui duikang zhengfu de shengli? *Deutsche Welle.* Retrieved July 12, 2010, from http://www.dw-world.de/dw/article/0,,4447683,00.html

Law, P.-L., & Chu, R. W. C. (2008). ICTs and China: An introduction. *Knowledge, Technology and Policy, 21*(1), 3–7.

Li, D. (2009, July 17). China's civil society: Breaching the Green Dam. *Open Democracy*. Retrieved July 10, 2010, from http://www.opendemocracy.net/article/china-s-civil-society-breaching-the-green-dam

Liang, S. (1987). *Zhongguo wenhua yaoyi*. Hong Kong: Sanlian.

MacKinnon, R. (2009, June 18). The Green Dam phenomenon. *Wall Street Journal*. Retrieved July 10, 2010, from http://online.wsj.com/article/SB124525992051023961.html

Metzger, T. A. (1994). Modern Chinese Utopianism and the Western concept of civil society. *Asian Perspectives, 18*(1), 1–6.

Metzger, T. A. (1998). *The Western concept of a civil society in the context of Chinese history*. Stanford, CA: Hoover Institution on War, Revolution and Peace.

Miao, Z. (2009, June 28). Teshu de 7–1: Guangfang shang Luba, wangmin yao fanqiang. *Deutsche Welle*. Retrieved July 9, 2010, from http://www.dw-world.de/dw/article/0,,4438800,00.html

New Tang Dynasty Television. (2010, January 8). Mei ruanjian gongsi zhengshi konggao Luba qinquan. *NTDTV*. Retrieved July 12, 2010, from http://ntdtv.com/xtr/b5/2010/01/08/a385993.html

OGRM BBS. (2009). 2009 niming wangmin xuanyan. *OGRM*. Retrieved July 12, 2010, from http://ogrm.net/bbs/showtopic-3924.aspx

Tan, K. (2009, June 24). Declaration of the Anonymous Netizens 2009. *Shanghaiist*. Retrieved July 10, 2010, from http://shanghaiist.com/2009/06/24/declaration_of_the_anonymous_netize.php

Wu, X. (2007). Chinese cybernationalism: Evolution, characteristics, and implications. Lanham, MD: Lexington Books.

Yan, X., & Pitt, D. (2002). *Chinese communications policy*. Boston and London: Artech House.

Yang, G. (2003a). The Internet and civil society in China: A preliminary assessment. *Journal of Contemporary China, 12*(36), 453–475.

Yang, G. (2003b). The co-evolution of the Internet and civil society in China. *Asian Survey, 43*(3), 405–422.

Yang, G. (2009a, July 1). 'Green Dam' as a case of online activism in China. *Columbia University Press blog*. Retrieved July 10, 2010, from http://www.cupblog.org/?p=663

Yang, G. (2009b). *The power of the Internet in China: Citizen activism online*. New York: Columbia University Press.

Yu, L., & Graham-Harrison, E. (2009, June 22). Yishujia Ai Weiwei huyu ba wang yi tian kangyi Luba. *Reuters China*. Retrieved July 12, 2010, from http://cn.reuters.com/article/wtNews/idCNChina-4811320090622

Yu, L., & Tng, T. H. (2003). Culture and design for mobile phones for China. In J. E. Katz (Ed.), *Machines that become us: The social context of personal communication technology* (pp. 187–200). New Brunswick: Transaction Publishers.

Yu, Y. S. (1984). Cong jiazhi xitong kan Zhongguo wenhua de xiandaiyiyi: Zhongguo wenhua yi xiandai shenghuo zonglun. Taibei: China Times Publication Company.

Zhao, Y. (2007). After mobile phones, what? Re-embedding the social in China's digital revolution. *International Journal of Communication, 1*(1), 92–120.

Zhao, Z. (2009). *Prisoner of the state: The secret journal of Chinese premier Zhao Ziyang*. London: Simon & Schuster.

Zheng, Y. (2008). *Technological empowerment: The Internet, state, and society in China*. Palo Alto, CA: Stanford University Press.

# 2 The Internet police in China

## Regulation, scope and myths

*Xiaoyan Chen and Peng Hwa Ang*

## Introduction

The Internet has grown phenomenally in China. In 1997, two years after its introduction in 1995, there were just over 600,000 Internet users, some 4,000 domain
names, 1,500 .cn websites, and the total bandwidth capacity of the Chinese Internet
was 25Mbps (CNNIC, 1997). At the end of December 2009, 12 years later, the
number of Internet users in China totalled 384 million, larger than the population
of the United States, where the Internet was invented. There were 16.82 million
domain names and 3.23 million websites registered under .cn, and the international connection bandwidth was 866 Gbps (CNNIC, 2010). Given China's size,
how it responds to the Internet will have an impact on the rest of the Internet
community.

The Internet poses a 'dual use problem' for the Chinese government. On the
one hand, the Internet is recognised as an essential tool in today's information
economy. On the other hand, the Chinese government worries that losing control
of the tool may not only harm the security and order of the Internet but may also
have spillover effects on the real world, perhaps even jeopardizing the legitimacy
of the Party or government to rule. To manage the potentially negative effects of
the Internet and harness the Internet to strengthen its rule, the Chinese government
has made great efforts to regulate the Internet.

Among the regulatory efforts of the Chinese government has been the formation of an Internet police force. This article investigates the creation of the Internet
police and its scope of work. The article concludes that the Chinese government
regards the Internet as an electronic public space in which a police force is needed
to keep order. Law and order are important to the Chinese psyche. While Internet
censorship, particularly of political expression, does exist, the Chinese government is also attempting to harness the Internet to bring popular grievances into
official channels. The Internet police and the regulatory mechanisms are therefore
intended to frame online content so that it is consistent with leadership goals and
thereby ensure that the Internet will not become a public space separate from the
Party-state.

**The formation of the Internet police**

The history of the Internet police can be traced back as far as the 1980s. In 1983, the Ministry of Public Security (MPS) took the initiative to set up the Computer Management and Supervision Bureau (CMSB) to oversee China's computer network security (International Centre for Human Rights and Democratic Development, 2001). In 1988, the MPS proposed in a national conference memo that such a bureau also needed to be established at provincial levels (Wu, 2009). However, at that time computer technology was just budding in China, used mostly for academic research, and computer and Internet security were not a serious concern. And so the proposal languished.

In 1993 the Chinese government began the Golden Bridge Project to build China's information highway (CNNIC, 2004). The project was timely because, a year later, in 1994, the Internet arrived in China (CNNIC, 2003). As might be expected in a centrally planned economy and society, Chinese officials almost immediately sprang into action to explore ways to regulate the new medium (Ang, 1997). In 1994, the State Council of China issued 'Regulations of the People's Republic of China for the Protection of the Safety of Computer Information Systems' (hereafter '1994 Regulations') and tasked the MPS with the security protection work of computer information systems in general, while the Ministry of State Security (MSS), the National Secrets Bureau (NSB) and other relevant ministries and commissions of the State Council, such as the Ministry of the Information Industry (MII), the Ministry of Culture (MC), etc. were tasked with aspects of security protection of computer information systems within their jurisdiction.

Article 17 of the 1994 Regulations states that the MPS is to supervise, examine and guide the security protection work of computer information systems and investigate and handle illegal and criminal acts endangering the safety of computer information systems. In 1995, the regular police force was empowered by the People's Police Law 'to supervise and administer the work of protecting the computer information system' (Standing Committee of the National People's Congress, 1995: Article 6(12)).

In 1998, 10 years after the proposal was first mooted, the Ministry of Public Security set up the Public Information and Internet Security Supervision Bureau (PIISS). This bureau was intended as a special police unit – the Internet police of China (Wu, 2009). The number of Internet police personnel may be calculated based on the fact that the bureau was to be established at provincial, prefecture and county levels. According to a senior Public Security Bureau officer in Sichuan, at the provincial level there should be 40 to 60 Internet police at each PIISSB; at the prefecture level there may perhaps be 30 to 40, while at the county level three to four (personal communication, December 20, 2004).

With 33 province-level divisions (including 22 provinces, five autonomous regions, four municipalities), 333 prefecture-level divisions (including 283 cities, 17 prefectures, 30 autonomous prefectures, and three leagues), and 2,862 county-level divisions (including 851 districts, 374 cities, 1,465 counties, 117 autonomous counties, 49 banners, three autonomous banners, two special regions and one forestry area) in mainland China, there should be between 20,000 and 26,750 Internet police. Keeping in mind that every location that the first author visited had a shortfall of the establishment strength, in all probability the number of Internet police is closer to 20,000. It should also be noted that this number includes janitorial staff.

## The legal basis for the Internet police

The first administrative regulation that was aimed at the Internet and that provided the legal basis for regulating its infrastructure was the 1996 'Provisional Regulations of the People's Republic of China on International Interconnection of Computer-based Information Networks' (State Council of China, 1996, hereafter '1996 Provisional Regulations') issued by the State Council, the central administrative body of the country. They were amended in 1997 (State Council of China, 1997a), and in 1998 implementation measures of the Provisional Regulations were issued (State Council of China, 1997a – Appendix). The 1996 Provisional Regulations divided China's Internet networks into two categories: interconnecting networks and access networks. Interconnecting networks are networks directly linked to the Internet through international leased circuits. Access networks are comparable to Internet Service Providers (ISPs) and are the only authorized means of access by individual users. An access network, in turn, accesses the Internet via an interconnection network directly controlled and administered by one of the following government agencies approved by the State Council: the Ministry of Information Industry (MII), the State Education Commission (SEC), or the Chinese Academy of Sciences (CAS). All interconnection networks must use international gateway channels provided by the MII to connect with the global network. While the Informatization Leading Group of the State Council is responsible for regulating, supervising, inspecting and resolving issues related to Internet connections (State Council of China, 1996: Article 5), the Public Security Bureau is authorized to punish violators with fines of up to RMB15, 000 (Article 14).

In 1997, the MPS clarified the mandate of the CMSB to include not only the protection of 'the public security of computer information networks and the Internet' but also 'the legal rights of Internet service providers and individuals, as well as the public interest' (Legislative Affairs Office of the State Council, 2001, Article 3, Measures for Security Protection of International Interconnection of Computer-based Information Networks).

## Scope of Internet police work

In general, Internet police work can be understood as supervision of the safety of the computer network and Internet systems, administrative regulation on Internet activities and detection of computer and Internet crimes (Zhang, 2008).

*Supervision of computer network and Internet systems*

For supervision, the Internet police is required to guarantee the security of the computer network and the security of the Internet systems, such as virus control, providing guidance for the security of computer information systems, training security personnel and supervising the research, production, sale and use of special products for the security of computer information systems.

In 1991, the MPS through its 'Measures of the Administration of Prohibiting Computer Virus' tasked the Public Security Bureau (PSB) at all levels with responsibility for investigating and prosecuting the intentional production and transmission of computer viruses or the circulation of false virus warnings. Administrative regulations since then have reiterated the PSB's virus-prevention role. Most websites of the Internet police have information on combating viruses.

In the 1994 regulation (State Council of China, 1994), the MPS is required to supervise, examine and guide the security protection work of computer information systems (Article 17). As the scope of computer information systems security is wide, the focus is on important areas related to state affairs, economic development, national defence and top science and technology. Institutions in these important areas, such as government offices, banks, transportation units and hospitals are recommended to use their own intranet and set up firewalls. They have to register their Internet connection with the PSB and report the safety measures taken.

The 1994 Regulation also required security products for computer systems to be licensed before entering the market (Article 16). In 1998, the MPS established a centre to test and evaluate security products. The Internet police's role is to supervise the sale and use of such products. For example, ISPs, ICPs and Internet cafés must install keyword-filtering and security programs designated by the relevant PSB.

In 2006, a new Law of the People's Republic of China on Public Security Administration Punishments was enacted that stipulates that the police can detain those who intrude into computer information systems and cause harm: deleting, revising, adding, disturbing the functions of computer information systems, and causing a malfunction of computer information systems; adding, deleting, or altering materials stored, processed or being transmitted through the networks; and intentionally producing or spreading destructive programs such as computer viruses and causing the malfunction of computer information systems.

*Administrative regulation of Internet activities*

The Public Security Administration Punishments empower the police to handle misbehaviour such as disturbing the social order, harming public security, violating citizens' individual rights or infringing upon public or private property (Article 2). The police's conventional role of maintaining social order and public security is extended to the Internet. This means that the myriad actors and activities on the Internet – ISPs, content providers, websites, blogs, BBS, Internet cafes, and individual Internet users – are all under the jurisdiction of the Internet police.

## Content regulation

The Chinese government has expressed concern about the Internet from the earliest days, as the new medium was seen to have the potential to undermine strict rules concerning the media. In the 1996 Provisional Regulations (State Council of China, 1996), Article 13 prohibits the disclosure of state secrets as well as the production, review and dissemination of pornography and information hindering public order, through international interconnection. The rules appeared to have been passed hurriedly. They did not specify any punishment in the event of breach, and the definition of what was to be considered 'information hindering public order' was ambiguous. The ambiguities were removed in the 1997 amendments (State Council of China, 1997). The new rules specified that no one (Internet service or content providers as well as individual Internet users) was allowed to produce, replicate, retrieve or disseminate nine types of content, and the police were empowered to punish violators.

The nine types of content include sedition, discrimination, defamation, pornography, and violence:

1   Information that incites resistance or disruption of the implementation of the constitution, laws and administrative regulations;
2   Information that incites the subversion of the state political power and the overthrow of the socialist system;
3   Information that incites the splitting up of the country and the sabotage of national unity;
4   Information that incites hatred and discrimination among ethnic groups or sabotages solidarity among ethnic groups;
5   Information that fabricates or distorts facts, spreads rumours and disrupts the social order;
6   Information that propagates feudal superstitions, obscenity, pornography, gambling, violence, murder and terror and instigates crimes;
7   Information that openly insults others or fabricates facts to slander others;
8   Information that damages the reputation and credibility of state organs; and
9   Other information that violates the constitution, laws and administrative regulations.
        (Legislative Affairs Office of the State Council, 2001: III-04-06-202, 2)

Subsequent regulations passed since 2000 and dealing with Internet content generally reiterated these nine types of prohibited content, e.g. the Administrative Measures on Internet Information Services (State Council of China, 2000), Article 15; the State Secrecy Regulations for Computer Information Systems on the Internet (State Secrecy Bureau, 2000), Article 9; the Measures for Managing Internet Information Services (State Council of China, 2000a), Article 13; the Administrative Measures on Internet Information Services (State Council of China, 2000), Article 12. These later regulations are virtually word for word the same as the earlier ones, except for one change. In the post-2000 regulations, 'damages the reputation and credibility of State organs' (no. 8 above) was deleted and the prohibition of cults and superstitions was emphasized in a separate clause. Enforcement of the regulations was handled by the PSB. Since 2000 the nine forbidden types of content have been:

1 Content that is against the basic principles determined by the constitution;
2 Content that impairs national security, divulges state secrets, subverts state sovereignty or jeopardizes national unity;
3 Content that damages the reputation and interests of the state;
4 Content that incites ethnic hostility and ethnic discrimination or jeopardizes unity among ethnic groups;
5 Content that damages state religious policies or that advocates sects or feudal superstitions;
6 Content that disseminates rumours, disturbs the social order or damages social stability;
7 Content that disseminates obscenity, pornography, gambling, violence, homicide and terror, or incites crime;
8 Content that insults or slanders others or that infringes their legal rights and interests; and
9 Other content prohibited by laws or administrative regulations.

(State Council of China, 2000)

On 25 December 2001, the revised Regulations on Publication Administration, which came into force 1 February 2002, added 'endangering social morality or outstanding national cultural tradition' (Article 26) to the list of prohibited types of content. In 2005, the State Council Information Office and MII promulgated the Provisions on Administration of Internet News Information Service, which added 'carrying out activities in the name of any illegal civil organization' as the 11th type of prohibited content.

### Internet café regulation

China's first Internet café (or *wangba*, literally 'Internet bar'), Shihuakai Internet Café, was opened by the Shihuakai Corporation on 15 November 1996, next to the capital gymnasium in Beijing (CNNIC, 2004). They spread so quickly all over China that, two years later, in 1998, the Chinese government, through the MPS, MII, the Ministry of Culture (MC), and the State Administration for Industry and Commerce (SAIC), attempted to regulate these 'wangba' by jointly passing the 'Notice on the operation of net bars and on strengthening operations security' (hereafter the 1998 Notice). In addition to the requirement to ensure computer and technician compliance, and the general adherence to all relevant laws and administrative regulations, Article 1 of the 1998 Notice listed three security requirements: safe business sites and corresponding safety protection compliance, comprehensive management system for security, and full-time or part-time personnel for security management. Articles 3 and 5 of the notice tasked the PSB with enforcement of these security requirements.

In 2001, the law was refined through the Measures on the Administration of Business Sites of Internet Access Services (Ministry of Information Industry,

2001 – hereafter 2001 Measures), which reiterated the PSB's responsibility for 'security inspection' and clarified the ambiguity of 'security' in the 1998 Notice to include environmental, technical and information security. In February 2001 the MPS authorized the first filtering software, 'Internet police 110', aimed at filtering out content related to the Falun Gong, a religious sect banned in China, pornography and violent and anti-government content (Beijing Daily, 2001). A special version was soon widely adopted by the PSB to regulate Internet cafés. Instead of the ambiguous 1998 provision that 'Internet bar proprietors must take the responsibility to inspect, report and stop the transmission or viewing of illegal information', Internet café proprietors were not only explicitly prohibited from making use of their business sites to produce, replicate, review, publish and transmit such forbidden content, they were also tasked with stopping their patrons' violations. The PSB could punish the proprietors for inaction or ineffective supervision and administration of their patrons' behaviour.

Internet café regulations were tightened in the wake of a fire in 2002. On 16 June a fire broke out at an unlicensed Internet café in Beijing, killing 25 people and injuring 12 others. Most were teenagers from nearby universities and middle schools, surfing the Web or playing games (China Daily 2002, June 17). The fire brought the poor security condition of Internet cafés to public attention and also raised questions about the efficacy of Internet café regulations.

Three months after the fire, the State Council promulgated the 'Regulations on the Administration of Business Sites Providing Internet Services' (State Council, 2002 – hereafter 2002 Regulations), which was promulgated on 29 September 2002, and came into force on 15 November 2002, while the earlier 'Measures for the management of business sites of Internet accessing services' released by MC, MPS, MII and SATC in 2001, were repealed on the same day. This empowered the MC to oversee Internet cafés, while the jurisdiction of the MPS to oversee security issues, especially issues concerning minors and fire prevention, remained in place.

According to the 2002 Regulations, Internet cafés are prohibited from operating within 200 metres of middle and primary schools, and a 'No Minors' sign has to be displayed at the entrance. Internet cafés must be closed between midnight and 8am, smoking and open fire for lighting are not allowed, a 'No Smoking' sign has to be hung on the wall, inflammable or explosive articles are not allowed within the café and doors and windows must not be dead-bolted. This last measure was to prevent what happened at the unlicensed Internet café: it had no fire exits, the door was locked and the windows were secured with iron grilles. MC and cultural administrative departments above county levels are authorized to enforce the provision, but the PSB may issue a warning, impose a fine or close the Internet café temporarily in the event of a breach, while in serious cases the licence may be revoked.

### Detection of computer and Internet crimes

Computer and Internet crimes may be divided into two broad categories: crimes committed against the computer and Internet systems, and conventional crimes using the computer and the Internet. China updated its laws in 1997, soon after the Internet became publicly available. In the 1997 Criminal Law, three articles – 285,

286 and 287 – address computer-related crimes; violators can be sentenced to five years' imprisonment. Article 285 forbids the intrusion into computer information systems of state, national defence, and top scientific and technological institutions. Article 286 forbids deleting, revising, adding to and disturbing the functions of computer information systems, and causing malfunctions of computer information systems. As many computer or Internet-related crimes are extensions of offline crimes, Article 287 makes it an offence to use a computer for financial fraud, theft, corruption, and misappropriation of public funds, stealing state secrets or other crimes.

The 2000 'Decision of the Standing Committee of the National People's Congress on Maintaining Internet Security' further specified the following as criminal offences subject to state prosecution:

A   Invading computer information systems containing information about state affairs, state defense and the most advanced science and technology of the state;
B   Deliberately producing and spreading computer viruses and establishing destructive programs to attack computer systems or communication networks, thus causing damage to such systems or networks;
C   Violating relevant state laws, arbitrarily stopping the operation of computer networks or communication services, thereby interrupting normal operations of such networks or services.

(Standing Committee of the National People's Congress, 2000)

As for offline offences using the computer or the Internet, the 'Decision of the Standing Committee of the National People's Congress on Maintaining Internet Security' gave a long list of possible criminal activities committed using the Internet and said that penalties for such crimes were analogous to those in the respective provisions of criminal law. That is, the offline laws applied to crime committed using the Internet as a means of commission.

For all these computer- or Internet-related crimes, the Internet police were required to investigate the cases first or to provide coordination (usually technical support) in investigating these offences, and then coordinate with or instruct other police to act (Zhang, 2008). For example, on 6 May 2008, the Water Resources Department of Jiangsu Province found its website hacked and reported this to the Internet police in Nanjing. The Internet police immediately coordinated with other regular police and investigated the case. They found out that two young men had hired many hackers to create and plant Trojan worms into websites to steal virtual property such as QQ money, and facilities for online games. The website of the Water Resources Department was only one of their victims (Meng, 2009).

## Mechanisms used by the Internet police

With almost 300 million Internet users in 2009 and a veritable ocean of information, it is a monumental task for the PSB to police the Internet. Most of the time therefore, the Internet police depend on blocking and filtering mechanisms to do their job; they also delegate some responsibilities to ISPs. Besides these measures, reporting webpages, hotlines and sweeps are also widely used by the Internet police.

At the national level, blocking takes place on the routers of the interconnecting networks. The 1996 Provisional Regulations require that Internet access be through points and networks controlled, however loosely, by the government. All established interconnecting networks are directly controlled and administered by MII, the SEC and the CAS. The establishment of new interconnection networks must be approved by the State Council. Each level of users (be they wholesalers or individuals) is responsible for preventing its own units and patrons from committing illegal acts. Therefore, from individual users to ISPs, self-policing, including self-discipline and self-censorship, is expected.

At the institutional level, according to the 33rd Directive of the MPS, 'connecting network units, entry units and corporations that use computer information networks and the Internet' must do the following:

1    Assume responsibility for network security, protection and management and establish a thoroughly secure, protected and well managed network.
2    Carry out technical measures for network security and protection. Ensure network operational security and information security.
3    Assume responsibility for the security education and training of network users.
4    Register units and individuals to whom information is provided. Provide information according to the stipulations of Article 5.
5    Establish a system for registering the users of electronic bulletin board systems on the computer information network as well as a system for managing bulletin board information.
6    If a violation of Articles 4, 5, 6 or 7 is discovered, then an unaltered record of the violation should be kept and reported to the local Public Security organization.
7    According to the relevant state regulations, remove from the network an address, directory or server which has content in violation of Article 5.

(State Council of China, 1997)

As a result of these fine-grained regulations, ISPs and ICPs have to install blocking and filtering software and hire staff to monitor information they or their users provide.

From the MPS to local levels, hotlines and reporting websites have been established to encourage reports of forbidden information as well as illegal activities. For example, the MPS's webpage for reporting illegal content (http://www.cyber-police.cn/alarm/pre_alarm.jsp) lists the following categories: conducting evil-cult activities and inciting national security; spreading rumours, insults and making up stories to disturb the public order; transmitting pornography and sexually explicit information, organizing pornographic shows via the Internet; gambling, fraud, and blackmailing; infringing on other people's freedom and privacy of correspondence; intruding and hacking; unauthorized deleting, altering and adding of data on other people's computers; other illegal activities and crimes related to the Internet.

To give the law a friendlier face, the Internet police in Shenzhen (Guangdong province, near Hong Kong) created two icons, 'Jingjing' and 'Chacha', in January 2006. (The word '*jing cha*' means police in Chinese.) The icons were posted on websites in Shenzhen (China Youth Daily, 2006). Clicking the 'Jingjing' or 'Chacha' characters would take the user to the Shenzhen Internet police's webpage, where a form was available to report online gambling, pornography and obscene content, online fraud and theft, and other Internet-related illegal activities. The Shenzhen Internet police were also available to answer queries about relevant internet laws and regulations. Reportedly, there was a decline in the amount of 'unlawful and harmful' information on Shenzhen websites. Not surprisingly, six months later the MPS took the Shenzhen pilot test to eight cities – Chongqing, Hangzhou, Ningbo, Qingdao, Xiamen, Guangzhou, Wuhan and Chengdu. The aims were to make more transparent the Internet police's work and to solicit cooperation from the public, thereby increasing the 'satisfaction' of users. The presence of the virtual police appeared to have worked in Qingdao: public awareness of the virtual police network rose from 12.6% to 83.7% in the 12 months ending mid-2006 and the satisfaction of users rose from 87.8% to 96.5% over the same period. With the reported success in the eight cities, the virtual police, allowing online reporting of illegal Internet activities and harmful content, went national from June 2007 (Hu, 2007).

As might be expected, the number of complaints about online offences increased with the availability of reporting. In Beijing, the virtual police were introduced in September 2007. After four months they had received 10,893 reports, including 400 pornographic cases, 4,647 fraud cases, 23 cases of gambling, and 221 virus attacks. The numbers reflected a fourfold increase over those during the same period before the 'virtual police' was created (Wu & Wen, 2008).

The Internet police also conduct regular sweeps or 'specialized rectification' to handle certain issues. Usually these kinds of sweeps occur at special occasions, such as before the Chinese New Year, National Day, or when some illegal activities or harmful content become a serious issue. For example, because a lot of people take trains to return home for family reunions for the Chinese New Year, ticket scalpers buy up the tickets months before the holiday. Before the 2009 Chinese New Year, many ticket scalpers went online to sell the tickets. Internet police in Guangdong, together with those in Hunan and Hainan, patrolled the Internet every day to prevent ticket scalping. With their help, during the 2009 Chinese New Year Guangzhou railway police detected 48 Internet scalping cases, arrested 63 suspects and confiscated 1,967 tickets worth of 190,000 Yuan (US$28,000) (Xiao, 2009). In August 2009, MPS and seven other government departments cooperated to conduct a three months' sweep against Internet porn in China. At the end of the sweep they made 1,179 arrests and closed 6,972 porn websites and posts (Xinhua Wang, 2009).

## Conclusion

China's reputation for regulation and control has tended to precede it, and here a similar pattern recurs. This article has attempted to demonstrate that there are some valid reasons for the creation of the Internet police in China. With the diffusion of the Internet, cyber crime has increased rapidly in China. Activities on the Internet are not confined to the virtual world but also affect the real world (Ang, 2005). Many, but not all, illegal activities that are committed online or via the Internet are reflections or extensions of offline illegal activities.

In 1999, the PSB all over China handled an estimated 400 computer-related crimes. The figure jumped to 2,700 in 2000 and nearly doubled to 4,500 cases in 2001. Among these cases, 90% were Internet related (Wong & Wong 2005: 62). The most recent statistics indicated more than 20,000 reported cyber crime cases in 2005, a compounded annual growth rate of more than 45% from 2001; officials estimated that unreported cases would be likely to have crossed the one million mark in 2005 (Guo, 2006). In this context, the Internet police, with computer and legal knowledge to counter online crimes, have been welcome. For example, Internet police in Beijing are required to have knowledge of information technology, detection and law. In their daily work they have used their specialities to detect crimes and trace criminals (Wu & Wen, 2008).

The Internet police's role in regulating Internet cafés is also understandable from a perspective of welfare and safety concern, especially after the fire in Beijing: more than 20% of middle school and primary school students access the Internet at cafés (Beijing Youth Daily, 2002; CERNIC, 2002) because families and schools cannot afford Internet access. According to the Ministry of Education, there are more than 200 million middle and primary school students in China, but fewer than 1.6 million computers in schools. The Chinese government's concern over Internet cafés and the measures to regulate Internet cafés are not exceptional. In the US, Los Angeles and Orange County have taken similar actions for the sake of minors, such as school-time curfews, camera surveillance and identity card checking (Leyden, 2004; McKee, 2004).

Of concern to the Internet community is the definition of what constitute offences or crimes. The Council of Europe's Convention on Cybercrime has set the *de facto* standard for what constitutes cyber crime, but at the time of writing this paper in early 2010, China is still not among the non-European countries intending to ratify the Convention (Council of Europe, 2010). The ratification of the CoE's Convention on Cybercrime by China would blunt much of the criticism that the Chinese Internet police was set up to curtail free speech rather than online crime. That is, for the most part at this stage, a myth that should be shattered.

## References

Ang, P. H. (1997). How countries are regulating Internet content. *Internet Society*. Retrieved August 7, 2010, from http://www.isoc.org/inet97/proceedings/B1/B1_3.HTM

Ang, P. H. (2005). *Ordering chaos: Regulating the Internet*. Thomson: Singapore.

Beijing Daily. (2001, February 26). 'Wangluo jingcha 110' ruanjian jin faxing. *Zhonghua Wang*. Retrieved July 14, 2010, from http://tech.china.com/zh_cn/news/product/891/20010226/126456.html

Beijing Youth Daily. (2002, July 3). Wu chengshi genzong diaocha baogao: Qingshaonian zhengzai chu wang. *Renmin Wang*. Retrieved July 14, 2010, from http://www.people.com.cn/GB/kejiao/41/20020703/766727.html

CERNIC. (2002, March 12). Quan guo putong zhong- xiaoxue xuexiao jiben qingkuang. *Chinese Education and Research Network*. Retrieved July 14, 2010, from http://www. edu.cn/20020312/3022424.shtml

China Daily. (2002, June 17). 24 Die in Beijing Internet cafe fire. *China.org.cn*. Retrieved July 14, 2010, from http://www.china.org.cn/english/2002/Jun/34723.htm

China Youth Daily. (2006, January 4). 'Jingjing' he 'Chacha'; Shenzhen shou she xuni jingcha weihu Wangluo zhixu. *Renmin Wang*. Retrieved July 14, 2010, from http:// politics.people.com.cn/GB/14562/3995632.html

CNNIC. (1997). *The First Statistical Survey Report on the Internet Development in China*. Beijing: CNNIC.

CNNIC. (2003, December 12). The Internet Timeline of China 1997~2000. *China Internet Network Information Center*. Retrieved July 14, 2010, from http://www.cnnic.net.cn/ html/Dir/2003/12/12/2001.htm

CNNIC. (2004, June 24). The Internet Timeline of China 1986~1996. *China Internet Network Information Center*. Retrieved July 14, 2010, from http://www.cnnic.cn/html/ Dir/2003/12/12/2000.htm

CNNIC. (2010). China Internet Network Information Center. *China Internet Network Information Center*. Retrieved July 14, 2010, from http://www.cnnic.net.cn/en/ index/0O/index.htm

Council of Europe. (2010, July 14). Convention on Cybercrime – CETS No.: 185. *Council of Europe – Documents*. Retrieved July 14, 2010, from http://conventions.coe.int/treaty/ Commun/ChercheSig.asp?NT=185&CM=8&DF=&CL=ENG

Guo, G. (2006, April 5). Gonganbu guanyuan xiangjie Wangluo fanzui. *Sina News*. Retrieved July 14, 2010, from http://news.sina.com.cn/c/2006–04–05/16119539870.shtml

Hu, M. (2007, April 28). 'Xuni jingcha' shanggang ji. *Renmin Wang*. Retrieved July 14, 2010, from http://npc.people.com.cn/GB/28320/41246/41339/5678749.html

International Centre for Human Rights and Democratic Development. (2001). *Review of China's Internet Regulations and Domestic Legislation*. Retrieved August 8, 2010, from http://www.dd-rd.ca/site/publications/index.php?page=12&subsection=catalogue

Legislative Affairs Office of the State Council. (2001). *Laws and Regulations of the People's Republic of China*. Beijing: China Legal Publishing House.

Leyden, J. (2004, July 8). LA plans cybercafe teen curfew. *The Register*. Retrieved July 14, 2010, from http://www.theregister.co.uk/2004/07/08/la_cybercafe_curfew/

McKee, M. (2004, February 2). Internet cafe ordinance sparks war of words. *Law.com*. Retrieved July 14, 2010, from http://www.law.com/jsp/article.jsp?id=1075219841269.

Meng, Y. (2009, September 1). Heike zhishou 'da xiaojie' kuang dao xuni caichan shang qianwan. *Fazhi Kuai Bao*. Retrieved July 14, 2010, from http://www.fzkb.cn/ news/20090901/fz8b/101532.htm

Ministry of Information Industry (MII). (2001). Measures on the Administration of Business Sites of Internet Access Services. *Ministry of Culture of the People's Republic of China*. Retrieved November 15, 2010, from http://www.ccnt.gov.cn/English/laws/ Regulations/200808/t20080806_62332.html

Standing Committee of the National People's Congress. (1995). People's Police Law of the People's Republic of China. *Law Info China*. Retrieved August 7, 2010, from http:// www.lawinfochina.com/law/display.asp?id=123

Standing Committee of the National People's Congress. (2000). The Decision of the Standing Committee of the National People's Congress on Maintaining Internet Security. *Canada–China Procuratorate Reform Cooperation Project*. Retrieved August 7, 2010, from http://www.icclr.law.ubc.ca/china_ccprcp/reports/index.html

State Council of China. (1994). Regulations of the People's Republic of China for Safety Protection of Computer Information Systems. *Laws of the People's Republic of China*. Retrieved November 15, 2010, from http://www.asianlii.org/cn/legis/cen/laws/rfspocis719/

State Council of China. (1996). Provisional Regulations of the People's Republic of China on the Management of International Networking of Computer Information Networks. *English Law Texts*. Retrieved August 7, 2010, from http://www.86148.com/englishlaw/shownews.asp?id=1092

State Council of China. (1997). Computer Information Network and Internet Security, Protection and Management Regulations. *Cryptome*. Retrieved August 7, 2010, from http://cryptome.quintessenz.at/mirror/cn/cn-netreg.htm

State Council of China. (1997a). Decision of the State Council Regarding the Revision of the Interim Provisions Governing the Management of the Computer Information Networks in the People's Republic of China Connecting to the International Network. *Laws of the People's Republic of China*. Retrieved November 15, 2010, from http://www.asianlii.org/cn/legis/cen/laws/dotscrtrotipgtmotcinitproccttin1993/

State Council of China. (2000). Administrative Measures on Internet Information Services. *China IT Law*. Retrieved August 7, 2010, from http://www.chinaitlaw.org/?p1=print&p2=050306173518

State Council of China. (2000a). Measures for Managing Internet Information Services. *Laws of the People's Republic of China*. Retrieved November 15, 2010, from http://www.asianlii.org/cn/legis/cen/laws/mfmiis499/

State Secrecy Bureau. (2000). State Secrecy Protection Regulations for Computer Information Systems on the Internet. *Laws of the People's Republic of China*. Retrieved November 15, 2010, from http://www.asianlii.org/cn/legis/cen/laws/ssprfcisoti915/

State Council of China. (2002). Regulations on the Administration of Business Sites Providing Internet Services. *ISINOLAW*. Retrieved November 15, 2010, from http://hk.isinolaw.com/gate/big5/www.isinolaw.com/isinolaw/english/detail.jsp?iscatalog=0&statutes_id=2003485&skind=110

Wong, K. C., & Wong, G. (2005). Cyberspace governance and Internet regulation in China. In R. Broadhurst & P. Grabovsky (Eds.), *Cyber-crime: The challenge of Asia* (pp. 57–79). Hong Kong: Hong Kong University Press.

Wu, D. (2009). Strengthening the construction of Internet police in China. *Journal of Chinese People's Public Security University, 1*, 41–44.

Wu, L., & Wen, J. (2008). Disclose the mysterious veil of Internet police. *Outlook Weekly*, 6–7, 28–29.

Xiao, Y. (2009). Internet police all out to sweep online scalpers. *China Internet, 3*, 86–87.

Xinhua Wang. (2009, November 14). Gonganbu bushu daji zhengzhi yinhui seqing shouji wangzhan zhuanxiang xingdong. *Xinhua Wang*. Retrieved July 14, 2010, from http://news.xinhuanet.com/legal/2009–11/24/content_12533328.htm

Zhang, Y. (2008). Internet police's power: Centering on protecting citizens' legal rights. *Legal System and Society, 10*, 10–13.

# 3 Grassroots agency in a civil sphere?

## Rethinking Internet control in China

*Peter Marolt*

## Introduction

Ever since China's Internet was first opened to the general public in 1997, the relationship between Chinese authorities and cyberspace has developed in a complex and oftentimes puzzling fashion, vacillating between periods of intense control and times of more permissive tolerance. Western (and in particular Anglo-American) scholarship, however, has only slowly come to appreciate the complexities and idiosyncrasies of the Chinese Internet. From the 1990s onwards, scholarly publications tended to connote the belief (or hope) that the introduction of the Internet would bring about a democratic shift in the Chinese system of governance, and academic research was often conceptualized and interpreted in terms of this desired change. In recent years, though, the emphasis has switched to the other side of the technologically deterministic pendulum, with analyses reflecting the Chinese party-state's increasingly successful efforts in both curbing and exploiting the growing power of the Internet.

Faster than academics could analyse online discourses and the party-state's reactions to these discourses, Chinese Internet use and control adapted to changing circumstances and diversified, employing ever new network technologies. Western research on the Internet in China focused primarily on questions of censorship, the blocking of websites, the use of the Internet by dissident groups, and its democratizing effects on Chinese society (Damm, 2006; MacKinnon, 2007; Kluver, 2008). At the same time, the Chinese party-state continued to adopt and refine ever-changing mechanisms designed to affect both Chinese consciousnesses in general and online discourses and actions in particular. Only very recently have academic scholars accepted that the Internet per se will not be the cause of political change in China, but that change might materialize as the result of broader social, economic, and political processes (e.g. MacKinnon, 2007; Kluver, 2008; Zhou, 2005, 2006).

This chapter provides a synopsis of the dynamic and complex nature of Chinese Internet control and the wide variety of strategies adopted by Chinese netizens to counter them, arguing that the widely used dichotomies of 'authoritarian/control versus democratic/ freedom', or 'virtual/online versus physical/ offline', have crowded out research into the many shapes of and possibilities for grassroots agency claiming liminal, performative spaces that are characteristic for China's Internet. The Chinese state and its censorship regime are an important context for the mapping of contested spaces within which state agents and other actors operate. Yet instead of attempting to map out and characterize these spaces, this chapter will suggest alternative approaches to a study of the Chinese Internet that would allow us to heed the grassroots agency visible in myriad narratives of creative power that have become ubiquitous on the Chinese-language Internet.

## State vs. netizens and the obsolescence of dichotomies

### *The dynamic and complex nature of Internet control in China*

In China, the media have long been the main tool for political control and ideological propaganda and education. After the arrival of the Internet in China, though, previously employed methods of control were fast becoming obsolete in the face of mostly young and increasingly vocal discontented urbanites that developed their own online strategies of resistance. In response, the Chinese party-state adapted its multi-scalar methods of control to meet the changing forms of dissent by urban citizens, and became both more creative and subtle in its endeavours to promote and preserve a so-called 'harmonious society' (*hexie shehui*). In the process, the free flow of credible and independent information and opinion available on the Internet was altered through *direct censorship, self-censorship*, and the *dynamic manipulation* of online discourse, resulting in a disquieting shift towards hegemonic forms of manipulation of Chinese minds.

Direct censorship strategies adopted by the Chinese regime range from the blocking of individual sites to general filtering techniques and physical incarceration. The party-state censors, deletes, or blocks politically outspoken websites, blog posts or comments publishing opinions that are not deemed appropriate. It also manages content availability by passing Internet traffic through the so-called 'Great Firewall', designed to deny access to international websites such as Wikipedia, BBC, or Technorati, or the blogs hosted by the blog provider Blogspot. Alternatively known as the 'Cyber Nanny', the 'Great Firewall' also blocks content containing a long list of keywords such as 'Tiananmen' or 'democracy' (*minzhuzhuyi*), content related to the new religious group Falun Gong, corruption among selected officials, Taiwan's and Tibet's independence movements, various human rights issues, or citizens' uprisings and demonstrations. From time to time the regime arrests individual Chinese citizens on charges of 'inciting subversion' for posting or disseminating articles critical of the Communist Party of China (CPC), etc. Suffice it to say that the censorship system has become so sophisticated that researchers, activists, and observers are concerned it may become a model for other countries looking to control the Internet use of their citizens (cf. Krim, 2005).

Thus far, direct forms of censorship have largely been restricted to websites or postings that either criticize China's party-state and its policies directly or advocate collective political action. This has resulted in many web commentators adapting their postings, following the popular saying 'Speaking truth the opposite way' (*zhenghua fanshuo*), using irony, humour, hyperbole, satire, implicit criticism through indirect expressions, or explicit but guarded criticism (cf. Esarey & Xiao, 2008). These forms of expression, although not undetectable by the censors, have thus far evaded extreme forms of censorship or repression, and for the time being netizens are mostly free to debate any issues that interest them as long as they do not step beyond the (deliberately) ambiguous line of what the party-state considers excessive criticism or a direct challenge of state power (see also Herold, 2008).

A far more insidious tool for control than direct censorship, though, is the Chinese regime's second weapon in the fight for public opinion online: the encouragement to self-censorship. Tasked with the enforcement of conformity through the promotion of 'harmony' in social interactions, the Information Office of China's State Council consistently emphasizes the importance of propaganda control, or what it refers to as 'grasping correct guidance' (*bawo zhengque daoxiang*). This euphemism for the encouragement to self-censorship is actively promoted among both Chinese individuals and organizations such as the Internet Content Providers (ICPs). The Internet Society of China, to mention just one example, presents Self-Discipline Awards to those Internet firms (including ICPs) that show '*excellence in self-censorship*' (Thompson, 2006, 23 April).

It is also no secret that the main function of the cuddly anime-style cartoon 'Internet Police' mascots 'Jingjing' and 'Chacha' ('Jingcha' meaning 'police') is to intimidate the visitors of websites displaying them on their pages. The *Beijing Youth Daily* explained that the function of the two 'mascots' is 'to publicly remind all Netizens to be conscious of safe and healthy use of the Internet, self-regulate their online behavior and maintain harmonious Internet order together' (quoted as in Thompson, 2006). The active endorsement, but lack of a clear definition of self-censorship is very effective in its impact on Chinese Internet users, as authorities retain 'maximum discretion to pursue almost anyone for almost any Internet-related activity' (Hachigian, 2003: 48) and, in doing so, create a climate of apprehension and self-censorship through vague prohibitions against content that 'causes spiritual pollution' (Deibert, 2002: 147), 'disturbs social order' (Hachigian, 2003: 48), or harms China's 'honor' (ibid.). The deliberately vague wording supports the individual Internet user's perception that one can never feel safe, as one never exactly knows where the authorities draw the line between the acceptable and the illegal. Although often imperceptible and not measurable by outside observers, the adoption of 'political mindreading' by individual netizens that self-censorship requires has to be classified as far more effective than overt or technical forms of censorship.

During the 20th century, China's citizens had to learn to anticipate and interpret sudden shifts in political orthodoxy, which were invariably followed by the persecution of all who did not adapt fast enough. In this context, self-censorship, or to use blogging pioneer Isaac Mao's term, China's 'mental firewall' has helped to protect individuals from punishment for 'wrong thinking'. It has, however, also had the more problematic effect of stifling the development of creativity, self-expression, and the diversity of thought that form the basis for genuine social development.

China's complex overt control and censorship systems, termed the 'Golden Shield Project', would find it difficult to deal with China's vast numbers of Internet users needing to be supervised, while also being forced to coordinate between the large number of state actors at all levels struggling for control and power over their 'own' corners of the Internet. Consequently, the only way for the 'Golden Shield Project' to succeed may well be the creation of an online 'harmony' through the active shaping of the behaviour of netizens in cyberspace. Such a process produces legitimacy for the surveillance of netizens through their own self-regulation, while fostering a climate of fear and insecurity and eliminating the need for the maintenance of expensive institutionalized and embodied mechanisms capable of detecting and censoring individual communications. This is further supported by the consistent portrayal of the Internet by China's mass media as dangerous because it is addictive, entertainment-centred, dull, supportive of mindless escapism, unproductive, or encouraging passivity (in its consumption of games, sex, or violence). Since 2006, the widespread promotion of self-regulation and self-censorship has drastically reduced the need for the party-state to actively interfere in online debates (see also Herold, 2008).

A third method to control Internet content is what I call the 'dynamic manipulation' of online discourse. As the Asia Times reported in a piece titled 'China's Internet awash with state spies':

> The huge number of official web commentators is evidence that the Communist Party of China (CPC) has attached great importance to the Internet. In President Hu Jintao's words the Internet is 'an increasingly important channel of public opinions'. So far the CPC's policy has been to control and manipulate public opinion, and its grip on the Internet is increasingly tight.
>
> (Zhong, 2008, August 14)

With an estimated 280,000 outsourced 'web commentators' (*wangluo pinglunyuan*) nationwide, better known as 'Fifty-Cent-Party' or 'Five-Mao-Party' (*wumaodang*), the Chinese party-state fights what David Bandurski has aptly termed a 'Guerilla war for the Web' (Bandurski, 2008, July). In other words, the regime actively manipulates Internet discourse on public opinion.

> China's growing armies of Web commentators – instigated, trained and financed by party organizations – have just one mission: to safeguard the interests of the Communist Party by infiltrating and policing a rapidly growing Chinese Internet. They set out to neutralize undesirable public opinion by pushing pro-Party views through chat rooms and Web forums, reporting dangerous content to authorities.
>
> (Ibid.)

Statistics show that this infiltration has worked: according to a survey about Internet use in China between 2000 and 2007, almost 85 percent of Chinese said they approved of Internet control and management, and more than 80 percent said their government should be responsible for this control (Guo, 2007; see also

Fallows, 2008, March 27). The survey noted that 41 percent of the respondents believed that online content linked to 'politics' (*zhengzhi*) in particular should be controlled or managed, which in the Chinese context includes not only questions of political rights or the competition for political control, but also concerns larger questions of public morality and social values. This strong belief in the authority of the state is hardly surprising for a country in which the authoritarian state has traditionally assumed responsibility for the management and definition of public morality and social values. Yet, the successful, active, and intentional manipulation of online discourse has certainly been a contributing factor to the belief's surviving the advent of the Internet and its communicative possibilities in China.

In conclusion, the combination of all three tools for the supervision and censorship of online behaviour makes it difficult to differentiate posts, comments, or even whole websites that merely consist of the (remunerated) regurgitation of the hegemonic views of the party-state, from content based on independent, conscious, and critical thought processes. While the ordinary Chinese netizen has the liberty to judge intuitively what content he wants to trust, for 'experts' studying the Chinese Internet there remain many issues and possibilities to consider and research. For example, how does China's party-state apparatus decide whether it is better merely to observe or when to discredit specific netizens if they are becoming too active, critical, or influential? How do state agents decide when to seek to undermine the netizens' trust in the Internet or popular network technologies (such as bulletin boards or blogging) in general, and when to damage the reputation of a specific critical individual or institution? What hidden or personal agendas do state agents have and how do those agendas impact their 'mission'? To what extent do individual netizens recognize and how do they respond to such agendas? To what extent are netizens persuaded to spend considerable efforts to voluntarily perpetuate or expand hegemonic narratives online?

The sheer variety of permutations and effects of the control mechanisms available to the Chinese party-state cannot be satisfactorily explained using a 'censorship versus freedom' dichotomy. Internet control in China cannot be properly understood without investigating the multitude of possible variations of Internet control available to the Chinese party-state and its online agents. Nor can Chinese netizens be rendered merely as un-free, docile, and passive recipients or simple 'resisters' of the party-state's efforts to control them. Just as the regime is deploying highly flexible, multi-pronged, and increasingly subtle forms of control and censorship to prevent the spread of undesirable content, so are Chinese netizens creating ever more imaginative ways in which individual Internet users bypass (rather than engage) the hegemonic narratives of censorship and control.

### Chinese netizens and the bypassing of narratives of censorship and control

Forces that are too powerful to overcome have to be avoided, or their effects have to be circumvented, if resistance is not to become futile. Such bypassing of the censorship and control mechanisms of the Chinese party-state is common practice among the Chinese netizens I have observed and spoken to over the years. Many of them have received online comments critical of their views, whose tone suggested that they were written by members of the Five-Mao-Party. Chinese netizens who are actively expressing their views online work with the basic assumption that it is virtually impossible to avoid the near-ubiquitous interference from actors who are controlled or influenced by the state. Netizens are, however, not particularly bothered by this interference, and while direct denunciations of the current regime or its leaders are rare, implicit criticism of state policies is common and widespread. Chinese netizens are both eager to and adept at finding trustworthy partners for the exchange of information and thoughts who do not merely reproduce the narratives of official policy statements, which are often regarded as insulting to the intelligence of 'real' netizens.

Most Chinese netizens voicing their views on social or political issues online are well aware that in China honest self-expression can result in dire consequences, and so self-censorship has turned into the widely practised art of reading and writing 'between the lines', similar to the subversion of Communist propaganda in the formerly Communist Eastern Europe. As Foucault demonstrated (1995), people who know they are monitored or under surveillance will adapt their behaviour or conduct, both in their thoughts and in their actions. However, this idea of assimilated conduct when under observation can also be turned upside down: not thinking or worrying about actually existing censorship and surveillance creates freedom. Whoever feels free is free. Put differently, individual Chinese netizens have adapted themselves to the censorship and surveillance of their online activities to such an extent that it has become meaningless, as the constant observation fades into the background and ceases to be a motivating or influencing factor for the individual Internet user.

Additionally, many Chinese netizens see censorship and other forms of manipulation as a necessary trade-off required to obtain the right to interact online. We need to keep in mind that, before the advent of the Internet, in China public dissent has had to stay largely underground (Goldman, 2000). This situation has improved a lot in cyberspace. As a result, the practice of censorship in China might be a less rewarding topic for research today, and instead researchers should focus on how change is initiated and implemented in spite of the state's pervasive surveillance (see also MacKinnon, 2007).

Many Chinese netizens no longer complain about censorship as such, as it has ceased to feel relevant to them. China's most famous political blogger, Zhao Jing (known by his 'pen' name, Michael Anti), felt that he intuitively knew where to draw the line between the acceptable and the potentially censored, and that he was safe as long as he kept to making speeches and did not organize actual *offline* protest events (Thompson, 2006, April 23). Zhao told the New York Times Magazine why even behaviour within the party-state's vague limits was already highly stimulating:

> Before, the party controlled every single piece of media, but then Chinese began logging onto discussion boards and setting up blogs, and it was as if a bell jar had lifted. Even if you were still too cautious to talk about politics, the mere idea that you could publicly state your opinion about anything – the weather, the local sports scene – felt like a bit of a revolution.
>
> (cited in Thompson, 2006, April 23)

This attitude, common among Chinese netizens, explains why advances in network technologies like blogging or micro-blogging are immediately popular with Chinese netizens – to the dismay of the party-state and the institutions tasked with the supervision of the Internet. In China, self-expression is a contested practice, and is thus influenced by conscious and subconscious forms of self-censorship, which ever new interactive Internet tools help to turn irrelevant. While online content in China 'reflects a compromise between what people want to say and what the regime is willing to permit them to say' (Esarey & Xiao, 2008), many of China's online public spaces are created, shaped, and abandoned by Chinese netizens, depending on their ability to transcend or avoid attempts at informational manipulation. The Internet has provided them with the tools necessary to think and associate in new ways through the creation of new social spaces and practices of communication and organization that allow their voices to be heard, and which carry over into their offline, everyday lives. As Arsenault & Castells (2006) show in the case of the social production of misinformation in the United States, it is possible to bypass such media and to influence the dominant political agenda and players, if two necessary transformations are effected: 1) the rise of a concerned citizenry more interested and involved in public affairs; and 2) the continuing development of horizontal communication networks that circumvent the party-state's controlled media and provide appropriate levels of authority and trust for the creators of content, and thus credibility in the content of these media. The capacity of Chinese netizens to bypass hegemonic narratives and to transcend narratives of censorship and control hinges on exactly the same transformations. A scholarly focus on the 'old battlegrounds' of control vs. freedom tends to overlook or marginalize the creative powers of grassroots agency, which is constantly creating new performative spaces online that alter the landscape of public discourse and enable netizens to engage in online interactions immune to the strict control mechanisms of the party-state.

## Online China and the emergence of a civil sphere

### *Chinese netizens and the inappropriateness of applying European theories*

Chinese citizens are able to transcend attempts at informational manipulation, and the resulting specific phenomena visible online might lead to trust, shared meanings, state–society intermediations, and broader, enduring societal change. Indeed, it could be argued that Chinese netizens have begun to create a *civil sphere* online that is populated by informed and aspiring actors and new institutional forms.

> The magic of the Internet is that it is a technology that puts cultural acts, symbolizations in all forms, in the hands of all participants; it radically decentralizes the positions of speech, publishing, filmmaking, radio and television broadcasting, in short the apparatuses of cultural production.
>
> (Poster, 1999: 222)

Scholarly discourse has long debated how to apply the European concepts of 'civil society' and 'public sphere' to China and its Internet (e.g. Ma, 1994; Tai, 2006; Yang, 2003a, 2003b, 2003c, 2009), ending in the general consensus that some form of 'nascent' or 'embryonic' civil society 'is taking shape in China outside the sphere of influence of the once all-powerful and all-inclusive state' (Tai, 2006: 79), but that a more general application remains highly problematic (e.g. Gu, 1999; Zhao, 2008). Within the framework created by Habermas (1989), the 'public sphere' is conceptualized as a homogenous space of embodied subjects pursuing consensus through the rational critique of arguments and the presentation of validity claims. Normative tradition views 'civil society' and 'public sphere' activity as mechanisms that enable public debate, which then in turn influence the formulation of policy and the legitimization of the nation state. In the era of mass communication and the Internet, Manuel Castells and others argued that these negotiations of political legitimacy shifted into the communicative space, and communication networks built around mass media which have since become the 'new public sphere' (Castells, 2007, 2008; see also Habermas, 1996; Hartley, 1992; Virilio, 1994).

This 'new public sphere' is built around the assumptions that the dichotomies between the state and the people, the governing and the governed, are universally applicable, and determinant of the behaviour of individual agents who enter shared communicative spaces regardless of their cultural backgrounds. However, empirical observations of Chinese netizens show that they do *not* define themselves in opposition to China's party-state or its censorship regime. They are *not* engaged in negotiations of political legitimacy, and are neither supporting nor rebelling openly against the party-state in China. Instead, as shown above, they are ignoring or avoiding such discourses of legitimacy and their attendant narratives of control and censorship. This suggests that the Chinese Internet and its users cannot be adequately explained or even framed with the European concepts of the 'civil society' or the 'public sphere', and that an explanation must look beyond adaptations of theoretical frameworks to the specific Chinese 'case'. The Chinese Internet is a highly complex *public space* inhabited by myriad individuals and groups, permeated with subspaces – particular places of playful and serious consent and dissent, with thoughts and ideas that are continuously produced, remixed, and reproduced across space and time.

China, unlike more democratic countries, lacks large, free public spaces such as workplaces and schools, government bureaucracies, corporate media institutions, etc. This is politically significant because such free public spaces are where people talk to each other, learn to define a situation on their own terms, and ultimately develop a capacity for independent thought and concerted action (Goldfarb, 2006). China additionally has a mass media system that largely remains uniformly homogenous in its dissemination of information. Both the media system and China's lack of public spaces create resistances and these resistances find their expression on the Internet. The Internet creates for Chinese people a space and the places to express what cannot be expressed elsewhere.

Following de Certeau (1984), a state aims to force people to play the game by its rules, just as the public continually seek to find or create their own places. Resistance thus emerges not from specific places with overpowering practices of domination, but rather from the state's exertion of power on everyday life and its practices of survival, enjoyment, etc. These practices, according to de Certeau, are constantly 'refashioned by this combination of manipulation and enjoyment' (de Certeau, 1984: 18). My experience with Chinese netizens shows that they do not wish to oppose the party-state's narratives of control and censorship, but instead hope to operate largely outside the state–society framework, redefining their values and identities based not on some structural 'given', or in opposition to the state, but as expressions of individual perceptions, opinions, and goals – while the forming of associations and building of institutions they trust is largely incidental. Chinese netizens are not interested in contesting the control of the Chinese state over Chinese society, but rather in avoiding and bypassing the surveillance and control mechanisms of the state in their own everyday lives, thus dodging unwanted influences on their thoughts, practices, and actions.

## *Everyday 'small politics' and the Chinese civil sphere*

It is impossible to capture China's specific decentralized and decentralizing qualities of electronic forms of interaction with the European concepts of a 'civil society' or a 'public sphere' as outlined by Habermas (1985, 1989, 1996). The attempts by many scholars studying China and its Internet have led to the underplaying of the reversibility of authorial power and their failing to recognize the existence of new forms of individual agency rooted in place-based everyday realities.

> Civil society is often idealized by philosophers and by lay members alike as a universalistic and abstract space, an open world without limits, an endless horizon. In fact, however, territory is basic to any real existing society. Territory converts the space of civil society into a particular place. Indeed, civil society can become unique and meaningful only as a particular place.
> (Alexander, 2006: 4)

In an attempt to critically assess the usefulness of Habermas' concepts in the context of China, Michael Keane (2001) provides an interesting alternative model of analysis based on people's everyday life practices. Keane argues that, in order to explain why people in China have (at least pre-2001) generally failed to organize themselves into pressure groups to influence policy, we need to understand the problematic of 'big and small' (*da yu xiao*). Using the example of the controversial 1994 television serial 'Chicken Feathers' (*yi di jimao*), Keane (2001) argues that in China there are two modes of political participation: 'big' (official) politics and 'small' (everyday life) politics. The programme's central theme 'revolved around the question of agency; in particular, how ideas about peoples' place in society and their relationships to authority are fashioned by the quotidian practices of everyday life as much as by political discourses' (ibid.: 790). Following on from this observation is the notion that, in China, 'small' politics, i.e. the ability and cultivation of strategies that influence associates and officials, can be a more functional (and smarter) strategy than overt political lobbying or activism – which may lead to the identification of the individual as a troublemaker by the party-state.

Keane concludes his insightful analysis with the argument that China's political sphere and its resulting policies are not only fashioned by official 'big' politics, but to a significant extent by everyday life practices, i.e. the cultivation of strategies to seek personal outcomes: 'small' politics. Whereas in the Western tradition policy is formulated as precise and specific rules and legal regulations, the formulation of policies is merely the beginning of the political process in China, but not its completion. The process, often initiated through the formulation of new governance policies by important political figures, is then circumscribed by various layers of written documents, reports, oral communication and speeches (Shi, 1997; also Keane, 2001). Permeated with 'policy rhetoric', these documents are often (deliberately?) imprecise and vague in language and are the outcome of a process of institutionalized bargaining of various actors, at various levels associated with 'small' politics (Shi, 1997; Ure & Liang, 2000). As a result of this convoluted nature of the policy formulation process, 'while cultural producers and intellectuals do not play any substantive role in policy formulation, they do have the capacity to influence policy interpretation and implementation' (Keane, 2001: 784) through their interactions with the main state actors involved.

In order to emphasize the rootedness in everyday life of both the nature of political participation in China and the Chinese-language Internet, it seems helpful to me to introduce the historicized and geographical concept of the *civil sphere* proposed by Jeffrey Alexander and to apply this social theory framework to China and its Internet. Alexander's notion of a 'civil sphere' is the core part of his project to develop a philosophical-sociological frame that could serve as a meeting point for normative and empirical sciences. The 'civil sphere' is imagined as a 'world of values and institutions that generates the capacity for social criticism and democratic integration at the same time' (Alexander, 2006: 4). Instead of depending on communicative action based on rational experience and self-interest as sole motivation (Habermas), Alexander's 'civil sphere' 'relies on solidarity, on feelings for others whom we do not know but whom we respect out of principle' (ibid.). The civil sphere swims in a world of public opinion, and public opinion is the 'middle ground between the generalities of high-flown discourse and the ongoing, concrete events of everyday life' (ibid.: 4–5). Consequently, the structure of the resulting civil sphere is not merely a discursive space, but it is also filled with groups and institutions, organizations of communication and of regulation. In societies not solely governed by power it is groups and institutions that create shared meanings necessary for a democratic life based on agreement in difference. These communicative institutions, e.g. mass media, non-mass media, fictional media, civil associations, etc., create and constantly alter public opinion.

If we are to avoid the state vs. civil society dichotomy, it is paramount to conceptualize civil society as an independent sphere, with its own institutions and ethics. Since a civil sphere is created by social actors located in everyday space and time, such spheres are also necessarily contradictory and fragmented, continuously

> delimited by such worlds as state, economy, religion, family, and community. These spheres are fundamental to the quality of life and to the vitality of a

plural order, and their independence must be nurtured and protected. At the same time, their concerns and interests often seem to threaten the civil sphere. The goods they produce and the powers they sustain are sectoral not societal, particularistic not universalistic. The hierarchies in these non-civil spheres often interfere with the construction of the wider solidarity that is the sine qua non of civil life.

(Ibid.: 7)

Delimitations and hierarchies of these competing and interacting spheres are never final. Those who are excluded from civil society and its networks – and thus constructed and stigmatized as anti-civil or 'irrelevant' (Castells, 2008) – can actually regain access not only through social movements but also through 'more indirect and incremental processes of incorporation' (Alexander, 2006: 7–8), assimilating themselves into membership by learning to 'wear the primordial camouflage of the core group' (ibid.: 8). Both civil and non-civil forces are engaged in constant negotiation, in which no side can completely coerce or be completely suppressed, and '[a]s the multicultural mode of incorporation becomes more than merely a theoretical possibility, the language of incorporation changes from integration to diversity' (ibid.) and both kinds of forces become acceptable parts of the developing civil sphere. Ultimately, the dynamic civil sphere remains an unfinished, ever-changing project that can never be completed.

In the context of China, this is in line with the analysis of the Chinese political sphere by the eminent and outspoken Chinese intellectual and (now imprisoned) human rights activist Liu Xiaobo who sees China's emerging grassroots resistances as the main factor in the growing pressure from the people on their government (cf. Liu, 2006). Liu argues that this power stems from people's increasing awareness and 'hunger for rights', and from the diversification of ideas and values in contemporary Chinese society (ibid.). Known as an insightful and incisive commentator on Chinese politics, Liu confirms that a focus merely on the 'big' politics in *Zhongnanhai* (an area in central Beijing that serves as the headquarters for China's top leadership figures) does not reflect China's realities, and that in order to appreciate 'the thinness of the superficial stability under authoritarian power' (Ibid.: 126), it is necessary to heed the importance of another logic – that of 'the spontaneous market system and the people's awareness of their own interest' (ibid.: 124). China's 'small politics' centre around ordinary Chinese people's growing rights awareness and their sense of justice, and thus around the discrepancy between the rights of officials and of the people (ibid.). While reform is led from above, Liu argues that the 'real force that pushes for the reform is society's logic, and the action in favor [*sic*] or against reform by the officials depends on the fact that it yields to or opposes society's pressure' (Liu, 2006: 125).

In a combination of the notions of 'big' and 'small' politics with Alexander's concept of the civil sphere, the Chinese Internet can be interpreted as a diverse and ever-changing civil sphere that, rooted in subjectivity, fosters people's awareness and agency. It is an independent sphere where civil and non-civil voices intermingle and share thoughts and ideas, thus creating multitudes of alternative possibilities that have the potential of eventually turning into proposals and actions

– pressure for actual political reform. The emerging forms of agency, discourses, negotiations, and institutions will hinge to a large extent on the netizens' capacity to develop and cultivate strategies that induce social and political transformation at the level of 'small', everyday-life politics.

## Concluding remarks and outlook

China's relatively short Internet history demonstrates the importance of individual and shared intellectual agency. Within 15 years, key agents of change, along-side myriad others, have turned the Chinese Internet into the huge, poly-vocal space it is today. In the process they have demonstrated not only the limits of traditional censorship but also the importance of free expression for human and social development. They have also revealed the courage and determination of young, educated, and politically astute individuals who are willing to expose their thoughts to the Orwellian surveillance and censorship mechanisms of the Chinese party-state.

In China, cyberspace is a space of relative freedom where people can develop their faculty to think independently. In an environment of countless professional limitations, especially for China's media, legal, and academic professionals, neti-zens look for everyday spaces where they can vent or express their own views that may not fit accepted norms of the hegemonic political production of knowl-edge. This online civil sphere provides Chinese people with encouragement by creating an awareness in them that they are not alone. It also provides the basis for the knowledge of the existence and availability of a far wider range of possible thoughts and ideas than espoused and perpetuated by traditional mass media under the direction of the party-state.

Far from the gaze of scholarly investigations, Chinese people have begun to create a civil sphere populated by informed and aspiring actors and new insti-tutional forms. The actual shape of and possibilities for grassroots agency and the creation of related liminal spaces on China's Internet should be studied from a fresh perspective, without recourse to simplistic dichotomies built around the presumed conflict between 'the state' and people, censorship and resistance. China's cyberspace is a space where politics is reinvented through celebrating difference and diversity, and not solely through resistance against given structures.

Emerging technological and societal realities, as well as the complexity of the present-day online–offline fabric demand a greater degree of flexibility and adaptability in academic thinking. Academic research that focused on questions of digital access, or on the clash between a free flow of information and state control, have contributed to the misrepresentation and underestimation of the Chinese Internet as a space for entertainment and play. In any society that includes members who value heterogeneity over conformity, and creativity over propriety, the classification of discourses of resistance as reactions to the power and control narrative of a state apparatus has to be regarded as too simplistic and of limited value for an analysis of the various processes at play between different societal actors. Moreover, the excessive scholarly focus on the dichotomies of 'control' vs. 'freedom', or of networked forms of 'authoritarianism' vs. 'democracy', tends to underestimate the ever-changing meanings of these concepts as well as the Internet's potential to empower people and alter societal structures from below. The dichotomization of a homogenizing universality and the heterogeneity of the particular allows only for systemic resistance from within, while precluding particularistic forms of dissent that are rooted in local identities and the experiences and actions of free subjects.

While traditional renderings of Internet control and censorship in China remain an important area of investigation, a new focus is required to study the extent to which Chinese netizens are able to transcend attempts at informational manipulation, and how the expression of choices and specific phenomena visible online might lead to trust, shared meanings and institutional forms, state–society intermediations, and, ultimately, to broader, enduring societal transformation within the continuously changing civil spheres of the Chinese Internet and of Chinese society and state.

Studies of China's online society should attempt to excavate the diversity of voices and shared meanings that are essential as a basis for understanding the actions and interchanges that are rooted in consciousness and discourse but do not necessarily remain within these realms. Indeed, *people* remain the key agency to be studied (compare Hartford, 2000), as ultimately people, and not technology, will decide what kind of future we will live in. The concepts to be used to study views and behaviours might well be the ones people use to see and describe themselves. A renewed focus on Chinese netizens' agency and practices would facilitate the reframing of descriptions of Chinese politics and space and provide us with a fresh, more 'bottom-up' perspective that allows for the interpretation of changes to hegemonic views and power structures as rooted in individual meanings and agency – thus rekindling hope for a more humane and solidaristic civil sphere.

## Note

I would like to thank the Asia Research Institute of the National University of Singapore for hosting me while I was co-editing this volume, and David Kurt Herold for his invaluable comments on an earlier draft of my chapter.

## References

Alexander, J. C. (2006). *The Civil Sphere*. Oxford: Oxford University Press.

Arsenault, A., & Castells, M. (2006). Conquering the minds, conquering Iraq: The social production of misinformation in the United States – a case study. *Information, Communication, & Society, 9*(3), 284–307.

Bandurski, D. (2008, July). China's guerrilla war for the Web. *Far Eastern Economic Review*. Retrieved 4 August 2010 from http://www.feer.com/essays/2008/august/chinas-guerrilla-war-for-the-web

Castells, M. (2007). Communication, power and counter-power in the network society. *International Journal of Communication, 1*, 238–266.

Castells, M. (2008). The new public sphere: Global civil society, communication networks, and global governance. *Annals of the American Academy of Political & Social Science, 616* (March), 78–93.

Damm, J. (2006). *China's Internet as signifier: Contradicting discourses, paradigms, and interpretations*. Singapore: Singapore Internet Research Center (SIRC), NTU School of Communication and Information.

de Certeau, M. (1984). *The practice of everyday life*. Berkeley: University of California Press.

Deibert, R. (2002). Dark guests and Great Firewalls: The Internet and Chinese security policy. *Journal of Social Issues, 58* (1), 143–159.

Esarey, A., & Xiao, Q. (2008). Political expression in the Chinese blogosphere. *Asian Survey, 48*(5), 752–772.

Fallows, D. (2008, March 27). *Most Chinese say they approve of government Internet control*. Retrieved 4 August 2010 from http://www.pewinternet.org/Reports/2008/Most-Chinese-Say-They-Approve-of-Government-Internet-Control.aspx

Foucault, M. (1995). *Discipline and punish: The birth of the prison* (A. Sheridan, Trans. 2nd ed.). New York: Vintage Books.

Goldfarb, J. C. (2006). *The politics of small things: The power of the powerless in dark times*. Chicago: University of Chicago Press.

Goldman, M. (2000). Politically-engaged intellectuals in the 1990s. In R. L. Edmonds (Ed.), *The People's Republic of China after 50 years* (pp. 138–149). Oxford: Oxford University Press.

Gu, E. X. (1999). Cultural intellectuals and the politics of the cultural public space in Communist China (1979–1989): A case study of three intellectual groups. *The Journal of Asian Studies, 58*(2), 389–431.

Guo, L. (2007). Surveying Internet usage and its impact in seven Chinese cities (November 2007). Retrieved 4 August 2010 from http://www.markle.org/downloadable_assets/china_internet_survey_11.2007.pdf

Habermas, J. (1985). *Theory of communicative action, Vol. I & II*. Boston, MA: Beacon Press.

Habermas, J. (1989). *The structural transformation of the public sphere*. Cambridge, MA: MIT Press.

Habermas, J. (1996). *Between facts and norms: Contributions to a discourse theory of law and democracy*. Cambridge, MA: MIT Press.

Hachigian, N. (2003). *The information revolution in Asia*. Santa Monica, CA: RAND Corporation.

Hartford, K. (2000). cyberspace with Chinese characteristics. *Current History, Sept. 2000*. Retrieved 4 August 2010 from http://china-wired.com/pubs/ch/home.htm

Hartley, J. (1992). *The politics of pictures: The creation of the public in the age of popular media*. New York: Routledge.

Herold, D. K. (2008). Development of a civic society online? Internet vigilantism and state control in Chinese cyberspace. *Asia Journal of Global Studies, 2*(1), 26–37.

Keane, M. (2001). Broadcasting policy, creative compliance and the myth of civil society in China. *Media, Culture & Society, 23*(6), 783–798.

Kluver, R. (2008). *The logics of new media and the information society: Finding a theoretical base for understanding the impact of new media on the harmonious society and international relations.* Paper presented at the Beijing Forum: Cultural Diversity, Harmonious Society, and Alternative Modernity: New Media and Social Development, Beijing, China.

Krim, J. (2005, 14 April). Web censors in China find success: Falun Gong, Dalai Lama among blocked topics. *Washington Post*, p. A2020.

Liu, X. (2006). Reform in China: The role of civil society. *Social Research, 73*(1), 121–138.

Ma, S.-Y. (1994). The Chinese discourse on civil society. *The China Quarterly, 137*, 180–193.

MacKinnon, R. (2007). Flatter world and thicker walls? Blogs, censorship and civic discourse in China. *Public Choice, August 9, 2007.*

Poster, M. (1999). Databases as discourse, or electronic interpellations. In K. Racevskis (Ed.), *Critical essays on Michel Foucault* (pp. 271–285). New York: G. K. Hall & Co.

Shi, T. (1997). *Political participation in Beijing.* Cambridge, MA: Harvard University Press.

Tai, Z. (2006). *The Internet in China: cyberspace and civil society.* New York: Routledge.

Thompson, C. (2006, April 23). Google's China problem (and China's Google problem). *New York Times Magazine.*

Ure, J., & Liang, X.-J. (2000). Convergence and China's national information infrastructure. In M. Hukill, R. Ono, & C. Vallath (Eds.), *Electronic communication convergence: Policy challenges in Asia* (pp. 115–147). New Delhi: SAGE Publications.

Virilio, P. (1994). *The vision machine.* Bloomington, IN: Indiana University Press.

Yang, G. (2003a). The co-evolution of the Internet and civil society in China. *Asian Survey, 43*(3), 405–422.

Yang, G. (2003b). The Internet and civil society in China: A preliminary assessment. *Journal of Contemporary China, 12*(36), 453–475.

Yang, G. (2003c). Civil society in China: A dynamic field of study. *China Review International, 9*(1), 1–16.

Yang, G. (2009). *The power of the Internet in China: Citizen activism online.* New York (NY): Columbia University Press.

Zhao, Y. (2008). *Communication in China: Political economy, power, and conflict.* Lanham, MD: Rowman and Littlefield Publishers, Inc.

Zhong, W. (2008, August 14). China's Internet awash with state spies. *Asia Times Online.* Retrieved 4 August 2010 from http://www.atimes.com/atimes/China/JH14Ad01.html

Zhou, Y. (2005). Living on the cyber border: *Minjian* political writers in Chinese cyberspace. *Current Anthropology, 46*(5), 779–803.

Zhou, Y. (2006). *Historicizing online politics: Telegraphy, the Internet, and political participation in China.* Stanford, CA: Stanford University Press.

# Part II

# Celebrating the carnival

Fun, freak-shows and masquerades

# 4 Parody and resistance on the Chinese internet

*Hongmei Li*

Internet parody, called *egao* in Chinese, has become a fad in China during the past few years. Keyword searches on Google.com and Baidu.com, the largest search engine in China, on June 16, 2009 using the two Chinese characters '*e-gao*' resulted in tens of millions of hits. The word '*egao*' literarily means 'evil joking' but figuratively refers to messages that include elements of parody or spoof. This chapter analyzes *egao* and related phenomena on the Chinese Internet and their social and political implications. It first examines theories of hegemony and parody by looking at theorists ranging from Antonio Gramsci, to George Orwell, to Mikhail Bakhtin. It then analyzes influential *egao* cases, including the short film of the *Steamed Bun*, two cases involving the China Central Television (CCTV), the Green Dam software fiasco, and the Cao Ni Ma and Qi Shi Ma incidents, by paying particular attention to their development, the reactions from internet communities and the responses of Chinese regulators. The chapter concludes by exploring some of the social and political implications of these parodies.

It is important to study parody on the Chinese Internet because the Internet has been increasingly incorporated into the daily lives of hundreds of millions of Chinese. With the largest number of Internet users, China had 298 million netizens by 2008, with an Internet penetration rate reaching 22.6%, and an annual growth rate reaching 41.9% from 2000 to 2008 (CNNIC, 2009). Looking at online parody can provide us with a new window for understanding how netizens resist the established order in China, where there is only limited freedom of speech and press.

## Hegemony and resistance through parody and laughter

Various theorists have analyzed hegemony and resistance. Attempting to understand why a Marxist revolution did not occur in Western Europe, Antonio Gramsci (1971) argued that capitalism was able to maintain control not only through political, economic and military forces, but also through developing a hegemonic culture that made the working class identify with and accept capitalist values. Hegemony in the Gramscian sense can be understood as the normalization and naturalization of power by the dominant class through a combination of coercive forces and consent. The hegemonic authority is challenged at critical moments when 'masks of consent' are broken, leading to the exposure of the violent nature of the authority. If we relate Gramsci's idea of hegemony to George Orwell's and Mikhail Bakhtin's thoughts on parody, we can argue that parodies offer important opportunities to erode hegemony through their destructive and sometimes revolutionary nature. Novelist and political writer George Orwell (1945) stated, 'Every joke is a tiny revolution. [...] Whatever destroys dignity, and brings down the mighty from their seats, preferably with a bump, is funny. And the bigger the fall, the bigger the joke' (par. 7).

Mikhail Bakhtin is probably the most often cited theorist who systematically examined carnival as an inherent part of folk culture and its subversive nature to overthrow official ideologies and initiate bottom-up changes. Bakhtin (1984) stated that carnivalesque laughter 'builds its own world versus the official world, its own church versus the official church, its own state versus the official state' (p. 88). Carnival's ambivalent nature means that it is not only about destruction but also about 'regeneration', 'renewal' and new birth. The Renaissance carnival, according to Bakhtin, built a world that was different from the pretentious, hypocritical, hierarchical and serious official culture in the Medieval Age. Carnivalesque laughter is universal, all-human and open to everyone. And carnival

> does not acknowledge any distinction between actors and spectators ...
> Carnival is not a spectacle seen by the people; they live in it, and everyone
> participates because its very idea embraces all the people.
>
> (Bakhtin, 1984: 7)

Thus, carnival creates a context where power relationships can be temporarily suspended, allowing suppressed voices to be heard. Bakhtin (1984) stated that 'carnival celebrated temporary liberation from the prevailing truth and from the established order; it marked the suspension of all hierarchical rank, privileges, norms, and prohibitions' (p.10).

Bakhtin (1984) eulogized the revolutionary regenerating nature of laughter and emphasizes how it can produce 'free and critical *historical* consciousness' (p. 73, original emphasis). He pointed out that medieval seriousness was 'infused with elements of fear, weakness, humility, submission, falsehood, hypocrisy, or ... with violence, intimidation, threats, prohibitions' (p. 94). However, 'laughter created no dogmas and could not become authoritarian; it did not convey fear but a feeling of strength' (Bakhtin, 1984: 95).

Bakhtin's concept of carnival can be useful in analyzing online parody on the Chinese Internet because the Internet's decentralized nature allows temporary freedom for Chinese to express their voices, despite the Chinese government's systematic efforts to produce pretentious official culture. The public persona of a Chinese official is often serious, humorless and poker-faced, who uses distant languages to discuss stuffy ideologies. The following sections use the notion of parody to analyze a few Internet cases in China so as to understand the potential and limitations of laugher as a communicative power and resisting strategy.

## The case of *The Steamed Bun*

In early January 2006, an Internet film titled *A Bloody Case that Started from a Steamed Bun* (hereafter shortened as *The Steamed Bun*) attracted huge attention and became a big hit within days on the Chinese Internet. Produced by Hu Ge, a freelance media professional and blogger in Shanghai, the short film was intended to be a spoof of *The Promise*, a big-budget film directed by the famous Chinese filmmaker Chen Kaige. As the most expensive film that was ever made in China, Chen's extravaganza employed production members from China, the US, Japan and Korea. However, it failed to win over Chinese audiences and critics, and instead attracted overwhelming amounts of criticism. Hu Ge felt that the film was all appearance with no substance (*wu liao*). He then produced a spoof version using images from a pirated copy. He used images and sounds from *The Promise*, the Legal Channel of CCTV, and a few popular Chinese songs, and turned *The Promise* from a love story into a crime drama. His film centered on a poker-faced TV host who uses conventional communist terminology in his tongue-in-cheek report on the murder case surrounding a stolen bun. He finished the clip on New Year's Eve, shared it with several friends as a New Year greeting and also posted the video on his own blog.

Hu's *Steamed Bun* became popular immediately and millions viewed this spoof within days. Chen Kaige threatened to sue Hu Ge, but large numbers of netizens showed support for Hu. Some MSN users even changed their names to steamed bun-related words, such as '*The Steamed Bun* is better than *The Promise*,' 'support Hu Ge' and 'support *The Steamed Bun*.' Baidu opened a 'steamed bun bar.' Discussions of the case covered topics as diverse as the creativity and humor of the film, the embarrassment for Chen Kaige and copyright issues. The Chinese authorities also responded to the spoof. For example, in response to Chen Kaige's threat to sue Hu Ge, Wang Ziqiang, director of the copyright division of the China Copyright Bureau, stated that whether *The Steamed Bun* was beyond the scope of fair use 'should be decided by legal institutions' (*Xinhuanet*, 2006, February 15). *The Steamed Bun* and related parody phenomena became hot topics during the 2006 National Congress and the Chinese People's Political Consultative Conference (Wu, 2006, March 26). A creative company in Suzhou even registered trademarks for Hu Ge buns, coffees, drinks and other products. On February 24, a small tea house in Suzhou was reported to have sold Hu Ge steamed buns for the first time (Wu, 2006, March 26). Hu was also called a 'big master of steamed buns' (*mantou daxia*) and 'father of steamed buns' (*mantou zhi fu*). He was ranked as 'the No. 1 Internet star in 2006' (Wu, 2006, March 26). The case was also enthusiastically covered by Chinese newspapers and TV stations. Facing huge amounts of criticism, Chen later dropped the lawsuit.

The *Steamed Bun* case is a typical example of parody that has profound political implications in the Chinese context. Of course, such parody was not completely new in China, For example, Stephen Chow's *A Chinese Odyssey* (*Da Hua Xi You*), produced in the mid-1990s, was very popular among Chinese youth for its parody of the Chinese classic *Journey to the West*. The Backdorm Boys (Houshe Nansheng), two Chinese students whose lip-synching videos became a big hit on YouTube, existed before Hu Ge and still exist. They have been incorporated in many advertising and marketing campaigns in China and were able to make a career out of their parody talents. What is especially interesting about the *Steamed Bun* case, however, is that it popularized online parodies and afterwards prompted Chinese authorities to issue various regulations about online spoofs (Eimer, 2006, August 9).

The website of the *People's Daily* (www.people.com.cn), the highest-ranking party newspaper in China, opened a special forum for this debate called 'Mantou lawsuit: an ant-and-elephant fight between Hu Ge and Kaige.' The forum collected many articles from scholars, lawyers and media reports. The majority of the articles showed support for Hu Ge. Hecaitou, a columnist and blogger from Yunnan, published an article entitled 'Chen Kaige, how can you become so un-witty (*wu qu*)' as a parody response to Chen Kaige's accusation of Hu Ge being 'shameless (*wu chi*)' (Lee, 2006, February 13). Hecaitou expressed his liking of Hu Ge's clip and dislike of *The Promise* and stated that Chen's extravaganza indicated a huge gap between the artist and the audiences. In his view, the nonsensical plot of *The Promise* invited such an appropriation, and Hu Ge was an Internet hero who provided easily accessible entertainment to web surfers (Hecaitou, 2006, February 15).

All articles for the special forum allowed Internet users to leave comments. When I checked the website for comments on June 16, 2009, there were over 200 postings, with the majority supporting Hu Ge (*People's Daily*, 2006a). Internet users laughed at the stupidity and self-importance of Chen Kaige. They criticized him for blindly emulating Hollywood production styles and techniques and questioned Chen's title as a 'master of Chinese film.' Not only was Chen's film trashed for its disconnectedness with Chinese audiences, but Chen was also criticized as narrow minded, arrogant, heavy handed and lacking in wit, humour and wisdom. Many also stated that Chen Kaige should show his gratitude toward Hu Ge, without whose spoof many viewers would not have watched Chen's film at all. Some expressed their solidarity with Hu Ge and gloated about the power of the Internet. For example, one netizen remarked:

> Chen Kaige, you should find someone with true Internet knowledge ... to give you a lecture on how to avoid self-destruction. Even though some people say that you are an 'elephant' and that Hu Ge is an 'ant,' instead, in the online world, you are an 'ant' and Hu Ge is an 'elephant.' If you win the lawsuit, it will result in numerous Internet friends attacking you and thus lead to a hundred holes and a thousand scares in you.
> (qian chuang bai kong, as in People's Daily, 2006b)

The Internet is presented as having overthrown traditional power structures and made Hu Ge, an ordinary netizen, more powerful than Chen Kaige, a big filmmaker with enormous social influence. The popularity of file-sharing sites in China meant that Hu Ge was able to garner the support of a large number of netizens. According to a survey released in 2007, a majority of Chinese Internet users enjoyed visiting YouTube-like websites (BBC, 2007, March13) that often contain file sharing and user-produced parodies.

Tianya community, one of the most-viewed Chinese online forums, conducted an online live interview with Hu Ge on January 16, 2006 for more than two hours (Daxue feng shan, 2006). The interview attracted over a thousand posts, with the majority expressing either their support for Hu or their liking of the video clip. Participants asked questions about Hu's production techniques, his intended meanings and the possible lawsuit with Chen Kaige. Many expressed their unconditional support for Hu Ge. Several Internet users asked whether Hu planned to produce future films that criticized social reality and things that ordinary people (*lao baixing*) cared about, such as education, the healthcare system and housing reforms. Chinese Internet users further criticized the facts that Chinese film producers wasted huge investments to produce seemingly dazzling but meaningless films, that many film producers were very idiotic and that they mistreated and cheated Chinese audiences. Netizens felt that such producers have abused their own credibility and thus deserve to be ridiculed (Daxue feng shan, 2006).

Chinese authorities actively responded to the parody phenomenon. Representatives from the Chinese Internet Society (an offshoot of the Ministry of Information Industry), the 81 Film Studio (a military-affiliated film studio), *Guangming Daily* (a large official newspaper), the News Bureau of the State Council, several Chinese universities and other agencies gathered at a conference on August 10, 2006 to 'stop the *egao* phenomenon' and 'develop progressive culture' (Lin, 2006, August 11). They were especially concerned with the appropriation of revolutionary films and literature. For example, a ten-minute Internet satire appropriated images of a 1974 film entitled the *Sparkling Red Star (Shanshan de Hongxing)* and turns a very popular revolutionary film about the growth of a brave child soldier in the 1930s into a story of a pop star longing for his fame and fortune in a TV singing contest. The landlord who brutally exploited peasants and tenants in the original movie is made into a contest judge who takes bribes. The parody turns the protagonist's mother into a fan of a CCTV host and his father into a Beijing real-estate tycoon. The movie further cheapens the revolutionary zeal expressed in the original movie through changing the villagers into the protagonist's fans and cheering group (Zhao, J., 2008: 39).

According to Xinhua News Agency, the satire was widely criticized, with some commentators stating that such a distortion of China's revolutionary history was 'immoral and unacceptable' (*China Daily*, 2006, August 17). Showing his concern over such parodies, Ming Zhenjiang, director of the 81 Film Studio, stated at the conference:

> Revolutionary canons are true reflections and representations of the history of our party and our army. They propagate patriotism, collectivism and revolutionary heroism and are in-depth expressions of justice, ideals and beliefs.... They are related to cultural security of a country and a nation, and should not be profaned, tramped, distorted, overthrown or parodied in any form.
>
> (Lin, 2006, August 11)

Zhang Biyong from *Guangming Daily* stated that *egao* has a particularly bad influence on Chinese youth who are forming their worldviews and value systems

(Lin, 2006, August 11). The authorities expressed the necessity of developing 'a clean Internet culture'. In the same month, the State Administration of Radio, Film and Television (SARFT) announced its intention to regulate online *egao* by requesting individuals to get licenses when disseminating short films. Chongqing Municipality passed a rule stating that Internet users spreading defamatory information would be fined up to 5,000 Yuan (approximately US$625), and that only authorized websites such as sina.com, sohu.com and netease.com were allowed to disseminate short films (*China Daily*, 2006, August 17; *Xinhua News Agency*, 2006, October 16). SARFT issued more regulations in 2008, forcing online video sites in China such as Tudou and Youku to register as broadcasters and accept regulations similar to those for TV or radio broadcasting companies.

In the Chinese film industry, directors such as Chen Kaige, Zhang Yimou and Feng Xiaogang symbolize the mainstream of the Chinese film industry in specific and Chinese culture in general, and they represent the status quo. In the current market economy, money has almost become the only goal for most Chinese youth to pursue (Rosen, 2004). Chen Kaige, to some extent, represents the hegemonic commercial culture in China, where money plays a primary role in determining one's social status and political power. Indeed, since the 1990s, Chinese cultural elites who can marketize their knowledge and skills have increasingly acquired political and economic power in the Chinese market (Zhang, 2001). Cultural elites employ cultural capital to make money, and to convert money into future cultural capital. Zhao (Zhao, Y., 2008) argues that in contemporary China global capitalist and local elites work together to exploit the Chinese market.

Chinese films are increasingly characterized by expensive production and the emulation of Hollywood styles that indicate their loss of roots with ordinary Chinese audiences. In the last few decades, famous Chinese film directors have become increasingly interested in winning awards in the Western world and selling their films on the international market. Many of the movies directed by 'fifth-generation directors' have been produced with Western audiences in mind. Indeed, Chen Kaige launched advertising campaigns throughout the world for *The Promise*, indicating that he was targeting the global middle class, with whom many Chinese netizens might not be able to identify. The fact that tickets sold in China were very expensive is just one indicator of how ordinary people were excluded. For example, a regular ticket for *The Promise* was sold at 80 Yuan (approximately 11 dollars), which is equivalent to a day's salary for an average Chinese resident in large cities such as Beijing, Shanghai and Guangzhou, while the salary of an average rural resident is much lower. In big cities like Beijing and Shanghai, VIP tickets were sold for up to 1,888 Yuan (approximately US$300) (Xinhuanet, 2005, December 9). Thus, a large number of Chinese Internet users, who were students with no income (CNNIC, 2006), were actually excluded from the film's target audiences, which confirms the big distance between the film and the Chinese public. On the other hand, Hu Ge, whose short film was freely available on the Internet, provided easy and free entertainment. His humble background made him easily accessible to ordinary people. He symbolized the Chinese grassroots working for the mass. Additionally, his clip used concepts, institutions, and officials very familiar to ordinary Chinese. Because Hu Ge was turned into a symbol of resistance, his apology to Chen Kaige in early February (Lee, 2006, February 13) did not chime well with Chinese netizens, many of whom viewed Hu's concession as a form of weakness. Even though Hu intentionally avoided political issues, he was expected to criticize current issues like housing, medical reforms and corruption, as indicated in his online interview with Tianya.

A few months after the Beijing Olympics, Hu Ge produced another short film, about China Central Adult Video (CCAV), as a parody of CCTV. Using political terminology and bureaucratic jargon in the style of CCTV news, Hu anchors a news report on the residents' annual meeting, discussing various daily housing issues in a shared apartment that resonated with current social problems in China: the restricted access to an overcrowded toilet (alluding to driving restrictions for private car owners during the Beijing Olympics), the economic recession, unemployment of college students, conflict between the property management and the residents, and so on. The spoof criticizes CCTV as a party organ and comments on many problems that Chinese citizens are familiar with. The format of the program and the use of familiar clichés and jargon satirize what George Orwell in *1984* (Orwell, 1961) called 'newspeak,' a fictional language that helps to maintain systematic political control by making alternative thinking impossible.

The following sections examine several more recent parodies that were created as direct reactions to Internet censorship and government corruption. They include the two 'very yellow, very violent' incidents involving CCTV, the Green Dam software fiasco, and the Cao Ni Ma and Qi Shi Ma cases.

## Very yellow, very violent (hen huang hen baoli)

The phrase 'very yellow [pornographic], very violent' became one of the most popular phrases on the Chinese Internet in 2008. A keyword search of this phrase in Chinese language on Google.com and Baidu.com on August 3, 2009 resulted in millions of hits. This phrase originated with a Beijing-based Chinese primary school student who was interviewed by the CCTV *Network News* program on December 27, 2007 on Internet censorship. The Internet was useful, stated the hostess, but it was also full of violence, pornography and parody. The hostess further remarked that all related departments should establish laws and regulations to control the Internet. During the interview, the student stated, 'the last time when I was searching for information, one window popped up. It was very yellow and very violent. I hastily closed the page.'

The Mop Forum (Maopu Luntan), one of the most influential interactive entertainment platforms in Chinese Cyberspace, first posted the interview within 40 minutes (Soong, 2008, January 7). A Mopper named Gegege wrote a post entitled 'Tonight's *Network News* broadcast was awesome'. She repeated the girl's words and then stated, 'I was having dinner then and I could not help but laugh. Very yellow, very violent. That is like the MOP slogan of Very Good, Very Powerful.' Other comments questioned how such a little girl could tell whether materials were very yellow and very violent (Soong, 2008, January 7). The expression 'very yellow, very violent' immediately became a popular catchphrase. Videos, photographs, spoof cartoons and comments poured onto the Internet overnight. People compiled lists of the top ten 'very yellow very violent' movies and websites. Within days, a search of this phrase on Google.com resulted in millions of hits. Internet users laughed at the primary school student for using such a propagandistic phrase. Netizens started a human flesh search (*ren rou sou suo*) and posted her personal information and contact details on the Internet. Her father issued an open letter online, asking netizens not to blame and persecute his daughter. One widely circulated image depicted a crying cartoon version of the girl, wearing a ripped shirt and sobbing out the catchphrase 'very yellow, very violent,' with the CCTV logo in the background.

Various parodies followed using the phrase 'very yellow, very violent.' Many Internet users felt especially disturbed because they thought a primary school girl could not coin such an adult-like phrase on her own. She was ridiculed for being set up as a puppet for the Chinese government and CCTV. Not only were various parody characters created for the primary school student, but also a blogger produced a list of the top ten very yellow and very violent Chinese websites that included the most popular Chinese portals, with CCTV listed as No.1 (Ning, 2008). This list was then incorporated into Chinese Wikipedia (Wikipedia, 2010, July 1). A personal blog site was further created after the event (http://hen.huang.hen.bao.li, later redirected to the secure site https://hen.bao.li/), which has been developed from a site collecting pornographic images into a site devoted completely to political criticism. Traditional media, such as the *Southern Metropolis Daily* and the *Xinjing Bao*, and various websites covered the incident. The *Xinjing Bao* criticized the *egao* phenomenon as 'cultural abnormality' and stated that Internet subculture in China had developed from 'being interesting, to no substance to violence' (*Xinjing Bao*, 2008, January 10). Traditional media and Chinese authorities also criticized netizens for not respecting the privacy of this little girl and their infringement of her rights.

## Cao Ni Ma

A more recent Internet phenomenon in China was the creation of mythical creatures using nonsensical words that sound similar to abusive or indecent words in the Chinese language. 'Cao Ni Ma' (grass mud horse) has become the most influential of these newly created mythical creatures. Keyword searches for 'Cao Ni Ma' in Chinese on Google.com on June 20, 2009 resulted in more than 46 million hits. Cao Ni Ma is a pun for a Chinese phrase meaning 'motherf***r.' Having the appearance of an alpaca, the Cao Ni Ma is said to be a gentle, courageous, tenacious, grass-eating mythical animal living a carefree life in the Ma Le Ge Bi desert, which sounds similar to another obscene Chinese phrase. Sub-species of these animals were later created, e.g. Wo Cao Ni Ma, meaning 'I f*** your mother,' and Kuang Cao Ni Ma, meaning 'violently f***ing your mother.' According to Wikipedia (Wikipedia, 2010, July 13), the Cao Ni Ma emerged to fight the 'He Xie' (river crab), which sounds like 'harmony' in Chinese language and refers to the 'harmonious society' that the Chinese leadership has promoted during the past few years. He Xie, often portrayed as wearing wristwatches in reference to the 'Three Represents' promoted by former President Jiang Zemin, has now become a code word, an adjective and also a transitive verb in Chinese to describe censors who constantly 'harmonize' Internet blogs and forums.

The Cao Ni Ma phenomenon became so popular that many music videos, documentaries and cartoons appeared on *YouTube* and other places on the Internet. Stuffed toys and other merchandise were also produced for grass mud horses. The mythical animal was also widely discussed in the English world and blogs after the *New York Times* published an article on it on March 11, 2009 (Wines, 2009, March 11). An entry was also created on Baidu Baike in early 2009 containing a list of ten mythical creatures on the Chinese Internet, with Cao Ni Ma listed as the No.1 creature (Wikipedia, 2010, June 7). Additionally, the list included animals such as Fa Ke You (literarily meaning 'French-Croatian squid' but actually referring to 'f*** you' in English), Ji Ba Mao (literally meaning 'Lucky Journey Cat' but a homophone with 'pubic hair'), Wei Shen Jing (literally meaning 'Stretch-Tailed Whale' but actually referring to 'menstrual pads'), Yin Dao Yan (literally meaning 'Singing Field Goose' but actually referring to 'vagina infection'), and other creatures. The easy availability of homophones in the Chinese language contributed, to a large extent, to the production of such online parodies. Later on, images, videos and even songs of these mythical animals appeared on the Internet. In response, SARFT issued a notice on March 30, 2009 prohibiting 31 categories of online audio and video content, 'from violence to pornography, terrorism and content that might incite ethnic discrimination, hatred and undermine ethnic unity and social stability' (Wu, 2009, April 3). Many netizens believe that this directive was in response to the embarrassment caused by the popularity of Cao Ni Ma and related phenomena.

The creation of Cao Ni Ma and other mythical creatures has to be seen against the backdrop of the government's effort to censor the Internet. On November 28, 2008, the Center for Illegal and Bad Internet Information Exposure (CIIRC) issued a notice exposing and criticizing Baidu and several other sites that were said to contain vulgar information (CIIRC, 2008). A conference call was conducted a few days later by the News Bureau of the State Council and six other ministry-level departments to launch a movement to clean up 'vulgar Internet content,' to improve Internet culture and to protect Chinese minors from unhealthy influences (CIIRC, 2009). Google, Baidu, Sina, Sohu, Tengxun and several other sites were mentioned as bad examples that contained a large volume of vulgar and pornographic information but had taken no action to comply with the authorities. CIIRC also posted a list of many other websites during subsequent cleansing actions. During this period, Douban.com even censored many oil paintings of the Renaissance period as vulgar and pornographic. Internet users subsequently started a movement called 'Anti-vulgarity, let's put clothing on famous paintings,' which garnered a lot of support. Faced with pressure, Douban.com later restored access to these images (Dayang Wang, 2009, February 10).

bullog.cn, a Chinese blog site that hosts some of the most influential and politically critical blogs, was also shut down, even though the site had little to do with pornography, which further confirmed people's suspicions that the government intended to censor politically sensitive content in the name of cleansing pornography and vulgar content. Cao Ni Ma and other examples are interesting because they indicate the ingenuity of netizens in bypassing Internet censors by combining innocuous Chinese words to mean things that have subversive meanings. The successful circulation of Cao Ni Ma online produced triumphant laughter that united netizens in laughing together.

## Gao Ye: the adult version of being 'very yellow, very violent'

A recent incident involving CCTV is often labelled the adult version of being 'very yellow, very violent.' On June 18, 2009, CCTV, in its *Network News*, *Focus Discussion*, and *News 1+1* programmes, singled out Google China and accused it of disseminating large amounts of pornographic and vulgar information. The Center for Illegal and Bad Internet Information Exposure strongly condemned Google and demanded that it clean up its search engine. Gao Ye, a college student, was interviewed by *Focus Discussions* and stated:

> I think pornographic Internet information is very harmful, especially materials accessed through Google links. I have a classmate who is very curious about such materials. He viewed pornographic websites and felt very restless (*xin shen bu ning*). After the government cracked down on pornographic websites, he could not access them anymore and became better. However, he later found that he could still access these websites through Google, and he became restless again.

The interview with Gao Ye spread instantly on the Internet and various parody comments were posted about him. Gao Ye's phrase '*xin shen bu ning*' (restless, lacking concentration) became popular overnight. Gao Ye also became a victim of a human-flesh search engine. Within days, his personal information, including his birthplace, cell phone number, personal blog, the name of his university and his girlfriend, was revealed online. What outraged netizens was that Gao was later found to have been an intern at CCTV's *Focus Discussions* program. Gao received hundreds of harassing messages questioning his motivation in speaking for the government.

Netizens also created the phrase 'you should not be too Gao Ye as a human being,' which equates Gao Ye with someone who is shameless. Apparently, Gao Ye was set up as an instrument to promote Internet censorship. Many netizens stated that Baidu profited from the movement to cleanse Google and might have been behind it, or at least somehow involved. Indeed, Baidu, the No. 1 search engine in China, which takes 60% of the market, has been tamer in China than Google.cn, the censored Chinese version of Google.com, in terms of filtering out sensitive political content. As a company founded by a Chinese, Baidu is often viewed as more 'politically trustworthy' than global companies (Peh, 2009, April 20). Google's withdrawal from China in 2010 somewhat confirmed Google's defiant stance toward the Chinese authorities and its philosophy of 'do no evil', despite comments from critics that Google had pulled out of China mainly for business reasons.

## The Green Dam software fiasco

An attempt at censorship by the Chinese government was to require the installation of the Green Dam-Youth Escort software on all computers sold in China, starting from July 1, 2009. While government authorities stated that the software aimed to filter pornographic information in China, critics argued that it was meant to censor politically sensitive information. The Green Dam software has also been found by researchers at the University of Michigan to have various bugs (Wolchok, Yao, & Halderman, 2009), and its developers are under legal attack by a California-based company that accused the Chinese developers of stealing its programming code (Wong & Vance, 2009, June 18). Facing strong protests from the international media, computer retailers and Chinese Internet users, the Chinese authorities decided to delay the required installation of the software. Nevertheless, several large PC makers had already voluntarily installed the software on new computers, indicating that the defeat is not as absolute as it appears.

Chinese netizens created 'Green Dam Girl' to ridicule the government's efforts to censor the Internet. There are at least twelve versions of the Green Dam Girl (Hecaitou, 2009). One version of the cartoon girl holds a rabbit (the Green Dam software's mascot), wears a hat with a River Crab logo (referring to the 'harmonious society') and a red badge asserting ethical and moral conformity (*zuofeng*) (alluding to various government regulators hired to promote ethical and moral principles during the last few decades), and carries a bucket of glue, together with banners to close down profane websites (Goldkorn, 2009, June 14). Another version features the Green Dam Girl dragging the grass mud horse along in chains, suggesting that the latter has been tamed, with the Green Dam Girl saying 'I am a rich girl worth 400 million Yuan [alluding to the amount of money the government paid for the Gram Dam software] and the no-good information is very disgusting,' while the grass mud horse states 'I am just an alpaca.' By turning something that the government considers serious into something funny, netizens successfully downplay the importance of what the government considers significant and reveal the stupidity and hypocrisy of official culture.

## Qi Shi Ma

In May 2009, Chinese Internet users created a new mythical animal called 'Qi Shi Ma,' meaning 70 kilometres per hour (kph), while using Chinese characters meaning 'the horse bullying the honest [of the world]'. The parody mocks a case in Hangzhou on May 7, 2009 where a Chinese pedestrian, Tan Zhuo, was killed on a downtown Hangzhou crosswalk by a rich college student speeding his Mitsubishi through a red light. The young driver's dangerous speeding and the reactions of his friends, who joked with each other after the accident, soon sparked public outrage. What especially angered the public was that the police did not arrest the driver immediately, but instead announced in a rush after interviewing his two friends that the driver was driving at 70 kph when he hit the victim in a zone where the speed limit was 50 kph. The police announcement contradicted the reports of many eyewitnesses who stated that Tan Zhuo was thrown into the air a long way before hitting the ground. Eyewitnesses estimated that the speed of the car was at least 100 kph. Well-known blogger and professional racing driver Han Han stated on his blog that the speed was at least over 120 kph (Chan, 2009, May 13). There was wild speculation that the driver's mother was a high-ranking official in Hangzhou, and Internet users expressed their concern that the driver's rich and powerful family might have already bought off the police. In addition, the police did not make a clear statement about the fact that Tan Zhuo was killed while he was crossing the road on a green pedestrian light. After public outrage flooded the Internet, Qi Shi Ma was created. According to Hudong.com, a user-editable online Chinese encyclopedia, Qi Shi Ma was a cross-breed of a grass mud horse and a river crab. It stated:

> A legend goes that in ancient Qiantang, the current Hangzhou, there was an old well called jiao jing [phonetically sounding like traffic police], and the well was said to have suppressed unnamed evils sealed by grass mud horses' excrement. The rich at that time in Qiantang observed a custom: whenever they encountered disasters, they would throw their treasures into this well to protect themselves from evils and disasters. The amounts that they threw into the well ranged from tens of thousands of Yuan to tons of money. What was strange was that the well did not become less deep. Throughout the years, its cold air has greatly scared ordinary people. In May 2009, the unnamed evil ruptured out of jiao jing through the seals of grass mud horses' excrement that had been there for thousands of years and brought disasters to human beings again. According to the opinions of brick masters [phonetically sounding like experts] and teaching monsters [phonetically sounding like professors], such an evil was the Qi Shi Ma.
>
> (Hudong Baike, 2009)

The creation of this mythical creature shows people's resentment and anger towards the police in particular and the Chinese authorities in general. There is a general resentment in China towards the rich and powerful. Again, Qi Shi Ma products and merchandising were made available over the Internet. T-shirts with '70 ma' were sold in stores in Hangzhou (China Daily, 2009, May 16).

Facing public outrage, the police had to change their position. The police arrested the driver, publicly apologized for the initial handling of the case, and announced that the driver was driving at a speed between 84 and 101 kph when the accident happened, so that the driver should take full responsibility. Later, an agreement was reached between Tan Zhuo's family and the driver, who agreed to pay over one million Yuan in compensation (Wang, 2009, May 21).

In the Qi Shi Ma parody, the police are described as evils who always ask for bribery and bring disasters on the world. Even experts and professors are ridiculed, partially because some experts supported the police's initial conclusion, which indicates a credibility crisis for authorities in Chinese society. Chinese officials, because of their widespread corruption, are viewed as people who do not take the public good into consideration.

## Parodies on the Chinese Internet

The power of parody serving political purposes can be seen in the above cases that mock the establishment, including but not limited to government authorities, the police, experts, cultural figures, revolutionary films, literary classics and celebrated heroes of the Chinese past. Criticizing the established order can certainly cause grins and laughter among Chinese Internet users, the majority of whom are young students who are often associated with rebelliousness against authorities (CNNIC, 2009). Speier (1998) pointed out that wit can be 'a weapon' to make the targeted look ridiculous. The simple laughter helps to create ties and form a coalition among a vast number of netizens who view themselves as individually weak and collectively strong when opposing the established political, cultural and social order.

These cases can also be understood in the context of the online carnival in the Bakhtinian sense that celebrates the turning of kings into clowns and clowns into kings. In the *Steamed Bun* case, Chen Kaige, as a symbol of the established order, was revealed as weak, while Hu Ge, a symbol of the powerless in China, turned out to be powerful. In the struggle for social influence, only the merits of *The Steamed Bun* and *The Promise* are determining factors. CCTV, as the most powerful media organization in China, and Chinese censors and authorities were ridiculed in several cases, and their stupidity was revealed, in order to reverse the hierarchy. Social status matters far less in the online context than in offline society. The temporary suspension of power hierarchies creates a context allowing individuals to express opinions in a freer way, and provides the only context in China that allows the Chinese public to become organized without the immediate intervention of the state. As a form of carnival, the Internet provides potential for resistance and social change.

In the online parody games, users become prod-users through commenting on and producing spoofs themselves. Everyone can become a target and everyone can target others. Similar to carnival participants in the Bakhtinian sense, Chinese netizens are not always rational, logical, coherent or ideal. Bakhtin's folk 'are blasphemous rather than adoring, cunning rather than intelligent; they are coarse, dirty, and rampantly physical, revelling in oceans of strong drink … and endless coupling of bodies' (Holquist, 1984: xix). Despite or because of all their shortcomings, carnivals can recreate an ideal but simultaneous realistic context for producing renewed human relations. Parodies produce laughter that helps to create a sense of belonging among people laughing together (Duncan, 1982; Lorenz, 1963; Meyer, 2000; Speier, 1998).

In this sense, Internet users who distrust Chinese media and the Chinese government distance themselves from Chinese propagandists and their colluders and laugh at their stupidities. Meyer (2000) argues that 'Humor use unites communicators through mutual identification and clarification of positions and values, while dividing them through enforcement of norms and differentiation of acceptable versus unacceptable behaviors or people.' (310). Lorenz (1963) also pointed out that laughter 'produces simultaneously a strong fellow-feeling among participants and joint aggressiveness against outsiders' (p. 253). Tracing multicultural historical fiction and building on theorists such as Freud, Bergson and Bakhtin, Bussie (2007) argues that for those who suffer and are exploited, 'laughter interrupts the system and state of oppression, and creatively attests to hope, resistance, and protest in the face of the shattering of language and traditional frameworks of thought and belief' (p.4).

It is possible to link the creation of mythical creatures to Bakhtin's 'images of the material bodily lower stratum' that can sufficiently expose the hypocrisy of official ideology and create a common baseline for people to communicate. Creatures referring to 'motherf***r,' 'pubic hair,' 'f*** you,' 'menstrual pads' and 'vagina infection' direct the readers' attention to human bodies. The use of abusive and obscene words, as a strategy of resistance, frees netizens from seriousness, traditional decency, piousness and official languages. Since Mandarin Chinese uses tone and written characters to differentiate words, it provides easily available homophones with myriad different meanings. While using homophones as a resistance strategy had existed long before the emergence of the Internet, cyberspace has popularized these kinds of parodies. As indicated by cases such as Cao Ni Ma, Qi Shi Ma and other mythical creatures, memorable catchphrases or short anecdotes are created to encapsulate the views of those who are being made into laughing stocks and those who are laughing at them. In the cat-and-mouse games, the powerless successfully get their message out that they are frustrated with seemingly unsolvable issues such as corruption, environmental pollution, lack of media freedom, lack of assembly rights and the increasing gaps between the rich and the poor.

Just as carnival culture built a world different from official culture for medieval Europeans, the Chinese Internet constitutes a second world that is different from the pretentious, hypocritical and serious official culture in China, partially due to the lack of separation between low and high culture online and the loss of credibility of official ideology. According to Bakhtin, laughter can help us to see the world 'anew, no less (and perhaps more) profoundly than when seen from the serious standpoint' (1984: 66).

While Bakhtin did not deal with commercial interests involved in parody, cases mentioned in this chapter indicate that commercial profits can become a part of the stories. In the Hu Ge and Qi Shi Ma cases, commercial entities acted very quickly to profit from the parodies. During the past few years, parodies have also been appropriated by advertisers, who now produce fake spoof videos and post them on the Internet as viral advertising. In the censorship campaign against Google, there was always a suspicion among the Chinese Internet community that Baidu, Google's main rival, was behind the movement, indicating that political resistance cannot be treated separately from all-pervasive commercialism in today's China.

As a backdrop to parodies in Chinese cyberspace, it also has to be pointed out that netizens enjoy only very limited freedom in China. Not only has China created the 'Great Firewall,' which filters out information from outside of China, but China has also implemented numerous measures to control information within the Great Firewall. An estimated 30,000 to 50,000 internet police have been employed to monitor Internet sites and the government has also contracted voluntary undergraduate students to monitor school discussion boards and to report 'negative conversations,' as well as to insert 'politically correct or innocuous themes for discussions' on the school boards (French, 2006, May 8). Freedom House's assessment of Internet freedom in 15 countries, based on three overall categories, including obstacles to access, limits on content and violations of user rights, through a set of 19 questions and 90 sub-questions, concludes that China ranks 13th, with a score of 78 (with 0 representing the most free, and 100 the least free) and is in the 'not free' category, in contrast to Estonia, which scores 10 and is in the 'free' group (Karlekar & Cook, 2009).

Online parody can be seen as a response to Chinese authorities' efforts to produce a docile Internet culture in particular and a tamed public culture in general. The Chinese Internet has become a contested space for power, for either the maintenance of power or the emergence of new power structures supported by a large number of netizens. The establishment has recognized the power of parody as a strategy of resistance and has revised its counter-strategy against it, for example by condemning parody as vulgar and threatening to Chinese cultural values in order to garner support for Internet control and censorship. The fact that traditional media participate in reporting and commenting on *egao* and related phenomena indicates that they are attempting to take advantage of online parodies to reshape themselves so as to gain new advantages and market share.

It is unrealistic to oversimplify the Chinese Internet as a space for resistance. While satire is a way of resisting censorship and challenging the Chinese authorities, it has limited effectiveness because it softens and lessens its critique. Laughter can function as a 'safety valve' for people in an authoritarian society that makes their suffering less intolerable (Meyer, 2000; Speier, 1998). Speier (1998) pointed out that

> Humor does not change the circumstances that it illuminates, although it is able to lessen the discontent and even the despair that these circumstances produce [...] It helps one only to bear somewhat better the unalterable; sometimes it reminds both the mighty and the weak that they are not to be taken seriously.
>
> (Speier, 1998: 1358)

## Conclusion

Chinese Internet users have creatively produced new words, images and imaginary creatures to defy the current regime and to mock the lack of social justice and freedom in China. Their creations are responsive to and criticize problems ranging from pervasive commercialism, corruption, inequality and Internet censorship, to issues of cultural, social and political hegemony. Netizens are tired of government propaganda and of its many colluders. Many do not trust Chinese authorities or political, cultural or economic experts. Netizens engage in parody and criticize problems by uniting behind regenerating laughter on the Internet. The embracing laughter means there is no pre-conceived agenda, but rather ideas are contested on the spot on their own merits. Even though the movement surrounding each specific incident may be short lived, the cumulative effect demonstrates the power that Internet users enjoy and the potential for social change.

Parody means the possibility of word play and *double entendre* to defy government censorship in general, and various Chinese authorities in particular. Chinese netizens exploit abusive language in parodies for its communicative power and as a strategy of resistance, which helps to reveal the hypocrisy of official culture and to establish common denominators for the vast majority of netizens to communicate with each other. Through the Internet, netizens are empowered to function as a collective and are bound together in cat-and-mouse parody games with government authorities. As a form of carnival, the Internet reverses the power hierarchy temporarily and turns the kings into beggars and beggars into kings.

While the Chinese Internet provides a limited space for the emergence of new voices, the establishment, to some extent, can still manipulate the Internet space and use symbolic or real violence to remove alternative voices, which indicates the complexities and difficulties in challenging the established order in China even in the age of information. While carnivals celebrate the folk's shortcomings as a baseline for the establishment of renewed human relationships, the authorities can take measures to marginalize and censor parodies. As a result, there is a constant struggle between serious, hypocritical and fearful official ideologies and participatory, cheerful, celebratory and humorous folk culture on the Chinese Internet.

# References

Bakhtin, M. (1984). *Rabelais and his world*. Trans. Helene Iswolsky. Bloomington: Indiana University Press.

BBC (2007, March 13). *China to tighten control over blogs, webcasts – media watchdog head*. Accessed through LexisNexis, May 23, 2009.

Bussie, J. A. (2007). *The laughter of the oppressed: Ethical and theological resistance in Wiesel, Morrison, and Endo*. New York: T. & T. Clark Publishers.

Chan, K (2009, May 13). Public anger at fatal accident. *South China Morning Post*. News, p. 7.

China Daily. (2006, August 17). New regulation to monitor online video spoof craze. *People's Daily Online*. Retrieved July 15, 2010, from http://english.peopledaily.com.cn/200608/17/eng20060817_293895.html

China Daily. (2009, May 16). A cry for safer roads. *China Daily*. Retrieved July 15, 2010, from http://www.chinadaily.com.cn/cndy/2009-05/16/content_7783562.htm

CIIRC (China Internet Illegal Information Reporting Centre). (2008, November 28). Dui chuanbo disu neirong wangzhan de puguang yu qianze (No. 5). *CIIRC*. Retrieved July 15, 2010, from http://net.china.com.cn/qzl/txt/2008-11/28/content_2604476.htm

CIIRC. (2009, January 5). Guoxinban deng qi buwei kaizhan zhengzhi Hulianwang disuzhifeng zhuanxiang xingdong. *CIIRC*. Retrieved July 15, 2010, from http://net.china.com.cn/ywdt/txt/2009-01/05/content_2668979.htm

CNNIC (2006). *Zhongguo Hulian Wangluo fazhan tongji baogao*, Beijing: CNNIC.

CNNIC (2009). *The 23rd Statistical Survey Report on the Internet Development in China*. Beijing: CNNIC.

Daxue feng shan. (2006, January 16). 'Yi ge mantou yinfa de xuean' zuozhe Hu Ge fangtan xianchang. *Tianya BBS*. Retrieved July 15, 2010, from http://www.tianya.cn/publicforum/Content/free/1/467604.shtml

Dayang Wang. (2009, February 10). Wangyou xiangying fan disu haozhao gei ji minghua 'chuanshang' yifu (zutu). *Sina News*. Retrieved July 15, 2010, from http://news.163.com/09/0210/08/51PEPTVI00011229.html

Duncan, W. J. (1982). Humor in management: Prospects for administrative practice and research. *Academy of Management Review, 7*(1), 136–142.

Eimer, D. (2006, August 9). The great parody craze. *South China Morning Post*. News, the Red Lantern, p.13

French, H. (2006, May 9). As Chinese students go online, Little Sister is watching. *New York Times*. Retrieved July 15, 2010, from http://www.nytimes.com/2006/05/09/world/asia/09internet.html?_r=1

Goldkorn, J. (2009, June 14). Green Dam Girl. *Danwei*. Retrieved August 1, 2010, from http://www.danwei.org/net_nanny_follies/green_dam_girl.php

Gramsci, A. (1971). *Selection from Prison Notebooks* (Q. Hoare & G. Nowell-Smith, Trans.). London: Lawrence & Wishart.

Hecaitou. (2006, February 15). Chen Kaige, ni zenneng wuqu dao zheyang de dibu. *Renmin Wang*. Retrieved July 15, 2010, from http://culture.people.com.cn/GB/27296/4106253.html

Hecaitou. (2009, June 14). 80hou zhi manhua nixi: Luba tiaojiao. *Cao bian wangshi*. Retrieved July 15, 2010, from http://www.hecaitou.net/?p=5770

Holquist, M. (1984). Prologue. In M. Bakhtin, *Rabelais and his world*. H. Iswolsky, Trans. (pp. xiii–xxiii). Bloomington: Indiana University Press.

Hudong Baike. (2009). Qishi Ma. *Hudong Baike*. Retrieved July 15, 2010, from http://www.hudong.com/wiki/%E6%AC%BA%E5%AE%9E%E9%A9%AC

Karlekar, K. D., & Cook, S. G. (2009). *Chinese Internet freedom in a comparative perspective: Select findings from Freedom House's 2009 Freedom on the Net index*. Paper presented at the 7th Chinese Internet Research Conference, Annenberg School for Communication, University of Pennsylvania, May 27–29, 2009.

Lee, M. (2006, Feb. 13). *Chinese director Chen Kaige calls parody of new movie immoral*. Associated Press. Section: International News. Accessed through LexisNexis June 1, 2009.

Lin, Y. (2006, August 11). Shazhu 'egao' zhi feng fazhan xianjin wenhua. *Guangming Daily*. Retrieved July 15, 2010, from http://www.gmw.cn/01gmrb/2006-08/11/content_462888.htm

Lorenz, K. (1963). *On aggression*. New York: Harcourt.

Meyer, J. C. (2000). Humor as a double-edged sword: Four functions of humor in communication. *Communication Theory, 10*(3), 310–331.

Ning. (2008, January 7). Hen huang hen baoli de shi ge wangzhan. *Ning's Blog*. Retrieved July 15, 2010, from http://nings.cn/2008/01/07/very-yellow-and-very-violent.html

Orwell, G. (1945). Funny, but not vulgar. *Edward Lear Homepage*. Retrieved July 15, 2010, from http://www.nonsenselit.org/Lear/essays/orwell_2.html

Orwell, G. (1961). *1984*. New American Library.

Peh, S. H. (2009, April 20). Welcome to China's parallel cyber universe. *The Straits Times*. Retrieved July 15, 2010, from http://www.straitstimes.com/vgn-ext-templating/v/index.jsp?vgnextoid=113da367b5fb0210VgnVCM100000430a0a0aRCRD&vgnextchannel=f511758920e39010VgnVCM1000000a35010aRCRD

People's Daily. (2006a). Mantou guansi: Hu Ge yi Chen Kaige de yi-xiang zhi zhan. *Renmin Wang*. Retrieved July 15, 2010, from http://culture.people.com.cn/GB/22226/58646/index.html

People's Daily. (2006b). Mantou guansi: Hu Ge yi Chen Kaige de yi-xiang zhi zhan – Discussion. *Renmin Wang BBS*. Retrieved July 15, 2010, from http://comments.people.com.cn/bbs_new/filepool/htdoc/html/e52dbb0bf0ab6558b31093dc9ebac3be0391b547/n58646/l_58646_4.html

Rosen, S. (2004). The victory of materialism: Aspirations to join China's urban moneyed classes and the commercialization of education. *The China Journal 51*, 27–51.

Soong, R. (2008, January 7). Very yellow, very violent. *EastSouthWestNorth*. Retrieved July 15, 2010, from http://www.zonaeuropa.com/20080107_1.htm

Speier, H. (1998). Wit and politics: An essay on laughter and power 1. *American Journal of Sociology, 103*(5), 1352–1401.

Wang, H. (2009, May 21). Deal can't bring his son back to life. *China Daily*. Retrieved July 15, 2010, from http://www.chinadaily.com.cn/china/2009-05/21/content_7913680.htm

Wikipedia. (2010, June 7). Baidu 10 mythical creatures. *Wikipedia*. Retrieved July 15, 2010, from http://en.wikipedia.org/wiki/Baidu_10_Mythical_Creatures

Wikipedia. (2010, July 1). Hen huang hen baoli. Wikipedia – China. Retrieved July 15, 2010, from http://zh.wikipedia.org/zh/%E5%BE%88%E9%BB%84%E5%BE%88%E6%9A%B4%E5%8A%9B

Wikipedia. (2010, July 13). Grass Mud Horse. *Wikipedia*. Retrieved July 15, 2010, from http://en.wikipedia.org/wiki/Grass_Mud_Horse

Wines, M. (2009, March 11). A dirty pun tweaks China's online censors. *New York Times*. Retrieved July 15, 2010, from http://www.nytimes.com/2009/03/12/world/asia/12beast.html

Wolchok, S., Yao, R., & Halderman, J. A. (2009, June 18). Analysis of the Green Dam Censorware System. *J. Alex Halderman's Website*. Retrieved July 15, 2010, from http://www.cse.umich.edu/~jhalderm/pub/gd/

Wong, E., & Vance, A. (2009, June 18). China intent on requiring Internet censor software. *New York Times*. Retrieved July 15, 2010, from http://www.nytimes.com/2009/06/19/business/global/19censor.html

Wu, J. (2006, March 26). Xin meiti 'Wuji shidai'! Ruhe queli 'fengxiangbiao'? *Xinhuanet*. Retrieved July 15, 2010, from http://news.xinhuanet.com/focus/2006-03/26/content_4334142.htm

Wu, V. (2009, April 3). Censors strike at internet content after hit parody. *South China Morning Post*. News, p. 8

Xinhua News Agency. (2006, October 16). SW Chinese city issues regulations banning on-line defamation. *Sina English*. Retrieved July 15, 2010, from http://english.sina.com/china/1/2006/1016/91972.html

Xinhuanet. (2005, December 9). 1888 Yuan kan *Wuji* shouying, 'tijian dianyingpiao' yin zhengyi. *Xinhuanet*. Retrieved August 2, 2010, from http://news.xinhuanet.com/ent/2005-12/09/content_3898856.htm

Xinhuanet. (2006, February 15). 'Mantou xuean' qinquan? Guojia Banquanju you sifajiguan jiejue. *Xinhuanet*. Retrieved July 15, 2010, from http://news.xinhuanet.com/society/2006-02/15/content_4184729.htm

Xinjing Bao. (2008, January 10). 'Hen huang hen baoli' shijian beihou de wenhua guaitai. *Xinhuanet*. Retrieved July 15, 2010, from http://news.xinhuanet.com/comments/2008-01/10/content_7396182.htm

Zhang, X. (2001). The making of the post-Tiananmen intellectual field: A critical overview. In X. Zhang (Ed.), *Whither China? Intellectual politics in contemporary China* (pp. 1–75). Durham and London: Duke University Press.

Zhao, J. (2008). A snapshot of Internet regulation in contemporary China: Censorship, profitability and responsibility. *China Media Research, 4*(3), 37–42.

Zhao, Y. (2008). *Communication in China: Political economy, power, and conflict*. Lanham, MD: Rowman & Littlefield Publishers.

# 5 China's many Internets

## Participation and digital game play across a changing technology landscape

*Silvia Lindtner and Marcella Szablewicz*

### Introduction

Internet technologies and sites of technology practice in China have undergone rapid transformation over the last ten years. Qiu (2009), for example, highlights how Internet cafés, which once served an elite market, are now discriminated against as sites that serve the lower class and breed Internet addiction. While the number of Chinese Internet users continues to increase, Internet policies and legislation, ranging from mass closings of Internet cafés to the installation of control mechanisms on computer terminals, have impacted technology practice. Changes in access to and control of online content have led to numerous debates over the social impact of Internet technology in China and the nation's image in a globalizing age. Consider, for example, recent events surrounding Google's announcement of its discontinuation of the censorship of search results on its local search engine in China, Google.cn, due to sophisticated cyber attacks that supposedly originated from within China. The announcement led to heated debates about the divergent values and ethics of Chinese and American politics. In a speech delivered at the Newseum in Washington, DC, Secretary of State Hillary Clinton, for example, referenced Google.cn to discuss China–US relations more broadly (e.g. Barmé, 2010; Chow, 2010; Eckert and Buckley, 2010; MacKinnon, 2010; Martinsen, 2010; Segal, 2010).

What the Google.cn case illustrates so well is that the interface, content and wider social meaning of Internet technologies today are not determined by software developers and designers alone, but rather by a complex web of actors, including, but not limited to, users, corporations, state actors and policy makers. As such, it is important to acknowledge that online practice, including such things as the use of search engines or the creation and modification of digital content, is not divorced from cultural processes, for example social discourses and political debates. Rather than portraying the rapid changes of the IT landscape in China as a single, unified process, we stress the importance of tracing 'multiple Internets,' the development of which are contingent upon broader cultural changes such as shifts in socio-economic class, political projects of modernization and economic reforms. Throughout this chapter, the notion of 'multiple Internets' thus serves as a playful reminder that Internet technologies shape and are shaped by these diverse forms of participation, values and interests.

We ground our explorations in findings from ethnographic research on digital gaming practices in urban China conducted over the last six years. Lindtner draws from research that was conducted during 2007 in collaboration with Bonnie Nardi, Jui-Lin Dai, He Jing and Wenjing Liang (see Lindtner et al. 2008; Lindtner et al. 2009), and from research in 2008 and 2009 that was conducted in collaboration with Ken Anderson and Intel Labs. Szablewicz draws from independent research conducted as a Master's student in 2004 (see Szablewicz, 2004) and from dissertation fieldwork conducted while a Fulbright Fellow during 2009–2010. Our research reveals how urban youths and young professionals in China use digital games to position themselves amidst China's rapid economic and technological transformations. Digital games are not only inherently participatory but are also one of the most popular forms of Internet technology in China today, and as such they are particularly illustrative examples of relations between technological practice and social and economic change in China more broadly. Our goals in this article are twofold. First, we show how digital participation is not a priori defined by a single software application, but is a contingent process evolving in relation to wider social, economic and political developments in China. Second, we show how digital games become a means by which young Chinese engage with and express ideas about social belonging, identity and class.

Our ethnographic research spans both online and offline sites, including digital games such as World of Warcraft, Warcraft III, Counterstrike, Killer Games, QQ Games, the Legend of Miracle 2 and Fantasy Westward Journey. The offline sites of our fieldwork include Internet cafés, student dormitories, gaming clubs, tea houses, workplaces and homes. Data was collected from participant observation, informal conversation, many hours of game play, semi-structured interviews, gamer blogs, online comments and bulletin board systems (bbs), and focus groups. We offer insight into the digital gaming practices of young Chinese living in Shanghai, Beijing and Hangzhou. The ages of our informants ranged from 18 to 45, though the majority of them were in their 20s and 30s. Though we deal with a diversity of games and sites, the young people who contributed to our research share the unique position of living at the forefront of a rapidly changing technological environment in some of China's technologically most advanced cities. As such, a comparison of the distinctions and connections made by these different groups can offer a nuanced account of IT development and its impact on social change in urban China.

It is important to note that our definition of digital games is purposefully broad, including real-time strategy (RTS) games, first-person shooter (FPS) games, massively multiplayer online role playing games (MMORPG), social games and mixed-reality gaming. We trace connections and frictions between different games and urban sites of game play, the ways in which they emerged and developed across diverse material, social and cultural practices. This emphasis on the relations and frictions between multiple sites of gaming practice – physical, digital and social – is then also tied to our analytical commitment to treating Internet technologies as deeply intertwined with other spheres of life.

## A changing nation, a changing technology scene

In China, digital games are particularly illustrative examples of the aforementioned broader debates over the impact of technological development. While officials recognize the economic and creative potential of the gaming industry, digital gaming is also rendered as a site where Internet addiction and immoral attitudes thrive. In official rhetoric, Internet games and the Internet as a whole are often referred to as a 'double-edged sword.' This ambivalent discourse is mobilized with regard to both IT content and the greater impact that it poses for economy and society. CNNIC's 2008 report on Internet development, for example, recognizes the incredible economic potential of the Internet games industry at the same time as it cautions that many Chinese youth have 'submersed' themselves in games, a habit that negatively impacts their ability to function normally at work, at school and in everyday life.

Digital media like online games, and Internet cafés where games are predominantly played, have become subjects of heated debate in ongoing re-evaluations of cultural representation. Mainstream media and government officials have, for example, portrayed places of public Internet access as dens of iniquity that foster crime and immorality. The supposedly 'unhealthy' effects of excessive Internet use have become the main impetus behind the Chinese government's efforts to control the industry. Online games, while not being considered politically motivated, are still rendered as a threat to the healthy development of China's youth (CNNIC, 2008: 52–55) and, by extension, the future of a harmonious Chinese society. Various scholars have referred to this crisis over Internet addiction in China as a 'moral panic' (Golub and Lingley, 2008; Qiu, 2009; Szablewicz, 2010).

Responding to the purported negative effects of Internet games and Internet cafés, the state initiated a series of interventions to control the two industries: Internet cafés have been subject to raids and mass closings, control mechanisms have been installed on café computer terminals, Internet companies have been encouraged to take a 'public pledge of self-discipline' and Internet Games companies are subject to 'service standards' that stress the production of 'healthy' games (for details see Chen, 2008; Ernkvist and Strom, 2008; Human Rights in China, 2005; Liang & Lu, 2010; Qiu, 2009; Qiu & Zhou, 2005; Tsui, 2003; Weber & Lu, 2007).

The post-1980s generation experienced these changes first hand, as the popular emergence and maturation of the Internet coincided with this generation's own shift from adolescence into adulthood. However, despite increases in private access and the stigmatization and regulation of public access sites, Szablewicz found that the Internet café is a nostalgic site for many post-1980s-generation gamers, most of whom recall a period between middle and high school when the Internet café was the prime site of game play and online activity.

In many ways, Chinese gamers' reminiscences about sneaking into the cafés parallel American students' stories about sneaking into bars. For example, Feijie, a Tongji University student, recalled that she and her friends would create fake IDs so as to get around the age restriction in the Internet cafés. Xiaobo, a Caijing University student, recalls a police raid in a café where he and his under-age friends had frequently been playing games. His friend was caught by the police and brought into the police station, where his parents were informed, while he himself 'ran relatively fast' and was able to escape.

The Internet café also played an important role as a site of leisure practice outside the confines of parental control and an often stressful and monotonous educational career. Xiaozhu, a Fudan University student, for example, highlighted the extreme pressure during his time in high school, a competitive boarding school that was known for its rigorous and successful program prepping students for the college entrance exam. He and his friends would frequent Internet cafés almost daily after class:

> Because when you are in high school studies are extremely intense, and so the school won't allow for Internet [in the dormitories], we also didn't have a television, we had nothing, just a dorm, so therefore you had to go to an Internet café … but you had to find a café that was further away … if you went to one near the school the teachers would find you.

For the post-1980s generation, then, these shared sites of nostalgia are a form of collective identity; visits to Internet cafés played an important part in these young people's adolescence, just as Internet cafés themselves play an important role in the adolescent phase of Internet development in China. As such, reminiscences about Internet cafés serve not only to preserve the memory of a unique period of time in China's Internet development, but also to define and unite groups of young Chinese around shared experiences.

Today, perceptions of the Internet café space are changing, in part because of this shift in sites of access and in part because of the pervasive stigmatization of the Internet café as a space that fosters crime and Internet addiction. The Internet is now readily available in college dormitories and many young people grow up with Internet access and private computers in their homes. The technological infrastructure has also ventured into other spaces and spheres of urban life, often being newly built alongside widespread urban redevelopment. Since 2008, Lindtner has traced the development of such a new site of urban digital technology use, a series of up-scale entertainment clubs designed around a mixed-reality game called the Killer Game (*sharen youxi*). The socio-technical arrangement of these clubs differs quite significantly from those of the Internet cafés, constituting an exclusive space for young professionals and entrepreneurs. The clubs are equipped with high-end interactive displays and sensor network technology, as such, different from the Internet café, which offers single PC stations for individual use. The first Killer Game club opened in Beijing in 2004, designed and built by a transnational Chinese who had studied abroad for several years before returning to China. In 2007 the franchise spread into other major cities in China and accumulated about 80,000 members. The clubs Lindtner visited in Beijing, Shanghai and Hangzhou mostly attracted young professionals and entrepreneurs, who flexibly navigated China's urban hubs and regularly travelled outside China for business and studies. Many of the people new to the clubs were returning after years abroad, often from the US or the wider Pacific Rim.

In the following section, we show that increases in Internet access in China did not necessarily lead to a homogeneous space of online participation that eradicated the importance of socio-economic difference. Rather, we show how young Chinese dealt with technological transformation by distinguishing between sites of online participation and modes of play.

## Socio-technical distinction work

Alongside technological changes such as the increase in private computer ownership (CNNIC, 2009) and transformations of the public sites of Internet access in China, young people's own experiences and perceptions of technology have also changed. A pervasive trend that we observed across technological and social transformations over the last years was that sites of Internet access and choice of leisure activity are increasingly used as indicators of social status and class. Where one plays, what one plays and who one plays with were all ways in which urban Chinese distinguished their gaming practices from other, less respectable forms of play. We describe this form of technological participation for social purposes as socio-technical 'distinction work.' By this, we intend to illustrate how increasing access to technology does not necessarily lead to egalitarian use across distinct social geographies. Rather, participation is shaped by people's social positions and negotiations thereof. By distinction work, we refer to Amy Hanser's (2008) definition of the term 'as distinctions [that] emerge in the course of social interactions' and in relation to sites that play a key role in the construction and reproduction of broader social hierarchies. Hanser largely focused on service settings and the retail industry, e.g. private and state-owned department stores, and processes of consumption and production. Drawing on Pierre Bourdieu's seminal work, her approach links particular distinction-making processes to larger institutional settings. Just as Hanser shows that consumers emphasize class difference through the choice of sites of consumption, so too do we seek to show that sites and forms of technology practice have become markers of social and class identity. For the young people we studied, distinction making is a process that evolves at the intersection of social and technical practice and in relation to larger social and institutional changes, such as Internet regulations and Internet addiction discourse.

### Distinct sites of game play

Many who once used Internet cafés on a regular basis now avoid them. Sean, Szablewicz's main guide to Internet café culture in 2004, no longer frequents such spaces. Now, he describes himself as a shut-in (*zhai*) a term derived from the Japanese *otaku* (Li, 2009). He still occasionally plays games and is a self-proclaimed Internet 'addict,' but he prefers to log on from the confines of his home. 'Internet cafés are a place for the lower class now,' he explained; they are disappearing from the city centres and the lives of upwardly mobile young Chinese.

Indeed, while Internet cafés are a shared site of nostalgia for a large percentage of the post-1980s generation, some of the younger Chinese have grown up with Internet connections in their homes and have never had to rely upon Internet cafés for access. Rather than expressing a fond nostalgia for the places, some of these young gamers now express disapproval of them, echoing the negative attitudes of the press and state officials. One such student estimated that he had visited Internet cafés less than 14 times in his entire life. He stated:

> Sometimes I am a bit repulsed by Internet cafés because the interior is so chaotic; there are lots of people smoking, and then, inside, umm, inside there are people of so many different vocations, sometimes there are fighting incidents ... they are not very safe places.

These carefully guarded comments about 'different vocations' seem to mask an implicit commentary on the working-class status of many café patrons.

As a result of such attitudes and new modes of access, many young, educated Chinese have begun to eschew Internet cafés in favor of shared broadband connections in their dormitories and apartments. Despite these changes in attitude towards the Internet café, digital gaming remains a pervasive social practice among urban youth. Often, gamers turn their rooms into a kind of social gaming space, not unlike an Internet café, but open only to their select group of invited friends. For example, in a college apartment a group of seven Caijing University students crowded inside a single bedroom about 70 square feet in size. In the centre of the small room was a large table with five laptop computers. While the five at the table played World of Warcraft, the other two lounged on the bed, one playing a mobile gaming unit and the other playing games on his mobile phone. All described the bedroom as being more 'comfortable' than the Internet café.

The relational aspects of socio-technical distinction work become particularly evident when we look across multiple sites of technology practice. In her research on the design of new technology sites alongside urban redevelopment, Lindtner found that processes of socio-technical distinction making were also linked to the ways in which people situated themselves broadly in relation to social and economic transformations in China. For example, members of the Killer Game clubs actively distinguished themselves from the social and technological practices in the Internet cafés, and also in terms of their own status in society broadly. This was often expressed through a common rendering of status and class in China, *suzhi* (quality). Summer, a 27-year-old freelancer, for example, described other club members as 'people of high *suzhi* ... this game provides opportunities for you to meet people, people of a certain circle. Not everyone likes this game!' Similarly, Jordon, club owner of the Killer Game Club in Shanghai, regards his clientele as being of a certain 'level':

> For people here, they are more white collar workers or the like, or people who run their own businesses, it's not like, how should I say, not very mixed, only people of certain levels will be here to play.

*Suzhi*, invoked by Summer in the first quote, is a common rendering of status and class in China, which roughly translates into English as 'quality.' Discourses around *suzhi* are said to have originated at the time of the idea of population control in the 1980s, when China's failure to modernize was attributed to the low quality of its population. It later began to circulate more broadly as a general explanation for everything that held the Chinese nation back from achieving its rightful place in the world (Anagnost, 1997; Rofel, 2007). Anagnost points to more recent interpretations: as economic reforms increased privatization, so she suggests, *suzhi* appeared in new discourses of social distinction and the discursive production of middle classness – thus defining a 'person of quality' in practices of consumption and a middle-class desire for social mobility.

Notions of *suzhi*, people of a 'certain level,' personality and profession were brought up by club members and owners, their employees, and by players in the Internet cafés who knew about the Killer Game club scene. These distinctions, then, were also used to legitimize one's belonging to the clubs, especially in contrast to inhabitants and the spatial and technological infrastructures in the Internet café. Many of Lindtner's informants described that visitors to the Internet café, even if the café was located just down the hall from the Killer Game club, did not belong to the same social scene:

> I think, it might be related to education also. For example, there is a *wangba* out there, but it's for sure there, there are more of these youths, but here, for us here, the age ranges from 20 to 40, it's a group of people who are successful in their careers in society, or things like that … it has something to do with social status and their own education.

As this comment illustrates, being a participant in the gaming club not only provided a shared context for people of a distinct social class to connect with one another, but also produced and reproduced socio-economic positioning within society.

### Distinct modes of game play

Aside from differentiating based upon the site of game play, many also draw distinctions based upon the type of game played. Many gamers were quick to offer stereotypes of what kinds of people preferred what kinds of games. One of Szablewicz's informants, Xiaobo, illustrated this very point. When asked if he played games other than World of Warcraft, such as Korean MMORPGs, he dismissed them, noting that they were known for their cartoonish graphics and therefore appealed largely to females. By contrast, some gamers who chose to play Chinese games remarked that they chose them in part to support the domestic games industry.

In particular, players had a great deal to say about the differences between Warcraft III and World of Warcraft. Feijie, Yuan and Zhang, all devoted Warcraft III gamers, argued that Warcraft III, an RTS game, was a game that required one to *dong naozi* (use your brain). Yuan immediately differentiated it from 'Internet Games,' referring to it instead as 'electronic athletics,' and comparing it to the competitive sports of the Olympics. World of Warcraft is, by contrast an MMORPG, which, in the group's opinion, was more attractive to people who wanted to create a fantasy life for themselves and achieve a *chengjiu gan* (a sense of success) that seemed unachievable in real life. Also, because one could play a full game of Warcraft III in the space of half an hour, the group agreed that it wasn't as time consuming as RPG games, which require investments of both time and money for success.

Indeed, electronic athletics has been a recognized form of sports competition within China since 2003, and gamers can aspire to the professional level, sometimes going on to compete for prize money in national and international competitions. At such events, officials emphasize the need to separate these 'healthy' electronic athletics from other addictive online games. At the 2010 Esports Champion League Competition held in Beijing, one official remarked 'electronic athletics and Internet games must be strictly separated.' At this same event, Szablewicz was interviewed for the camera about her views on the industry and, prior to the interview, coached to carefully avoid any mention of Internet cafés and/or Internet games in her discussion.

Despite the distinctions made by those in the gaming industry or gaming community, parents and media sources often fail to acknowledge the differences between these games. When the Shanghai Zhonghua Vocational School announced plans to offer an electronic athletics elective in March 2010, the media was quick to report on the development, but much to the frustration of the school principal and students leading the class, the reports confused Warcraft III with World of Warcraft. For example, one web headline proclaimed 'A new experiment: A Shanghai vocational school initiates a "World of Warcraft" elective.' Similarly, reports about Internet addiction frequently bemoan 'Internet games' and their effects in general, not bothering to distinguish between the types of games with which they are concerned and the varying ways in which they are being played.

While the many different distinctions made by gamers about sites of play, game choice and social interactions within the games go largely unnoticed by the media, it is clear that such 'distinction work' is an important part of identity building and meaning making for our informants. In the case of 'electronic athletics,' distinction work is a necessary step in seeking legitimacy in the eyes of the government and public. These findings align with those of games studies scholar T. L. Taylor (2006), who noted that gamers do distinguish between different types of game play and many will go so far as to argue that certain types of 'casual' games are not 'real games' (p. 171). In urban China, we might add, it is not only about the choice of game and what constitutes a 'real game' but also about the contexts in which game play is situated, where the game is played and with whom.

We see this again in Lindtner's findings on the Killer Game clubs, where the type of game play was used to mark social distinction. Members of the clubs highlighted that the Killer Game itself attracted a particular personality type that was linked to one's ability for international networking or background in higher education. One of Lindtner's informants, Kevin, for example, who travels regularly between first- and second-tier cities in China and the United States for his trading business, described the linkages between his own personality, his profession and other members of the club:

The nature of the entertainment attracts certain kind of people, it matches certain personalities ... like me, my personality is very cheerful, lively, including a strong thinking ability, this is in line with my profession also. That's what attracts me most to the game, including your speech and those from others ... Only when people are more or less of the same level, can they be together. If there is a gap in terms of career or education level, aeh, then it might be very ... they can still play the game, but it is difficult for them to sit in the same room to play the game.

Similarly to Kevin, many of the club members worked in international corporations or had studied or worked abroad for many years. As such, they also distinguished their technology practices from those in the Internet café as being about international networking and helping to build a modern and international China. Zhen left China eight years ago for studies and work in the United States. Shortly after his return, one of his friends took him to one of the Killer Game clubs in Beijing, which Zhen described as not only a valuable resource to reconnect to local Beijing culture, but also – as he emphasized – to practice the kind of 'international thinking' he considers a necessary skill for employment in Chinese companies today:

I think this club really helps people to speak out, to speak their opinion. In Chinese enterprise, people are more and more outgoing these days, this is a good thing. This kind of club is a good thing ... This game is training you for international thinking ...

With their mix of computer-mediated game play and face-to-face social networking, Killer Game clubs thus became almost iconic representations of Chinese life style for an upper middle class of young professionals and entrepreneurs who maintained both local and international connections and professional ties. Participating in the clubs then not only entailed knowing how to play the Killer Game, but also how to position oneself within the new cultural climate of international networking, transnational business relations and/or education.

## Political and cultural discourse

The socio-technical distinctions made by Internet gamers, those within the electronic sports industry, and those who frequent Killer Game clubs are particularly important in light of the government's concerted effort to control and eradicate 'unhealthy' games. In recent years, the popular American online game World of Warcraft (WoW) has become the target of much negative media and government attention, as officials seek to control and restrict what is deemed to be its inappropriate content. In this section, we show that young WoW gamers exhibit multiple scales of participation through both their technology practice and their engagements with the broader political and social environment that surrounds their technology use. Specifically, we illustrate how the said gamers find new ways to creatively navigate game restrictions and respond to dominant discourses about Internet addiction.

### Engagement with local politics

While technological experience was in part shaped by the aforementioned inter-ventions, we found that Chinese youths developed numerous ways of circum-venting local restrictions of game software. For example, in 2007, the Chinese government required the local distributor of WoW to remove images of skele-tons from the game. The game graphics were changed so that skeletal characters were 'fleshed out' or replaced with large graves. The government's insistence on changing game graphics was widely disseminated in the local media as 'an effort to purify the Internet of anything that might affect national cultural information security or undermine the attempt to promote a harmonious society.' Many of Lindtner's informants commented on the narrative of harmonious society and its consequences for their game play, often rendering it as an abstract social force that they considered old fashioned or simply irritating. For many, the change in game graphics made visible a larger political project that was at stake:

> Bingwen: What's more, in China I am not quite clear about the reason [for the action], perhaps it's China's political situation. In the past when you died [in the game] there were bones and skeletons but now graves are used instead. What we were told is that the skeletons are frustrating and scaring people. But I feel graves are actually scarier.

> Xing: It's a grave, which didn't exist before. You see, there's a corpse drop-ping items. When you pick up those items, the corpse turns into a grave. Before ... there used to be a skeleton. It is a result from the upgrade, which is part of the governmental project to introduce harmony.

In the second quote, Xing describes how the new game upgrade suddenly led to changes of the game graphics – something he attributed to 'the governmental project to introduce harmony.' The irony, here, is that game players correlated the aforementioned changes in game graphics and the political reasoning behind it with exactly the feudal past from which the post-Mao government had tried to distance itself: We dislike the harmony such as the disappearance of skeletons. It is feudal and introduced as part of the whole cultural environment in China.

The change of game graphics constituted only one among many interven-tions into the online spaces of our informants. During fieldwork conducted by Lindtner in 2007, The Burning Crusade (TBC), an attractive expansion to WoW that introduced new features such as level cap increase and high-level in-game combat zones was released with a delay of over six months (in comparison to release dates in the US, Europe, Taiwan and Hong Kong for example). Players, however, not only discussed the changes of game graphics and the delay of TBC and the motivation behind these, but often took action. Several set up their own gamer servers, for example, using pirated versions accessed through the local media-pirate industry or logging into American or Taiwanese game servers (Lindtner, Nardi, Wang, Mainwaring, Jing, & Liang, 2008). Szablewicz's most recent research shows that little has changed since 2007, as gamers continue to migrate to foreign servers, due to disruption of service and restrictions on game play.

Aside from switching servers, WoW gamers have also found creative ways of responding to negative government and media representations and participating in political discourse. *War of Internet Addiction* is an hour-long machinima production that depicts WoW gamers' struggle to save their beloved game from government controls and Internet addiction 'experts' who seek to destroy it. The narrative is intricate, referencing government censorship and the issues surrounding the handover from The 9 to Netease, alongside other hot-button news items. The creator of the machinima, a self-proclaimed post-1980s-generation WoW player, made the film over the course of three months, with the help of over 100 WoW gamers who volunteered their time to the production. It was posted on video-sharing sites on January 21, 2010 and received millions of viewers and comments within days.

Following the release of the *War of Internet Addiction*, there was much speculation that the video would be banned. However, the video successfully harnessed what Yang (2009) has referred to as the 'playfulness' of the Chinese Internet. The genius of the video lies in its humorous take on many political issues, masking serious critique in Internet parody. Yet, while it managed for the most part to elude the censors, it did capture the attention of millions of Chinese gamers, successfully harnessing their passion for Internet games and directing it against government agencies, corporations and professionals who have interfered with game play.

In one of the final speeches of the video, Kan Ni Mei, the hero of the story, addresses Yang Yongxin, one of the Internet-addiction treatment specialists notorious for using shock therapy as a method to cure addiction. He states:

> Yang Yongxin, we are the generation that has grown up playing games. Over these many years people have changed and games have changed, but our love for games has not changed and the weak and disadvantaged status of the gamers within this society has also not changed ... What we are addicted to is not the game, but the feeling of belonging that games have given us. We are addicted to the friends and emotions we have shared over the past four years, to the nostalgia and the hopes and dreams we have placed on this game over the last four years.

It should be noted that *War of Internet Addiction* is not the first effort to promote 'gamer rights,' though it may well be the most successful, with over 10 million views in the space of one month. But 'gamer rights' is also a topic of discussion on online forums and bulletin board systems. For example, a member of Shanghai-based forum KDS Life commented on a much-publicized corporate battle over the hosting of WoW in China, connecting the disruption in service to larger issues of gamer rights and Internet addiction:

> Internet gamers also have rights.... In reality, despite their love of Internet games, there are many gamers whose work, life, emotional well being and

character go unaffected by them. As such, we cannot, just because of the existence of Internet addiction, cut out Internet games altogether.

(Liu, November 11, 2009)

For these gamers concerned about gamer rights, politics is not so much about disrupting or rejecting the state as it is about asserting the legitimacy of gamer identity and the gamer's right to play without restriction. The thousands who proclaimed support for the message of *War of Internet Addiction* did so in order to collectively acknowledge their participation in and affirmation of this virtual leisure culture. Similarly, gamers who build private servers and/or access VPNs (Virtual Private Networks) in order to log on to Taiwanese and European servers manage to subvert the authority of the state by circumventing it (see Lindtner et al., 2008 and 2009 for more details). While they do not necessarily seek to disrupt or overturn state policies, their actions are an indication of the creative ways in which gamers overcome game restrictions and forge new identities amidst constantly shifting technology sites and Internet policy.

### *Translocal engagements and identities*

Aside from illustrating the engagements of gamers in broader political and social discourse, gamer reactions to the video *War of Internet Addiction* also reveal the feelings of unity among the players; there was an overarching sense of *guishugan* (belonging) that spanned age, class and nation, among other things. The hundreds of thousands of comments left by viewers are a telling indication of this cama-raderie. Many affirmed their collective identity as a WoW gamer. Some replied in Chinese: 'We/I am a World of Warcraft Gamer!' Others used English to claim their identity as 'WoWers.' Still others chose to restate the climatic phrase '*ju shou*' or 'raise one's hands,' an expression of gamer solidarity that echoes the call made by the protagonist, Kan Ni Mei, in the final scenes of the film.

Most noticeably, the viewer comments reveal the emotional link that players share as a result of digital gaming. Some were moved to tears, while others stated that although they had long since quit playing WoW, they sympathized with the plight of the gamers and felt a connection to them. The comments had an unmis-takable air of 'once a gamer, always a gamer.' Many bloggers elaborated on this further, stressing the resonance of the film's message and the connections made through the game. Blogger Xiao Hami stated:

This is a rare and outstanding production; after viewing this [video], basi-cally every World of Warcraft gamer can sympathize [with its message] … in WoW everyone is equal, we can become friends with anyone, we can team up with anyone; … I love World of Warcraft, I love this game, and love the friends I have made in this game!

Another blogger, Aether, suggested that, beyond appealing to WoW gamers, the video speaks for an entire generation of Chinese youth:

Its [the video's] voice is the voice of the same yellow-skinned, black-eyed youth, the same logic and emotions flow through our blood; we grew up in the same environment and under the same circumstances.

The video also gained a following among overseas Chinese, many of whom re-posted it on YouTube and other video-sharing sites for fear that it would be banned in China. Szablewicz contacted three such overseas Chinese by email and conducted online interviews with them about their decision to re-post the video. Each of the three is located in a different part of the world, one in Japan, one in England and one in the United States. TheGreatestYang, who is credited with adding English subtitles to the video and posting it on YouTube, attends college in New York state. He states:

I was moved by this movie. I'm Chinese, immigrated to the US years ago. Although I've never played on the Chinese servers [*sic*], I know a lot of people who do and the necessary annoyance they face every day … I just feel bad for these players in China.

Johntxq, a 28-year-old overseas Chinese working in Japan, said about the video:

It reflects the innermost repressed feelings of the vast majority of Mainland gamers, its call has caused a lot of long-aggrieved gamers to experience a swell of emotion, and it has brought them to tears.

While gamers may engage in socio-technical distinction making in order to distinguish between different sites and types of game play, within these distinct sites of play gamers often share feelings of solidarity and belonging. As illustrated by these passionate affirmations of the video, *War of Internet Addiction* provides a unique example of gaming as a site of social connections and emotional bonding, also across geographical borders. As such, an important part of understanding digital media participation in China is to recognize online spaces as sites where ideas of self-hood and solidarity emerge in relation not only to the technology at hand but also to societal concerns and narratives that frame the technology practice, such as the discourse on Internet addiction.

## Discussion

Through the games young people in China play and the various sites, both urban and digital, they traverse in so doing, they also participate in wider social processes and discourses. In this chapter, we show that digital media participation is not confined to the production of new digital content or modifications of digital content, but also encompasses the creation of new meanings and socio-cultural values in relation to broader social developments. The creative ways in which gamers circumnavigate and respond to restrictions and the complex nature of socio-technical distinction work, through which new identities and social markers of difference are produced, serve as evidence of these various participatory processes.

By digital media participation we refer to recent works in new-media studies that have employed the notion of participation to speak to the ways in which users become co-producers of our Internet technologies today. New forms of Internet and communication technologies, ranging from online games and virtual worlds such as WoW and Second Life to online networking forums such as Facebook and Twitter, allow users to engage in active modification or creation of digital content. Across these platforms, the level of participation varies; some allow users to manipulate textual content and the visual interface while others require users to create virtual avatars or buildings. In the case of game mods, users actually modify software code, creating unscripted alterations of the program. Jenkins et al. (2006) describe digital participation as leading to a more broadly termed 'participatory culture, which is emerging as ... new media technologies make it possible for average consumers to archive, annotate, appropriate, and re-circulate media content in powerful new ways' (p. 8). Ito (2009) takes this one step further by situating media participation in relation not just to technological production, but also to cultural production and institutional processes such as the marketing and distribution of software, the production of class distinctions and cultural discourses.

In our work, we build on these prior studies, and use the notion of participation to encompass the production of both digital artifacts and cultural meanings. We show how digital media in China become sites of participation in changing social structures and cultural discourses of modernization.

Participation in digital media is often portrayed as a narrative of user empowerment, a method by which users may overcome social inequalities and gain agency (Jenkins, 2006). Our findings on socio-technical distinction making also serve as a note of caution, revealing that participatory platforms and new media are not simply distinct spaces that lead to the transcendence of social difference and power differentials. While gamers do form strong bonds and relationships across social and geographic boundaries, as in the case of WoW gamers' show of solidarity through *War of Internet Addiction*, users' participatory practices also reflect and reproduce dominant narratives and social inequalities. What this notion of participation allows us to see is that digital media practices must be read in conjunction with larger social, political and economic concerns.

The motivation behind this approach is to account for the highly distributed and contingent nature of media and its effects. As Ito (2009) puts it, 'new technologies never start out as separate or outside of existing structures. Change happens as a result of struggles between different discourses and institutions seeking to shape a new technology and set of genres' (p. 4). Such an approach is complemented by anthropological theory that recognizes media as sites of cultural production and identity formation (Appadurai, 1996; Ginsburg, Abu-Lughod, & Larkin, 2002). Media anthropologists have begun to track different forms of media participation as it shapes and is shaped by local cultures. Part of this project entails moving beyond media content to investigate the discourses, sites and practices that flow through and around technologies. For example, Brian Larkin (2002) conducted a historical study of cinema theatres in Nigeria, emphasizing the need to 'analyze the materiality of the theatre itself, theorizing its significance for an anthropology of the media that situates technologies in the wider social realms in which they take on significance' (p. 332). This chapter follows along these lines, emphasizing the identity politics implicated in gamers' choice of physical location, be it Internet café, dormitory or up-scale entertainment club. By engaging with these different sites, we have also shown that the transformation of technologies is not a single phenomenon. Rather, users are participants in many Internets, and technological change is experienced differently across these multiple spaces.

In much the same vein as Ito (2009), Larkin (2002) also notes that cinema theatres in Nigeria are entangled in larger discourses related to modernity, civilization and colonialism. The case of Internet cafés and digital gaming is no different. In the Chinese context, pervasive modernization discourses, ranging from efforts to promote a 'harmonious society' to efforts to combat 'Internet addiction,' both shape and are shaped by technology practice. As such, our research explores the various ways in which such discourses are absorbed and contested. On the one hand, increasing prejudice against Internet cafés and gamers' increasing willingness to label themselves 'addicts' indicates that such discourses do indeed affect identity and meaning making. On the other hand, our informants often contested such labels, as illustrated by the popularity of *War of Internet Addiction* and gamers' readiness to critique government claims that Internet addiction and Internet practices are harmful for the development of a harmonious society.

This contestation of labels and battle for legitimacy in the eyes of the Chinese government and media is in many ways reflective of struggles about digital gaming within the academic community. Indeed, game studies scholars have fought for many years to prove the legitimacy of game culture, which has led to a series of studies on the serious aspects of games and approaches which challenged the notion of a single Internet user or identity such as the Internet addict. T. L. Taylor (2006), for example, suggests that the concept of 'gamer' is fraught with stereotypes. She argues that gaming is often discussed in mass media outlets as highly anti-social, gendered and meaningless 'play.' Ian Bogost (2006) similarly argues that games are often seen in the context of amusement and distraction and challenges assumptions that a priori correlate games with fun or a waste of time. Mindful of these debates, we consider it crucial to acknowledge that the construction of a 'gamer' identity is entangled in complex webs of social, technological and economic change in China. Gamer identity is not simply shaped by the digital software one participates in, but rather emerges at the intersection of technological practice and participation in wider cultural discourses and debates, like the one on Internet addiction. We have shown in this chapter that the formation of identity is a contested process shaped both by people's practices, experiences and imaginations and by state discourse and pervasive media images. 'Game culture' or 'Internet culture' in China is not a monolithic entity, but an ever-changing conglomeration of participatory practices and identifications shaped by many diverse actors.

## Note

We would like to thank Paul Dourish, Bonnie Nardi, Ken Anderson, Tom Boellstorff and Mimi Ito for their valuable input and suggestions. We also thank our participants, the Intel's People and Practices Research Group, the Center for Organizational Research at UC Irvine and the U.S. Student Fulbright program, which supported part of this work. This research has also been supported in part by the National Science Foundation through awards 0921216, 0712890, 083860, 0838499 and 0917401.

Any opinions, findings, and conclusions or recommendations expressed in this material are those of the authors and do not necessarily reflect the views of Intel, the Fulbright Program, the U.S. Department of State or the National Science Foundation.

## References

Anagnost, A. (1997). *National past-times: Narrative, representation, and power in modern China*. Durham: Duke University Press.

Appadurai, A. (1996). *Modernity at large: Cultural dimensions of globalization*. Minneapolis: University of Minnesota Press.

Barmé, G. R. (2010, January 29). The harmonious evolution of information in China. *The China beat – blogging how the East is read*. Retrieved July 15, 2010, from http://www.thechinabeat.org/?p=1422

Bogost, I. (2006). *Unit operations: An approach to videogame criticism*. Cambridge, MA: MIT Press.

Chen, X. (2008, July 10). Zhuanjia jieshi wangyou hangye fuwu biaozhun. *Internet society of China*. Retrieved July 15, 2010, from http://www.isc.org.cn/ShowArticle.php?id=9623

Chow, E. (2010, January 13). Everything (almost) that's happened with Google + China so far. *Shanghaiist*. Retrieved July 15, 2010, from http://shanghaiist.com/2010/01/13/everything_almost_thats_been_happen.php

CNNIC (Chinese Internet Network Information Center) (2008). *Statistical Survey on the Internet Development in China (January 2008)*. Beijing: CNNIC.

CNNIC (2009). *The 23rd Statistical Survey on the Internet Development in China*. Beijing: CNNIC.

Eckert, P., & Buckley, C. (2010, January 13). U.S., Google and China square off over Internet. *Reuters*. Retrieved July 15, 2010, from http://www.reuters.com/article/idUSTRE60C1TR20100113

Ernkvist, M., & Strom, P. (2008). Enmeshed in games with the government: Governmental policies and the development of the Chinese online game industry. *Games and Culture, 3*(1), 98–126.

Ginsburg, F., Abu-Lughod, L., & Larkin, B. (Eds.). (2002). *Media worlds: Anthropology on a new terrain*. Berkeley, CA: University of California Press.

Golub, A., & Lingley, K. (2008). 'Just like the Qing empire': Internet addiction, MMOGs, and moral crisis in contemporary China. *Games and Culture, 3*(1), 59–75.

Hanser, A. (2008). *Service encounters: Class, gender, and the market for social distinction in urban China*. Stanford, CA: Stanford University Press.

Human Rights in China. (2005). Logging on in China's Internet cafés: An HRIC field survey. *China Rights Forum, 3*, 102–109.

Ito, M. (2009). *Engineering play: A cultural history of children's software*. Cambridge, MA: MIT Press.

Jenkins, H. (2006). *Convergence culture: Where old and new media collide*. New York: New York University Press.

Jenkins, H., Clinton, K., Purushotma, R., Robison, A. J., & Weigel, M. (2006). *Confronting the challenges of participatory culture: Media education for the 21st century*. White Paper, MacArthur Foundation. Retrieved from digitallearning.macfound.org.

Larkin, B. (2002). The Materiality of cinema theaters in Northern Nigeria. In F. Ginsburg, L. Abu-Lughod, & B. Larkin (Eds.), *Media worlds: Anthropology on a new terrain* (pp. 319–336). Berkeley: University of California Press.

Li, W. (2009) Zhaici Xinjie [A New Explanation of the Term 'Zhai']. *Journal of Shanxi Normal University (Social Science Edition) 36*(3):112–116.

Liang, B., & Lu, H. (2010). Internet development, censorship, and cyber crimes in China. *Journal of Contemporary Criminal Justice, 26*(1), 103–120.

Lindtner, S., Mainwaring, S., Dourish, P., & Wang, Y. (2009). Situating productive play: Online gaming practices and guanxi in China. *Human–computer interaction – INTERACT 2009*, 328–341.

Lindtner, S., Nardi, B., Wang, Y., Mainwaring, S., Jing, H., & Liang, W. (2008). A hybrid cultural ecology: World of warcraft in China. In *Proceedings of the ACM 2008 conference on Computer Supported Cooperative Work* (pp. 371–382). ACM.

Liu, Y. K. (2009, November 11). Moshou shengsi buming, shei lai baozhang wanjia de quanyi? *KDS Life*. Retrieved November 11, 2009 from http://club.pchome.net/thread_8_118_4749687__.html

MacKinnon, R. (2010, January 17). Google, China, and the future of freedom on the global Internet. *RConversation*. Retrieved July 15, 2010, from http://rconversation.blogs.com/rconversation/2010/01/google-china-and-the-future-of-freedom-on-the-global-internet.html

Martinsen, J. (2010, January 13). Google, Baidu, and wild speculation. *Danwei*. Retrieved July 15, 2010, from http://www.danwei.org/front_page_of_the_day/google_vs_baidu.php

Qiu, J. L. (2009). *Working-class network society. Communication Technology and the information have-less in urban China*. Cambridge, MA: MIT Press.

Qiu, J. L., & Zhou, L. N. (2005). Through the prism of the Internet café: Managing access in an ecology of games. *China Information, 19*(2), 261–297.

Rofel, L. (2007). *Desiring China: Experiments in neoliberalism, sexuality, and public culture*. Durham: Duke University Press.

Segal, A. (2010, January 26). The Chinese Internet century. *Foreign Policy*. Retrieved July 15, 2010, from http://www.foreignpolicy.com/articles/2010/01/26/the_chinese_internet_century

Szablewicz, M. (2004). *A space to be your virtual self: An introduction to the world of Internet gaming in the urban Chinese wangba*. MA thesis. Duke University, Durham.

Szablewicz, M. (2010). The ill effects of 'opium for the spirit': A critical cultural analysis of China's Internet addiction moral panic. *Chinese Journal of Communication, 3*(4).

Taylor, T. L. (2006). *Play between worlds: Exploring online game culture*. Cambridge, MA: MIT Press.

Tsui, L. (2003). The panopticon as the antithesis of a space of freedom: Control and regulation of the internet in China. *China Information. 17*(2): 65–82. DOI: 10.1177/0920203X0301700203

Weber, I., & Lu, J. (2007). Internet and self-regulation in China: The cultural logic of controlled commodification. *Media, Culture and Society, 29*(5), 772–789.

Yang, G. (2009). *The power of the Internet in China: Citizen activism online*. New York: Columbia University Press.

# 6 Lost in virtual carnival and masquerade

## In-game marriage on the Chinese Internet

*Weihua Wu and Xiying Wang*

### Introduction

A study of the 'in-game marriage' opens up a socio-cultural carnival and virtual masquerade of existing gender bias in online-game-based computer-mediated communication (CMC). This term, usually attached to the category of cyber marriage in Chinese language, refers to the virtual-marriage-making activity between two virtual avatars initiated by game players. Following text-based cyber marriages in the narratives of Multi-User Dungeon or Dimension (MUD) games, in-game marriage first appeared as an extra emotional bonus of different game reward systems, similar to virtual money and treasures in the MMOGs. The earliest form of cyber marriage was the text-based cyber marriage, which still exists and is quite popular on the present-day Chinese Internet. It usually involves getting married in online communities or chat rooms by typing set vows of marriage. The procedure of the text-based cyber marriage is relatively simple. Both potential spouses send messages to ask the forum organizer's permission to get married. After granting approval, the operator of the cyber marriage serving website will send the couple a greeting mail, host the virtual wedding, and issue a marriage certificate for public access. The couple's marriage names will be listed in the virtual community daily.

Another type of cyber marriage that needs to be mentioned here is weddings performed within MUD games, which involve

> [a] loosely binding agreement between two players to behave within a game as if they are married. Usually established with a formal ceremony (whatever that means in the specific game) attended by high ranking members of the game administration. Sometimes couples are afforded additional rights, such as having a private domain or house. A record of the marriages is generally publicized.
>
> (McDaniel, 2000)

Cyber weddings are often conducted in massively multiplayer online games (MMOG) and mostly remain online, benefitting from the promise of disembodied CMC, though occasionally the in-game marriage transcends online anonymity and identity and players explore an offline relationship. A 2007 research report found that

23% of teenagers between 14 and 18 years old had experienced in-game marriage at least once. The report showed that 56% of virtually married teenagers took additional steps to create an offline relationship, including dating, intimacy, and sometimes even sexual intercourse (China Central Television & The Base of Teenage Psychological Growth and Development of Beijing Military Hospital, 2007).

This paper attempts to reveal the cultural specificities that underpin the rise of the virtually defined marriage in Chinese MMOGs through understanding its local game codes and 'marriage' regulations. It also looks at the possibility of interaction and dialogue between virtual consumption and reality, by exploring the game players' gender performativity and how the 'imagined' or 'virtual' relationships impact on 'real' life.

This study is based on two periods of textual analysis, from January to April 2005 and from March to July 2009. It looks at the regulations and patterns of in-game marriage and its changes within the most popular Chinese-language online games as listed in the top 10 registered-users MMOGs in both 2004 and 2008, with special attention paid to the official websites and bulletin board services hosted on the game developers' servers, particularly on Swordsmen Online, Fantasy Westward Journey, Westward Journey II, and Audition Dance Battle Online.

The top 10 domestic MMOGs in 2004 were:

*   Swordsman Online (Jianxia qingyuan, http://jx.xoyo.com/)
*   Fantasy Westward Journey (Menghuan xiyou, http://xyq.163.com/)
*   Westward Journey Online II (Dahua xiyou 2, http://xy2.163.com/)
*   Monster and Me (Huanling youxia, http://hlyx.91.com/)
*   M2 China Online (Shenjia qibing, http://www.m2china.com.cn/)
*   World of Qin (Tian jia, http://www.m2china.com.cn/)
*   Chain of Life (Xuanyuan jian, http://swdol.joypark.com.cn)
*   Conquer (Zhenfu, http://zf.91.com/home.htm)
*   Meteor, Butterfly and a Blade (Liuxing hudie jian, http://www.mbs.com.cn/),
*   NetDream (Mengxiang, http://www.netdream.com.cn/).

(China Internet Research Center & 17173.com, 2005)

The top 10 domestic MMOGs in 2008 were:

*   Fantasy Westward Journey (Menghuan xiyou, http://xyq.163.com/)
*   The Condor and The Lovers (Tianlong babu, http://tl.sohu.com/)
*   Zhuxian (http://zhuxian.wanmei.com/),
*   March (Zhengtu, http://zt.ztgame.com/)
*   QQFantasy (QQ Huanxiang, http://fo.qq.com/)
*   Legend of Blood (Rexue chuangqi, http://home.mir2.sdo.com/NewWeb/Home/)
*   Audition Online (Jin wutuan, http://au.52pk.com/)
*   Westward Journey Online II (Dahua xiyou 2, http://xy2.163.com/)
*   World of Legend (Chuanqi shijie, http://home.woool.sdo.com/project/200907_intro/)

- Truth, Three Kingdom Unique (Zhen, Sanguo wushuang, http://bbs.wush-uangol.com/).

(China Internet Research Center & 17173.com, 2009)

The first author interviewed 15 game players (seven females and eight males) in March 2005, and the follow-up study in 2009 included 15 additional game players. These semi-structured interviews (usually around one hour each) were conducted online through two popular Internet Relay Chat (IRC) software programs: MSN and ISQ (same as ICQ, but available only for Chinese Mac Users). The ages of the game players ranged from 20 to 30, and all of them had been playing MMOGs for more than two years. Nineteen of them had experienced in-game marriage at least once, and all of them had experienced attending in-game weddings online. All quotations included in this paper were translated into English by the authors, and names mentioned are pseudonyms.

## The virtual nostalgia of in-game marriage

The gaming space of MMOGs has now extended beyond digital leisure activity, as it is significantly reconstructed within the socio-economic order under the state discourse. Since 2000, MMOGs have become one of the most important domains that the government nurtures, involving specific online-game related financial and economic policies (Zhang, J., 2005), in particular with a view to investment in the Chinese game market. The 2008 Report of the China Game Industry shows that 133 domestic game studios launched 286 Chinese-language MMOGs by the end of 2008, not to mention the numerous imported online games from Korea, Japan and the US. The online game market rose by 76.6% in 2008, compared to 2007 (GPC & IDC China, 2009). A survey conducted by China Internet Network Information Center (CNNIC) in 2009 also shows that more than 64.2% (217 million out of 338 million) Chinese Internet users had regularly been involved in online game entertainments by June 2009 (CNNIC, 2009). The survey in 2005 showed that more than 19.76% (18.5 million out of 94 million) Chinese Internet users had regularly been involved in online game entertainments before the end of December 2004 (CNNIC, 2005).The 2008 *Statistical Survey Report on the Internet Development in China* shows the total number of Internet users has increased to 298 million. MMOGs have becoming the most popular online forms of entertainment among Chinese young people, and the heated growth and popu-larity of MMOGs are expected to continue (CNNIC, 2009; GPC & IDC China, 2009; Xu & Tian, 2005; Zhang, J., 2005).

Meanwhile, China's leading online game operators, Netease.com and Kingsoft Inc., have developed massive game-related spaces through which millions of gamers have logged in to blog about their gaming experience, personal feelings and in-game love stories and to upload screenshots and personal photos. The website of Easy Blogger (Xiaoyao ke), hosted by Kingsoft Corp. at http://blog.xoyo.com/, encourages gamers to exchange gaming experiences with each other by blogging about their virtual lives. Other related websites, such as Easy Show (Xiaoyao xiu) at http://show.xoyo.com/, have offered services allowing gamers to upload personal photos and gaming snapshots. By July 2009, Easy Show had around 801,587 registered users, with 148,836 albums of photos including both real-life snapshots and in-game images (These numbers are increasing every day: on August 28, 2006, there were only 43,181 registered users, 18,408 albums, and 114,581 images). These extended spaces nurtured by MMOG gaming activities create a communicative platform for young people to experience interactive entertainment with animated features and filmic story lines. Moreover, they offer new possibilities for an ongoing integration between the Internet and the everyday life of the general public (Bakardjieva & Smith, 2001; Bargh, 2002; DiMaggion, Hargittai, Neuman, & Robinson, 2001; Howard & Jones, 2004; Wellman & Haythornthwaite, 2002).

Although criticism of in-game marriage systems has increased on MMOG servers in recent years, Chinese young people are actually rewriting the MMOG industry's plans to some extent.

> I kind of have the feeling that Chinese game players initiate many more possibilities than the in-game system created, because I remember it is really difficult to get a real 'in-game marriage' that was blasted by a NPC matchmaker and your virtual friends a few years ago. In-game marriage is a market, which attracted not only players, also the Bosses (the game designers and companies).
>
> (Xie, M, 28)

> It seems that in-game marriage is quite like a virtual daily routine, and lots of my gaming buddies found it irresistible. If you want to play a game, you have to get married at least once, and then you get the chance to upgrade your levels.
>
> (Xi, M, 22)

In-game marriage has recently become a 'compulsory' gaming setting in some domestic MMOGs. Looking at Chinese in-game marriage reveals cultural uniqueness with regard to the issue of computer-mediated relationships in its details. Compared to the simple procedure of text-based cyber marriage, the in-game marriage is far more complicated and is dominated by heterosexual ideology and gender bias because of the regulations built into the gaming systems on how to get married in the games.

As of 2008, all the top 10 domestic MMOGs have implemented their own particular and complex in-game marriage services (compared to 8 out of 10 in 2004). Most of them are also nostalgically embedded with ethnic folk culture and social context, and usually anchor storylines within traditional Chinese fairy tales such as Westward Journey (Xiyouji) and Romance of the Three Kingdoms (Sanguo yanyi) by following the classical narrative structure of heterosexual love stories which involve the sequence: 'the birth of the hero' (players create avatars), 'meeting the princess' (two players let their online avatars fall in love with each other), and 'hero getting married' (two players decide to let their online avatars get married). All these steps correspond with the assumptions of a typical narrative and imply heterosexual ideas. Since happy endings are a part of gender-biased storytelling, game players are required to follow the typical marriage instructions from Chinese folk and ethnic traditions. These regulations, rules, and marriage laws enacted within different Chinese-language MMOGs coincidentally bear striking similarities with and implications in relation to social rules and Chinese rituals.

Avatars with the same gender are not allowed to get married in the MMOGs. This principle seems to be a basic and rigid one in almost every MMOG, with the exception of one game called Chain of Life (I) that allowed same-sex avatars to get married as the system was not coded to differentiate between marriage of same-sex avatars and that of opposite sex avatars, and thus did not restrict homosexual relationships. However, after a short period of time, Dream of Mirror Online (the second net version of Chain of Life (I)) no longer supported online homosexual marriage. It seems that same-sex marriage is as big a taboo online as it is the reality in today's China. However, in 2008 Courage OL released its marriage system which allows two female avatars to get married (but not male avatars) and to play as couples online by completing quests suitable for virtual couples only.

Basically, all games encourage monogamy and offer some exclusive benefits to married avatars. They also all have policies discriminating against avatars who get married more than once. In the games World of Qin and Dream of Mirror online, every avatar has only one chance to take part in a wedding ceremony. In the game Swordsman Online, the matchmaker (*yuelao*) gives rings as gifts to the avatars for only their first marriage.

Avatars can also not get married until they have climbed into 'the middle class' by both earning experience points for their actions and accumulating enough wealth in in-game virtual money. Usually, avatars should spend a lot on their wedding, as in the game Westward Journey Online (II), which charges at least 100,000 in virtual money for a wedding ceremony. In the game World of Qin, the avatars pay for the wedding according to how long the ceremony lasts: for 10 minutes, the male avatars pay 1,000,000 in virtual money, and if the ceremony is to last for an hour, they pay 10,000,000. In the game Westward Journey Online, couples can choose different types of houses to live in after getting married, but the basic rule is that if you want a fancier house, then you will have to pay much more. An ordinary flat costs 400,000 in virtual money, while the VIP flats cost 5,000,000.

Another gender-biased aspect of in-game marriage is that male avatars have to take the initiative without exception – that is, the man should be the one to propose and the woman has the right to accept or reject the proposal. For example, Swordsman Online authorizes a matchmaker in charge of the weddings in the game. If a female avatar comes to the matchmaker and asks him to propose for her, the matchmaker will refuse and say, 'It's not good for a woman to propose. You should follow the tradition and ask your future groom to come here to initiate the proposal.' It is obvious that such regulations imply the gender-stereotypical roles of active men and passive women in romantic relationships, even in the Internet entertainment market.

It is noticeable that the above principles for constructing a virtual Chinese marriage in a traditional society provide a venue for young people in urban areas to marry and consume according to the ideology of a consumer society. The principles create a normative status of gender bias which produces a world biased systematically against women. The principles also copy the formulas for living everyday life in an urban Chinese society into a visual game and create a world regulated by money, hierarchy, and class which may be harsher than reality. These institutionalized regulatory hierarchies are hidden not only in the skeleton of online games and computer-mediated communication, but also in contemporary modern Chinese societies, providing the backdrop for the grand narrative of in-game marriage.

The in-game marriage forms a digital metaphor of Chinese society online. The individual experience of in-game gender performance sheds some light on the social transformations hidden behind the 'fun' spirit of online gaming.

## The gender battlefield of performed in-game marriage

The seduction of in-game marriage has succeeded in contributing to the development of Chinese MMOGs and boosted both absolute numbers and the diversity of game players from across China's rural and urban areas, which led to a highlighting of the gender issues coded into the socio-cultural settings of the games. In particular, gender is emphasized by the one of the most popular gaming activities accompanying in-game marriage, *dajia* (literally: fighting against everything artificial, faked, something that cannot happen in offline reality).

> I went to one of my friend's weddings, but he didn't get married successfully that time, because a group of avatars rushed into the banquet and began to slaughter guests, hosts and everybody in the name of *dajia*. All that happened when the leader of the group shouted, 'The bride is a man!'
>
> (De, F, 22)

Of course, within the game scene mentioned, the bride was a beautiful woman, but behind the bride was actually a male player disguised as a female avatar. Every embodied and gendered avatar in MMOGs may assume any age, gender, height, skin color, or other physical attributes, career and social status, etc., which raises the question why '*dajia* attacks are aimed only at fake gender. Why is it acceptable for female avatars to be manipulated by male players as long as they interact in the game space only as gaming icons, without getting involved in intimate dealings: love, sex, or marriage? In this context, it is important to explore the strong trend of homophobia on gaming platforms that is masked by the liveliness and diversity of gender performativity among players.

*Dajia* objections within games can be linked to the concept of *renyao*, a discriminatory and negative word which was originally used in Chinese to refer to trans-genders in Thailand. More recently, it has been used to describe a man disguised as a woman in Mainland China. The term *renyao* is used within MMOGs to describe in-game gender swapping in which male players employ a female avatar and proceed to play their avatar in a hyper-feminine way, aiming to get married to male players and even representing themselves as real women with online friends and husband. Gender swapping is one of the most debated issues in online gaming, though it allows players access to gender identities that are often socially prohibited or delegitimized offline. Butler (1990: 25) argues that 'gender proves to be performative – that is, constituting the identity it is purported to be. In this sense, gender is always a doing.' In the context of MMOGs, the game players' gender swapping turns into a masquerade which blurs the boundaries between 'appearing' and 'being' a virtual woman in cyberspace, and becomes a 'problematic expression and performativity' of femininity, with an implication of there being 'no fixed identities' (Butler, 1990; Salih, 2002).

The sociological study of gender swapping by Suler (2004) examines this in-game phenomenon in relation only to male players: why are males so interested in experimenting with a woman's identity? Suler offers some hypotheses for explaining the emergence of gender swapping, e.g. 'in some online games where participants assume imaginary identities, being a female may be advantageous'; or 'a male looking for intimacy, romance, and/or cybersex from another male may be acting upon conscious or unconscious homosexual feelings'; or 'in rare cases, gender-switching could be a sign of what would be diagnosed as "gender confusion" – i.e., a psychological disturbance where one's identity as a male or female has not fully developed'(ibid.: 149–52).

The phenomenon of *renyao* emerges in the context of more and more female game players entering this once male-dominated domain, with research for the US suggesting that over 50% of gamers are by now female (Cassell & Jenkins, 2008), which changes earlier set-ups in which both female and male avatars were manipulated by male gamers. It is worth noting that male avatars being played by female gamers are not included in the term *renyao*, and that this is not seen as problematic. This might be linked to all the Chinese fairytales about women who disguise themselves as men. The most popular female images are Mulan and Butterfly Lovers.

Mulan is a heroine who disguises herself as a man so as to serve in the army in her father's place. While serving, she is recognized as a courageous soldier and is offered a government post. Zhu Yingtai is the female protagonist in Butterfly Lovers who cross-dresses as a man in order to pursue formal education at a time when women were not allowed to go to school. She then falls in love with her classmate Liang. In order to resist the arranged marriage by her father, she commits suicide together with Liang and their spirits turn into butterflies, which symbolize freedom. Just like these archetypal images from Chinese history, women's gender swapping within the game space seems to find approval with the general gaming public, who tend to think that their performances in cyberspace are a display of autonomy and individuality. By contrast, male gamers involved in gender swapping are thought of differently from their female peers, and they are always despised and referred to as *renyao*.

Many female informants stated that they play female characters during most of their gaming time, and some of them take pride in being able to consistently play as women, as if to preserve the integrity of their identity.

I am a true girl! I hate it when people call me *renyao*.

(De, F, 22)

I never have the idea that I may play a female avatar in games. I cannot play as a boy in the cybercafé with my friends and perform as a girl in the game, I want to be relevantly 'true' to myself and my friends in online game, somehow, like in the Xiaonei and Facebook.

(Li, M, 24)

The above gamers' statements show a clear self-identification with their avatars and emphasize the consistency of their online and offline gender identities. Even if they clearly know that there is no true gender as such in Chinese MMOGs, they insist that it is better to be true to their own gender.

Here, there is no true gender! I have never thought to change my gender online. Beside, even if I say that I am a woman, others won't believe me 100 percent. It's just so exciting and cool to be a superwoman and so why would I bother to be a man?

(Mei, F, 23)

The 'superwoman' in the digital world successfully redraws the picture of the victimized woman into the model image of Chinese womanhood. She is good at fighting, hence, rich and attractive in the virtual world. The 'superwoman' in the Chinese context is often called Iron Lady, who is powerful, aggressive, and assertive, and therefore competent enough to compete with men. The Iron Lady invites criticism for her lack of femininity in real life, whereas the 'superwoman' in the game space is challenged on whether or not her gender is true to her offline gender.

Many female avatars are *renyao*, especially those who are very good at fight-ing. I know many male game players like to be female avatars in the game because it is easy for women to make use of their appearance to find husbands and cheat them for virtual money and equipment.

(Yun, F, 23)

This narrator is a 'virtuous woman' who plays MMOGs just for online dating with her boyfriend and to be immersed in a fantasy environment (Yee, 2005). These types of 'virtuous women' are not good at fighting, and 'forming a rela-tionship' is their first priority. Within the game space, the better an avatar is at fighting, the more beautiful her appearance will be. Thus, 'virtuous women' may become jealous of other female avatars' attractiveness, and employ the notion that 'fighting is in the domain of the men' to attack cute female avatars, which suggests that if a female avatar is good at fighting, she must be an impostor, and therefore *renyao*. Using fighting as the only criterion to classify gender roles, this notion based on stereotypes attacks not only *renyao* but also 'superwomen'. In response, one 'superwoman' pointed out:

Now I feel it's stupid to acknowledge that I am in fact a woman. It's nonsense to ask me to prove myself as a woman through the web camera. Why should I let them see my real face? I reject it always. I never ask for favors from others. I think women should be self-confident and self-respectful.

(Qing, F, 24)

Turkle (1996) and Bruckman (1999) argued that female characters are inundated with attention, sexual advances, and unrequested offers of assistance, based on the assumption that they cannot do things by themselves in the context of MUD games. To avoid being discriminated against as *renyao*, the 'superwomen' turn down all these offers and reject being classified as powerless women. Within the game spaces, 'superwomen' are like feminist activists in a conventional patriarchal society trying to raise the consciousness of fighting against gender dichotomies in cyberspace, though their endeavors are often ignored by others.

Some male interviewees find it uncomfortable to admit to being *renyao* or to gender swapping online, and they label their experience as a way of learning differences between genders.

Maybe it is not to enjoy, but just to try a different game experience brought by the other gender.

(Heng, M, 25)

For other male players, being *renyao* is an active choice.

Being a *renyao*, the most important thing is to be happy, if you are not happy, you'd better not be a *renyao*.

(Feng, M, 23)

I have been playing online games for six years. All the avatars I play are women. Yes, I am the so-called *renyao*. In the past six years, no one has believed that I am *renyao*, and no one doubts that I am not a woman in real life.

(Lei, M, 20)

Some male players assuming *renyao* roles outed themselves and shared their experiences with the general public, such as Cimeigui (literally, thorny rose), on the 'Netgame Special Community' hosted by pcgame.com, who reviewed all his strategies for playing a *renyao* and reflected on his five years of being a perfect virtual woman in MMOGs.

The first thing is to be ready for *renyao*, which means you should use a special mailbox for your female avatar with the profile of a virtual girl and a picture for 'security reason (in case somebody asks for an exchange of email addresses for further contact).' Then you need to learn the tricks of being a *renyao*, research women's habits, men's needs, and more importantly, the strategies – talking with girls and remembering how they respond to your questions, noting useful information such as chatting with your buddies about girls, and then 'developing' yourself in this way. Last, but not least, the netname, a catchy feminine name to take the boys' interest. Representing a sweet and tender female image of yourself, you should keep your mouth shut no matter what happens. As soon as you are inspirited by the treasurable strategies of being a *renyao*, nobody can reject the glamour.

(Cimeigui, M)

For these male-turned-female players, gender is merely a 'play of appearance,' a style, a disguise (Butler, 1990). During the journey towards becoming a successful female avatar, they are capable of 'parodic recitation to produce certain transgressive effects' (Lloyd, 2005: 108), such as having a sweet netname and performing in a feminine way. The reason that *renyao* are criticized so much is that people feel that they have used the virtual identity of a woman for their own benefit, e.g. getting 'money', equipment, and upgrade levels from helpful online male partners, and even getting married online. However, a successful *renyao*'s principle is 'I never ask things from others, but people are always willing to give me what I want' (Lei, M, 20). Bruckman (1999) argues that male players will often log on as female characters and behave suggestively, even encouraging sexual advances, while men playing women's roles in MMOGs have made remarks about other male players (real male characters) expecting sexual favours in return for technical assistance.

Actually, I chose the female fairy character as my avatar in the first place, simply because it was really beautiful. I work in my Lab all day and it is no harm for me to enjoy eye-candy happiness. I realized that the female avatar could be the blessed one when I joined a super Boss combating teamwork; other team members give me the first opportunity to collect combat-useful items. Ladies first – funnily enough … I never thought to be dishonest with my team members about my real gender .

(Lo, M, 29)

No matter how discriminatory the situation is for *renyao*, in Chinese MMOGs 'being *renyao*' means more than operating a sexy female avatar as a male player. Instead, *renyao* are a combination of seductive female avatars and happy virtual gender swapping.

On the in-game marriage market, the virtuality of the game space has produced three strong types competing in their femininity: 'virtuous woman', 'super-woman', and *renyao*. 'Virtuous women' use their stereotypical concepts of femininity in real life but fail to become virtually commodified 'super' avatars online, while trying to form relationships in the virtual world. 'Superwomen' create a new image of Chinese women who are assertive and aggressive, although their avatars have gorgeous appearances and great bodies, while nonetheless refusing to be gazed at or seduced. *Renyao* 'act out' fictional women's gender roles, have fabulous women's bodies and appearances online, and are good at making use of their virtual femininity to get whatever they want. In short, the three groups of feminine avatars employ different ways of performing their gender and exploring the virtual landscape of in-game marriage, which in turn is also defined by the virtual gender roles.

## The aftermath of virtual marriage

As players engage in in-game relationships, interact emotionally with others, promote a striking change in contemporary Chinese youth sub-culture, and define in-game marriage as a new paradigm of computer-mediated relationships, there remains the question why these young game players are so eager to enter into in-game marriages.

> Having in-game marriage is just like eating fruit, you can survive without eating it, but everyone just likes it.
>
> (Li, F, 28)

> It's just for fun, it's different from the reality, having a lot of fantasy – besides, it saves money. It's horrible to get married in reality.
>
> (Qing, F, 24)

> In-game marriage is only a game; you can play and get high, but you don't need to take it seriously.
>
> (Feng, M, 23)

> Just want to experience a thing that we haven't experienced before.
>
> (Hua, F, 27)

The reasons offered by interviewees varied, but they had a common theme: 'having fun'. In China, marriage is still too serious a topic for many young Chinese people because of the responsibilities that go with it. As one game player put it:

> Because in real life, we are all afraid of getting married; but in the game, we can do something we are afraid to do and take no responsibility for it.
>
> (Feng, M, 23)

Most interviews indicated that in-game marriage should be understood simi-larly to children's 'playing house', with the difference that players are adolescents and young adults. Another difference is that the players in the children's games portray the gender roles that are assigned to them and take up the associated social responsibilities, while in MMOGs they experiment with marriage, try to alleviate the responsibilities that go with married life, and make their choices in the spirit of play, in a free, independent, and spontaneous spirit that demonstrates anti-utilitarianism, joyful experiences, and imaged creativities (Cao, 2005). At present, many Chinese subversively discard and re-evaluate the spiritual and cultural burdens of a traditional and puritanical convention and the political ideology that was once deeply embedded in their lives and thoughts (Li, 2004), and in-game marriage has to be understood in this context.

Zhou (2004) argued that cyber marriage might result in a misunderstanding among young game players when they downplay the responsibilities involved in marriage. Studies showed that most game players do have a clear picture of the difference between offline life and online virtual games.

> I know the marriage in game will face its dead end finally. The so-called true love stories never exist, neither online nor offline.
>
> (Liu, F, 30)

> You can enjoy the dreaming-like intimacy in the game and explore the limit of virtual relationship that you would like to engage with. I found that intimate relationship in reality has been becoming more and more difficult, but you can easily have a bunch of sweet lovers and make excellent virtual career development with your online buddies. Whatever, my opinion is, it's virtual, different from real, no harm to anyone.
>
> (Jiang, M, 22)

For some game players, in-game marriage has a real function, that is, to enrich their dating relationships and experience.

> My boyfriend goes to college in another city, playing the game together, for us, is a kind of dating.
>
> (Yun, F, 23)

> I got married once online. I established an account for my girlfriend so that we could get married there. She didn't want to play. So I played the two avatars at the same time and let them get married.
>
> (Lin, M, 23)

These two informants found it difficult to get married offline, even though they had dated a stable boyfriend or girlfriend, respectively, for a very long time. This problem is being encountered not only by them, but also by many other young Chinese, especially those who are highly educated and live in urban areas. Although the marriage law stipulates that Chinese men and women can get married at the ages of 22 and 20, respectively, there are many factors that prevent them from getting married early. Usually, universities do not allow students to get married, neither undergraduates nor postgraduates. Workplaces once enforced the government's one child policy and encouraged their employees to get married and have babies at a later age (Tsui & Rich, 2002). Even without these restrictions, young people still have to consider many practical problems involving money, housing, etc. While getting married offline has become a distant or almost impossible goal in the short term, many young Chinese have discovered in-game marriage as an adequate alternative and see it as a celebration of their dating relationships and an affirmation of their commitments to each other.

> My dancing buddies in Audition Online fell in love and got married, though virtually. I can see they are happy. When we role-play together, they called

each other Laogong [husband] and Laopo [wife]. Crazy enough. Take it easy, no one gets hurt.

(Li, F, 21)

The Audition Online is simply evil, but we love it. I know my two virtual friends had been married two years, then they walked onto the 'real' real red carpet in the real world, but the husband ran away from their honeymoon. The real marriage is really scary.

(Lu, F, 30)

The playful and imagined adventure of in-game marriage is based on the promise that 'marriage' can be a game (Zhang, F., 2005; Zhou, 2004), both in reality or on the virtual playground. In-game marriage offers an attractive picture of self-discovery and adventure to young Chinese in cyberspace, and has become one of the forms of what is called 'the third sexual revolution' in China (Huang, 2002). The first sexual revolution in China happened after the establishment of the People's Republic of China, and should be called a prohibition rather than a revolution, as for almost 30 years the only privileged function of sex was reproduction. The second sexual revolution, after China's opening up in 1978, saw sex not only for reproduction, but for pleasure and the satisfaction of desires as well. The third sexual revolution began in the late 1990s, and stated that sex is a human right.

In-game marriage indeed mocks the perceived seriousness of real marriage by introducing the notion of a 'digital ethnography' practiced and experienced by millions of Chinese to pursue alternative dating forms and a virtual marital life on the Internet, both seriously and just playfully. According to the primary website organizer Lazhuo at Tianya Wedding Hall, between 2001 and July 2006 the Tianya community certified 1,156 cyber marriages, out of which 14 couples developed offline relationships leading to real marriages, while 239 cyber-married couples filed for divorce, as their computer-mediated relationship had become unbearable to them. In-game marriage has proved especially popular among those young Chinese labelled either the post-1980 or the post-1990 generations, who are often criticized by the general public and the media as irresponsible and self-centred 'lost generations' (Li, 2008).

The mass media severely criticize the concept of cyber marriage, arguing that it 'has encroached on social ethics and even violates the law' (Lu, 2004; Zhou, 2004) by perverting young people's understanding of marriage.

Some people call it as the danger zone. They believe that cyber marriage is innocuous as long as it is kept in cyberspace. But once you have the guts to bring it into the realm of reality, you will risk jeopardizing your real marriage.

(Zhou, 2004)

During the past few years, there have been many legal disputes involving game players and cyber marriage, as it has been viewed as destructive to real life marriages. Within such narratives, innocent husbands and wives suddenly discover that their spouses are engaging in another marriage on the Internet (having virtual sex or even giving birth to a virtual baby, e.g. in Fantasy Westward Journey), which is followed by them filing for divorce (Dai & Li, 2004; Fang, 2004; Wang & Gao, 2004). According to the Intermediate People's Court of Nanjing, Jiangsu Province, the first divorce case involving cyber marriage was filed in 2001. Since then, the numbers have continued to increase: in 2002, there were 20 cases reported, while in 2003 they totalled 80. During the first five months of 2004, 151 cases were documented. In Guangzhou, the Information Times reports that 30% of legal marital disputes were caused by cyber marriage (Yuan & Sivelle, 2005).

Most existing Chinese studies on MMOGs focus on the negative outcomes of gaming, e.g. aggressive behaviour, addiction, social isolation, or identity confusion (He & Liu, 2005; Li, 2004; Lu, 2004) of players rather than seeing it as an activity which forms an important part of many people's leisure lifestyles (Bryce & Rutter, 2003). However, in this study, game players are viewed as subjects with high mobility, flexibility, and a spirit of adventure, rather than as passive victims influenced by gaming.

Chinese MMOGs offer many benefits to married avatars, and sometimes getting married is a way for users to upgrade their levels or improve their online lives quickly.

> Most game players are male. Some of them will get married, even knowing very well that the other party is also a man in real life.
>
> (De, F, 22)

> Getting married online does not mean falling in love. I get married online just like finding a new friend in real life.
>
> (Li, F, 28)

Where upgrading levels is the main concern, in-game marriage becomes a means, not an end itself. One female informant's story can best explain this idea of relationship.

> When I met my online husband, Wan, for the first time, he had a wife called Nei, who is a man in the real life (*renyao* – I am joking). When I became close with Wan and felt that I could not live without him online, Nei volunteered to get a divorce with Wan and gave me a chance to marry him online. Nei became our best friend.
>
> (De, F, 22)

In reality, this type of romantic story seldom happens. Love is usually regarded as the basis of marriage and is always associated with exclusivity and jealousy. However, in-game marriage helps to shake off the exclusivity and jealousy and provides for the building up of friendships that are 'pleasurable, emotional and affective' (Roseneil & Budgeon, 2004: 139). Many game players think that 'making friends' becomes the most important function of online games, and in-game marriage is regarded as the ultimate form of friendship.

I just want to know more people through playing the game; many people emphasize the friendship.

(Lei, M, 25)

Previous Chinese studies on game players claimed that players become addicted to gaming and abandon physical ties and their offline social life (He & Liu, 2005; Yang & Xu, 2004). Here, we would argue that digital friendship is a method of communication and socialization (Taylor, 2003) and that this type of digital communication and socialization has become an indispensable part of young people's lives because of the impact of technology on the social lives of young Chinese. When asked to compare the quality of their MMOG friendships with their offline friendships, 39.4% of male respondents and 53.3% of female respondents stated that their MMOG friends were comparable to or better than their offline friends (Yee, 2005). The emotional bonding and interaction between game player and virtual avatars has become the key motivation for them to play the game and live their marriage online every day.

Regarding the general criticism that in-game marriage is the 'cool killer' (Zhou, 2004) of real marriage, one informant begged to differ.

I've been a game player for many years. According to my understanding of the Chinese Internet environment and Chinese netizens, I think that the possibility of in-game marriage turning into a real marriage is almost zero. Friendship is more rational and pervasive.

(Qian, M, 24)

According to this statement, most online in-game marriages do not lead to offline marriage but are useful for developing friendship networks online and then extending these networks to offline life. The possibility of turning an in-game marriage into an offline marriage relationship is quite small because young Chinese have such unrealistic expectations of their online spouses that, if and when they meet offline, they most probably receive a death blow of disappointment. *Jian guang si*, which means 'perish upon seeing light' (Zhou, 2004), is a Chinese term that refers to such fateful meetings. However, in most cases, even when the fantasy romance ends, friendship survives.

In-game marriage, conversely, has becomes a means to celebrate both online relationships and the possibility of their conversion into offline friendships, instead of remaining limited to the imagined virtual reality. Friendship undermines the interpretation of the marriage system as imagined nostalgia consisting of sexist gender roles. In this regard, the findings of this study are consistent with those of Roseneil and Budgeon (2004), who concluded that friendship is appreciated more highly than romantic love, and that there was a tendency to de-sexualize intimacy, thus making it more similar to friendship.

# Conclusion

Chinese MMOGs have become valuable exemplars to show how online gaming has influenced and changed relationships between young Chinese, in particular through the immensely popular MMOG-related in-game marriage. This not only offers a new perspective on forms of CMC, but also provides a new framework for understanding the attitudes and the behaviour of young Chinese regarding gender, sexuality, and daily life.

This study has focused on the social phenomenon of in-game marriage and fills a gap in research undertaken by Chinese academics, as an interdisciplinary study connecting new media, gender study, and youth culture. In-game marriage has become a digital metaphor of Chinese society on the Internet and the game players' exploration of visualized and institutionalized in-game marriage sheds light on the social transformation hidden behind the gaming spirit, on the mixture of the traditional cultural symbols and new media, and on the connections between gender, sexuality, and society.

This chapter has explored the rules and regulations of in-game marriage, which construct a symbolic world by coding a collage of gender hierarchies and gender expressions in the virtual space by changing them into more material-istic and ideological constructs than their offline counterparts. In this context, young Chinese game players demonstrate high mobility, flexibility, and a spirit of adventure. They are rebellious not only within the virtual world, but also in their real life. Existing studies have focused on online addiction, violence, and self-isolation of young Chinese through their immersion into game spaces. However, this over-emphasis on posited psychological effects neglects the assessment of the force of social transformation expressed in the young game players' practices.

This chapter has also elaborated on gender performativity and gender swapping as masquerade by male game players, which ultimately resulted in the classifica-tion of female avatars into three types, the 'superwoman', the 'virtuous woman' and the *renyao*. Each has been shown to have different strategies of performing their gender and femininity, thus creating an intense competition in the dating market, with the *renyao* emerging as the victor. Through the performances of visual masculinity and femininity by game players in in-game marriages, both female and male players and avatars interact with each other in various situations of everyday real and virtual lives, subvert the binary gender system, and develop relations between individuals and the digital network, and subvert individual behaviour within the consumer society. In China, the concepts of gender and sexuality are still deeply institutionalized in every aspect of daily life. However, as this study demonstrates, within the game space, these pre-embedded, institu-tionalized concepts of marriage and hierarchy fail to control gamer choices for their avatars' lives.

The adventure of in-game relationships and the emotional interactions with other gamers allow for an ethnographic understanding of contemporary Chinese youth culture and its struggles to find its own voice between the commercial, digital environment in which they play and the ideological surveillance of the commodified socialist society in which they live. Here, we have examined how practices of in-game marriage contribute to the challenges of existing gender stereotypes and hierarchies, both online and offline.

Chinese in-game marriage highlights the struggles between the marginalized subject and the mainstream objects of the commercial system, combining the pursuit of CMC and the surrender of offline hierarchies within the game's storytelling. Through the demystification of the offline legal marriage in China and its attack on the dichotomy of gender roles, albeit virtually, in-game marriage provides alternative discourses that represent the new generation's confusion and eagerness for seeking alternatives to the construction of relationships and pre-existing gender roles, employing the affordances of the gaming spaces provided on the platform of new media.

# References

Bakardjieva, M., & Smith, R. (2001). The internet in everyday life: Computer networking from the standpoint of the domestic user. *New Media & Society, 3*(1), 67.

Bargh, J. A. (2002). Beyond simple truths: The human–internet interaction. *Journal of Social Issues, 58*(1), 1–8.

Bruckman, A. (1999). Gender swapping on the Internet. In P. Ludlow (Ed.), *High noon on the electronic frontier: Conceptual issues in cyberspace* (3rd ed., pp. 317–325). Boston: MIT Press.

Bryce, J., & Rutter, J. (2003). The gendering of computer gaming: Experiences and space. In S. Fleming & I. Jones (Eds.), *Leisure cultures: Investigations in Sport, media and technology* (pp. 3–22). Eastbourne: Leisure Studies Association.

Butler, J. (1990). *Gender trouble: Feminism and the subversion of identity.* New York: Routledge.

Cao, H. (2005). When love encounters the spirit of play. *China News Weekly, 2005*(8), 63.

Cassell, J., & Jenkins, H. (2008). From Quake girls to desperate housewives: A decade of gender and computer games. In Y. B. Kafai, C. Heeter, J. Denner, & J. Y. Sun (Eds.), *Beyond Barbie and Mortal Kombat* (pp. 5–20). Cambridge, MA: MIT Press.

China Central Television, & The Base of Teenage Psychological Growth and Development of Beijing Military Hospital. (2007). *When marriage has became online business.* Beijing, China: China Central Television & The Base of Teenage Psychological Growth and Development of Beijing Military Hospital.

China Internet Research Center, & 17173.com. (2005). *The rank of top 10 domestic MMOGs.* Beijing, Shanghai, Shenzhen. China: Iresearch Consulting Group.

China Internet Research Center, & 17173.com. (2009). *The rank of top 10 domestic MMOGs.* Beijing, Shanghai, Shenzhen. China: Iresearch Consulting Group.

CNNIC (China Internet Network Information Center). (2005). *The 15th Statistical Survey Report on the Internet Development in China.* Beijing China: CNNIC.

CNNIC. (2009). *The 24th Statistical Survey Report on the Internet Development in China.* Beijing China: CNNIC.

Dai, X., & Li, C. (2004). Cyber marriage: Game or trap? *Community, 3–5,* 61.

DiMaggion, P., Hargittai, E., Neuman, W. R., & Robinson, J. P. (2001). Social implications of the Internet. *Annual Review of Sociology, 2001*(27), 307–336.

Fang, G. (2004). Cyber marriage encounters the legal vacuum. *The Western, 7,* 35–36.

GPC (Game Publishers Association), IDC China. (2009). *The 2008 Report of China Game Industry.* Beijing, China: GPC & IDC China.

He, H., & Liu, H. (2005). Internet love of the married group and role conflict. *Journal of South-Central University for Nationalities (Humanities and Social Science), 25*(2), 131–135.

Howard, P. N., & Jones, S. (2004). *Society online: The Internet in context.* Thousand Oaks: Sage.

Huang, X. (2002, 26 August). New revolution, sex revolution. *News Weekly*, 24–27.

Li, H. (2008). The influence of thirty-year opening-up in shaping the post-80s characteristic. *China Youth Research, 19*(11), 89–92.

Li, J. (2004). Virtual marriage once. *News Weekly*, 7, 48–53.

Lloyd, M. (2005). *Beyond identity politics: Feminism, power & politics,* London and Thousand Oaks: Sage.

Lu, L. (2004). Wangluo hunli, xianfeng haishi youxi? *Mental World, 97*, 4–6.

McDaniel III, H. (2000). Marriage. *Encyclopedia of MUDs.* Retrieved July 15, 2010, from http://www.iowa-mug.net/muddic/dic/M.html#MARRIAGE

Roseneil, S., & Budgeon, S. (2004). Culture of intimacy and care beyond 'the family': Personal life and social change in the early 21st century. *Current Sociology, 52*(2), 135–159.

Salih, S. (2002). *Judith Butler.* London and New York: Routledge.

Suler, J. R. (2004). Do boys (and girls) just wanna have fun? Gender switching in cyberspace. In A. Kunkel (ed.), *Gender Communication* (pp. 149–52). Dubuque: Kendall/ Hunt.

Taylor, T. L. (2003). Multiple pleasure: Women and online gaming. *Convergence, 9*(1), 21–46.

Tsui, M., & Rich, L. (2002). The only child and educational opportunity for girls in urban China. *Gender and Society, 16*(1), 74–92

Turkle, S. (1996). *Life on the screen : Identity in the age of the Internet.* London: Weidenfeld & Nicolson.

Wang, X., & Gao, X. (2004). How to judge the cyber marriage. *The Western*, 37–38.

Wellman, B., & Haythornthwaite, C. A. (2002). *The Internet in everyday life.* Malden, MA; Oxford: Blackwell.

Xu, L.-Y., & Tian, X. (2005). On the development of Internet game industries. *Journal of China Youth College for Political Science, 24*(2), 114–119.

Yang, H., & Xu, H. (2004). The disassimilation of digital game and social countermeasure. *Journal of Inner Mongolia Agricultural University (Social Science Edition), 6*(21), 121–123.

Yee, N. (2005). The psychology of massively multi-users online role-playing games: Motivations, emotional investment, relationships and problem usage. In R. Schroeder & A.-S. Axelsson (Eds.), *Avatars at work and play: collaboration and interaction in shared virtual environments* (pp. 187–207). Dordrecht: Springer.

Yuan, R., & Sivelle, K. (2005, June 7). On-line marriage can be a mixed blessing. *China Daily.* Retrieved July 15, 2010, from http://www.chinadaily.com.cn/english/doc/2005-06/07/content_449284.htm

Zhang, F. (2005). A divorce lawsuit caused by cyber-marriage. *China Society Periodical, 7*(30), 44–45.

Zhang, J. (2005). Policy suggestion to developing online game in China. *Science and China Youth and Technology 3*, 48–49.

Zhou, R. (2004, March 19). Marriage bells toll in cyber churches. *China Daily.* Retrieved July 15, 2010, from http://www.chinadaily.com.cn/english/doc/2004-03/19/content_316461.htm

# Part III

# Instrumentalizing the carnival

Rioting as activism

# 7 Human flesh search engines

## Carnivalesque riots as components of a 'Chinese democracy'

*David Kurt Herold*

## Introduction

Since Hu Jintao's ascension to the offices of President of China and General Secretary of the Chinese Communist Party, the creation and maintenance of a 'harmonious society' has been one of the main aims of the Chinese central government (see, e.g., Xinhua News Agency, 2005, June 27). The concept seeks to combine the continuing rapid development of the Chinese economy with gradual political reforms designed to 'forge an ever closer relationship between the people and the government', while promoting 'stability and unity' (ibid.). Put differently, it is the aim of the central government to maintain public order while pushing the country towards ever greater economic prosperity.

As a result of this aim, public protest is often met with force (e.g., Xiao, 2009, June 26), dissidents who criticize the government are placed under house arrest (e.g., Kahn, 2007, May 19), and news reports about events that might reflect badly on the government are suppressed (e.g., Washington Times, 2009, January 21). While the political structures in China are changing and officials at all levels of the Chinese state are showing a willingness to reform China (e.g., Buxi, 2008, July 10), any public outpouring of criticism against the Chinese Communist Party or the central government seems unacceptable. 'The people' are supposed to remain quiet and obedient, while the government figures out how to proceed.

Academic discourses on the Internet in China often discuss the online situation in the same terms, with Chinese netizens (Internet + citizens) being portrayed as attempting to circumvent the repressive actions of the Chinese government (e.g., Chase and Mulvenon, 2002; Giese, 2006; Hachigian, 2001; MacKinnon, 2008). The interaction between the two sides is seen almost as a contest, or as 'contention' (Yang, 2008; 2009), and outsiders, for example, multi-national Internet corporations, are portrayed as being co-opted by both sides in their struggle against each other (e.g., Goldsmith and Wu, 2006; MacKinnon, 2009).

A few academic studies point out that the situation is less clear cut and that the relationship between the Chinese state, in its various institutions, and Chinese netizens is far more complex and diverse. There are local officials who interact with the people under their jurisdiction via the Internet (Hartford, 2005), others who employ their knowledge of the Internet to further their own goals within the government's or Party's hierarchy (Lagerkvist, 2005), while the changing ICT landscape affects different individual officials differently, to create a far more nuanced situation (Damm and Thomas, 2006; Shie, 2004).

Against this background, statements made by Hu Jintao in his first online chat with Chinese netizens (see, e.g., Mu, 2008, June 20 for a video clip and an English summary, also for the quotes below), carry several interesting implications, in particular as the entire event was obviously scripted and the answers pre-planned. When asked what he did when online, he 'said the Internet is an important source of news', and that he perused both Chinese and international news sources, thus 'legitimizing' the access of foreign news sites by Chinese netizens. In contrast to the picture presented in European and American media reports (e.g., Daily Telegraph, 2009, August 14), Hu Jintao, and therefore the Chinese central government, seem to approve the accessing of international news websites by Chinese netizens.

He added that the Internet was also 'a channel where the president can find out what netizens' concerns are, and a way to gather their opinions', thereby creating the impression that the Internet in general and 'the People's Daily Strong Country Forum' in particular constituted legitimate and direct channels of communication between netizens and the central government, by-passing local levels of government. In effect, the statements made by Hu Jintao encouraged Chinese people to use the Internet (rather than the streets of China) to air their grievances with officials, and promised that the online posting of problems would receive the central government's attention.

The Chinese Internet, and the 'Human Flesh Search Engines' (*Renrou Sousuo*, below as RRSS) in particular, have to be studied and understood in this context. The Chinese Internet is a wild, carnivalesque place with many sites of contention (see Yang, 2009), but it is a place where such wildness is – within limits – permissible and even encouraged by the state, if it coincides with greater 'harmony' offline and if it can be used by the central government to improve the relationship between the Chinese state and its citizens. While the exact boundaries, rules, and limitations are still being negotiated (or 'contested', to use Yang's terminology), in China, the Internet appears to be an integral part of a new social contract between the state and its citizens that emphasizes the need for offline stability and 'harmony' while allowing for considerable leeway online and promising to listen to the criticism of citizens it is if aired online.

One unique feature of the Chinese Internet demonstrates this leeway more than any others: the RRSS, which would be a cause for legal action in most other countries but are an acceptable (and almost mainstream) part of the Chinese Internet. Even Google runs an RRSS in China (see Google China, 2009) in addition to its usual search engines for pictures, books, academic articles, etc. The largest and most popular RRSS in China (Mop.com, 2009a) receives hundreds of postings each day.

In this chapter, following a provisional working definition of RRSS, a number of examples will be provided to show that RRSS represent an integral part of the new social contract between the Chinese state and its citizens as outlined above. Chinese citizens are employing RRSS to address problems the official government structure is unable or unwilling to handle, which range from personal grievances, problems, or observations of individuals, to the outrage of large groups of Chinese people over specific events, to online protests against aspects of the political system or government officials.

## A working definition of RRSS

Simply put, RRSS aim to track down offline individuals by employing as many computer users as possible in the search. Baidu Baike (2009), the online encyclopaedia hosted on the webservers of China's largest search engine, compares RRSS to 'normal' search engines like Google or Baidu by pointing out that RRSS are far more reliable and far reaching, as they rely not on mere computer algorithms, but rather on the voluntary contributions of thousands of Chinese netizens who are contributing their own, personal, offline knowledge.

The encyclopaedia continues by pointing out that there is often not a lot of difference between forum debates of a topic and a case of RRSS, as both are started by an original poster who outlines the topic of the thread or the RRSS search. Other users respond to the original posting with their own (often irrelevant and off-topic) posts until the entire thread runs out of steam or the RRSS search comes to a successful conclusion. The main difference between a forum debate and an RRSS search can be found in their impact on offline individuals, though. While forum debates rarely have offline consequences, the aim of an RRSS search is to identify specific offline individuals, usually in order to target these individuals for some form of punishment, a point this chapter will return to later.

Baidu Baike (2009) also outlines an understanding upon which all RRSS are supposedly based (see for a similar description also Mop.com, 2009b). Among the 'rules' for RRSS, there is an attempt at a fine balance between the individual's need for privacy, which is to be respected by all netizens, and the collective's need to punish corruption or evil, which supersedes all individual rights. Individual netizens are expected to supervise their own behaviour, so as to ensure that no innocents are harmed through an RRSS, but the very nature of the RRSS makes a central control or clearing system impossible. RRSS work by enlisting as many people as possible to identify specific individuals, and the result is frequently that an online 'mob' forms, intent on 'hunting down' the 'target' provided by the original poster. Given these parameters, it is surprising how often the RRSS have worked over the past few years, and examples will be discussed in the next part.

A final 'rule' worth mentioning here is the first 'understanding' Baidu Baike (2009) mentions, i.e. the love of China as the motherland of all Chinese netizens, and the resulting obedience to Chinese laws this requires. While RRSS are very similar to the stirring-up and then running amok of a mob of people against individuals who are labelled 'evil', the encyclopaedia implies that the RRSS are more than just that; instead they are presented – whether correctly or not – as legitimate expressions of outrage of law-abiding citizens of the People's Republic of China. As mentioned in the introduction, RRSS have to be understood within the political framework of the PRC, not as an anarchistic (online) movement of disgruntled and oppressed (offline) citizens. Judging from the self-presentation of Chinese netizens, and the examples in this chapter, RRSS represent a new but legitimate form of political discourse in China, not a form of citizen resistance against a corrupt or over-powering state apparatus.

## From personal interest ...

The simplest form of RRSS are started by individuals trying to track down an individual they know, but with whom they have lost contact. Rather than going to the authorities, many Chinese now post their queries on RRSS websites, in the hope of faster success. They post all the information available to them, and might even include a picture of the person they are looking for. In some cases, the poster is only trying to get in contact with the person they are looking for, for example to thank someone who helped them in the past (Yunluo, 2008, December 17), or to get in contact with a run-away wife (Ante, 2009, March 11). Others intend to punish the person they are looking for and ask for the help of the online community. To this end they include details of that person's deeds in their search request, hoping to attract the sympathy of other netizens, for example in the post of a wife and mother of a one-year-old child, who is looking for her missing husband and his mistress, by including the accusation that the mistress was leading her husband into drug abuse (admin, 2009, June 14). Similarly, a man is looking for his younger brother who abandoned the family two years ago, leaving the older brother to care for their sick grandfather, who is now close to death (admin, 2009, November 23).

These latter posts by individual netizens seeking the help of the online community to punish someone who wronged them sometimes get out of hand. Occasionally, one of these personal requests for vengeance or punishment of an individual 'evil person' catches the imagination of the online community and causes the formation of large mobs of Chinese netizens who start to 'hunt' for the 'guilty' individual. Once the 'target' has been tracked down, this leads to a severe harassment of this individual, their family, their employer, etc., with often drastic consequences for the targeted individual.

One of the first RRSS hunts to inflame online opinion in Chinese cyberspace started with a 5,000-word post on a popular bulletin board (BBS) connected to the online game World of Warcraft (WoW). One game player posted on an entry in which he accused his wife of infidelity with a student she had met while playing WoW in April 2006 (French, 2006). After returning from a business trip, he checked some of his wife's log files, messages, and emails, and found several saved conversations between his wife and this student that hinted at an affair. Instead of confronting his wife directly, the enraged husband posted the 5,000-word entry on the BBS, publicly accusing his wife and the student of adultery. He included lengthy quotes from the logs he had found and asked fellow netizens for their help in identifying the offline user behind the WoW handle 'Bronze Mustache'.

Netizens responded in great numbers and within days the real name of the student behind the WoW handle that the betrayed husband had discovered was posted online, together with his address, phone number, etc. Enraged netizens started harassing the student and his family, to a degree that he and his entire family barricaded themselves into their home and disconnected all lines of communication to the outside world so as to escape the harassment and threats (Soong, 2006, April 17). The student's university and the parents' employers were contacted by netizens asking for their immediate dismissals, and extremist posters on blogs and BBS forums called for the public execution of the student and the unfaithful wife for breaking up a marriage.

Within the WoW game, users began to congregate in the area where the student could usually be found so as to protest the alleged affair, slowing down the Internet servers of the company behind WoW in China in the process. After several demonstration marches and 'sit-ins', a large number of users met and had their game characters commit suicide together in order to push their protest even further.

In addition to posts seeking support from netizens for the punishment of others, there are also posts of people who have been impressed by someone they have encountered, and who then turn to the Internet to share this with others. If many other netizens agree with the original poster's impressions, they proceed to spread the story across Chinese cyberspace and RRSS are started to identify the 'good person' the original poster encountered. One such event, of which a summary with links to further information can be found at Fauna (2009, February 8), was started when a netizen in Beijing heard a young woman playing the guitar and singing in the Xidan Underground tunnel. The netizen, called alucard77117, liked the performance so much that he videoed the girl twice and uploaded the videos to the Internet. The videos were watched by over 3 million people and netizens began asking for more information about the girl. The female performer soon disappeared, while a person claiming to be the original poster of the videos asked for netizens not to pursue her any longer, as she had been frightened by all the attention.

Besides talent, poverty is another reason for Chinese netizens to become interested in a person, often with the intention of either giving advice or attempting to help the person in need. In 2008, a female netizen using the name 'I am a peasant girl' posted her life's story to the Sina BBS, describing her desperate financial situation, her poor background, and hard life (summaries with links at Shaohua, 2008, September 25, and 2008, October 25). Her story was copied across many other sites and heavily commented upon by Chinese netizens. Some criticized her for complaining about her hard lot, others tried to encourage her or to give her advice, while yet others started an RRSS to find her, with the intention of helping her. The story became so widespread that it caught the attention of the national TV channel CCTV, and it ran a segment on her and on the changes that her blog entry had caused in her life.

While a number of personal RRSS requests received disproportionately numerous responses from Chinese netizens, a few caught the attention of the authorities as well, and one such case even became a matter for the Chinese legal system. The case occupied the Chinese Internet for most of the year 2008 and began with a young woman committing suicide. The young woman had recently discovered that her husband was having an affair with another woman and became so depressed that she decided to jump off a building in December 2007.

She left behind a suicide note on her own computer and her sister decided to post the suicide note on the dead woman's blog (see Soong, 2008a). Additionally, the sister decided to add a letter of her own to the blog, in which she attacked the cheating husband and provided the husband's real name as well as his place of work and place of residency (Buxi, 2008, July 19).

The information was used by netizens to start an RRSS that quickly produced the husband's phone numbers, exact addresses, etc. as well as those of the woman he was allegedly seeing. Netizens then began to harass both of them by calling all their known phone numbers, by phoning their colleagues and superiors at work, by painting rude messages on the side of the house of the parents of the husband, etc., which led to the dismissal of the husband from his job (Soong, 2008b).

Instead of going into hiding, the husband decided to counter-attack by suing three Internet sites, as well as a friend of the sister's who had helped her post the deceased's materials online (Buxi, 2008, July 19). The case caught the imagination of the media as the first RRSS trial in China and occupied many legal professionals throughout 2008 (ibid.), but ended with a disappointing result for the husband, when the People's Court in Beijing ruled on December 18, 2008, that one of the websites and the friend had to pay the widowed husband 3,000 and 5,000 RMB respectively for causing him emotional distress (Chinaview.cn, 2008, December 18). The other websites were judged innocent, as they had attempted to delete some of the information posted while the RRSS was going on.

The ruling is important within the context of this chapter, as it demonstrates that the judges did not condemn the posting of identifying information on the Internet, nor did they rule against RRSS in general. Instead, one of the people who made the RRSS possible was punished for causing emotional distress to the husband, and the website was punished for not attempting to regulate the RRSS while it ran. None of the netizens who harassed the husband was punished or censured, thus signalling to China's cyberspace that RRSS are legally acceptable as long as they are at least partially regulated by the website owners, and that participating in an RRSS and in the offline harassment that often accompany them is also not considered illegal by the Chinese legal system.

This verdict by a Chinese court legitimized the use of RRSS websites by individuals to punish others who had wronged them, as the sister of the deceased was not condemned, and absolved all those netizens who participated in the RRSS or the harassment that followed. 'The Chinese State' announced that it was not going to interfere with this practice beyond asking site owners to exercise a certain – but largely undefined – restraint when an RRSS is conducted on their websites. The victims of RRSS hunts were not protected by the court, and the compensation awarded to the husband of the deceased was for causing emotional distress, but not for causing him to lose his employment, or for the damage done to his parents' home. In short, if an individual netizen manages to attract large numbers of netizens to his/her cause, then they are free to begin harassing other Chinese individuals.

## ... to mob anger ...

The majority of RRSS are started by specific individuals who are trying to locate other specific individuals. However, most of the largest RRSS in Chinese cyberspace are not initiated by individual netizens, but by groups of netizens who become enraged over a story spreading on the Internet, and decide to do something about it.

In one early but very famous case in March 2006, a nurse from the north of China decided to rid herself of her frustrations over a failed marriage by allowing a camera man to video her while she crushed a small kitten's head with stiletto heels (Shanghai Daily, 2006, March 16). The video, and stills from the video, were uploaded to the Internet and caused a huge stir both in China and abroad (see e.g., Daily Telegraph, 2006, March 4). An RRSS was started and both the woman and the camera man were eventually identified by Chinese netizens. Both lost their jobs, due to intense harassment by netizens, and both had to publicly apologize for their behaviour, while the media and animal welfare activists used the episode to lobby the Chinese central government for the enactment of animal protection legislation.

Also in 2006, a foreign English teacher with the online name of Chinabounder began describing his sexual conquests of Chinese girls in Shanghai on the Blogspot blogging service. The blog's language was highly literary and the author described his sexual encounters with numerous Shanghainese women in great detail. Additionally, he used comments made by his female partners to criticize China, Chinese culture, Chinese politics, Chinese men, etc. on a wide range of issues. He displayed a detailed knowledge of China's history, which he used to defend his views against all who attempted to argue against him in comments left on his blog (Chinabounder, n.d. – the entries referred to here date to the time before September 2006).

Because Blogspot was blocked in China at the time he remained unnoticed by Chinese netizens for many months, although he became a household name among the more technologically savvy Internet users, especially among male expatriates living in China, who started chatting on- and offline about him. Once Blogspot was unblocked in China, though, this changed dramatically. Within a week, increasing numbers of Chinese netizens visited the site and started venting their anger about the posts on the blog in Chinese cyberspace.

At the end of August, 2006, Prof. Zhang Jiehai, a professor of psychology at the Department of Sociology in the Shanghai Academy of Social Sciences, called for all Chinese to join him in a hunt of this immoral foreigner and asked for help in identifying him so that the authorities could expel him from China (Soong, 2006, August 28; and Chen, 2006, August 31). The open call for help from Chinese netizens in hunting down a foreigner who was perceived as insulting all Chinese gained a lot of support on the Internet and resulted in widespread Western media attention as well. The online hunt slowed down very fast, though, once Chinabounder appeared to have left China and stopped blogging on his site. Additionally, expatriates blogging in China, as well as Western media organizations, confused the issue through the publication of several conflicting claims about Chinabounder's identity and purpose in blogging. Despite Western media attention, the involvement of Prof. Zhang, and widespread online hysteria about Chinabounder and his blog in September 2006, Chinese authorities ignored the entire affair and neither commented on it nor took any action.

In another incident, a Western woman stopped a car driver from entering a bicycle lane in Beijing. The Western woman had an altercation with the driver during which the Chinese man forcibly removed her bicycle from the road. The Western woman did not back down, however, and retrieved her bicycle to continue to block the car's entry into the bike lane. The event would not have been remarkable, except for the fact that a bystander had pointed his mobile phone at the developing situation and uploaded the resulting photos (Soong, 2006, October 27).

The photos show numerous Chinese bystanders who looked on but did not interfere in the scene to support either the Western woman or the Chinese driver, but reactions online were very different. Chinese netizens were outraged at first that a Western woman had dared tell a Chinese man how to behave in his own country, but this impulsive and nationalistic reaction soon changed to at first include, and later on focus solely on criticizing, the Chinese man in online debates. Netizens accused him of having embarrassed the entire Chinese nation, of having lost face for China, and wondered why a country with a history of 5,000 years kept producing such uncultured people. As the debates gathered steam online, netizens used the partly visible number plates in the photographs to track down the driver, and soon the driver's name and his personal details, including his phone numbers, were published online, at which point the online community started harassing him and his family until he publicly apologized for his behaviour and for having shamed China (China Daily, 2006, November 16).

The foreign woman in the pictures was never identified, nor did anyone try to track her down or to involve her in the debates. The driver's apology that the online community forced him to make was also not directed at her. The driver did not apologize for having threatened the foreign woman or for having thrown her bicycle to the side of the road, but instead he apologized to Chinese netizens for having embarrassed and shamed the Chinese nation in front of foreigners.

Another incident to be mentioned here was hardly noticed by Western news media, but created quite a stir in Chinese cyberspace in 2007 and provoked a response by Chinese government officials. This was the story of Beijing Boy, a video about students of an art school in Beijing whose videoed antics in the classroom met with intense criticism online after being uploaded to various video websites, among them YouTube and its Chinese counterpart, Tudou (Soong, 2007). The uploaded video shows two male students physically attacking a teacher during class while about half of the other students are cheering them on and the teacher tries to continue his lesson (Zhang, 2007, May 30). Netizens identified both the school and all the students involved within days and began a harassment campaign that only died down after both CCTV 2 and CCTV News delivered a response from the central government asking netizens to control themselves and to calm down while the government appointed a commission to investigate the matter (CCTV 2, 2007, May 31; CCTV News, 2007, June 1).

The government was seemingly not interested in getting involved in the affair. It never moved to protect the art school in Haidian, nor the students or their families while they were being targeted for harassment. Authorities were also strangely absent when a crowd of self-appointed reporters descended on the school and tried to enter its grounds during teaching hours, and they didn't stop the reporters from harassing all who entered or left the school campus. Netizens were lobbying for an increase in government control over education and over the behaviour of both teachers and students, but the official answer given via CCTV was to ask for more individual responsibility and self-restraint, while arguing against the need for stricter government control, both on the Internet and in real life.

In another incident that involved the stupid behaviour of an individual which outraged Chinese netizens, Chinese government officials got involved and decided to punish the target of the RRSS. A 21-year-old female called Gao Qianhui from Liaoning province recorded and uploaded a five-minute video (Zhouhaichuan0, 2008, May 22), in which she complained about the long period of mourning after the earthquake in Sichuan in May 2008 (Tan, 2008, May 22; and Tang, 2008, May 21). She made a number of highly rude remarks about the victims of the earthquake and about the survivors and blamed them for interrupting the TV schedule and causing her favourite online games to observe three days of mourning. Netizens across Chinese cyberspace became very incensed about her remarks, and several RRSS were started that soon identified her. Before she could be harassed, though, it emerged that the police had detained her pending further investigation.

> Yang Zhiyan, the chief instigator of the backlash against 21-year-old Gao Qianhui, was also quick to dismiss any notion of wrong doing. 'She just had to be stopped', the 27-year-old said simply. 'In the face of a catastrophe, we Chinese have to be of one heart.' 'Gao Qianhui publicly defamed the State Council's announcement of a national mourning period through the fastest and most effective avenue possible [the Internet] and she should be dealt with according to the laws on public order.' He added, proudly: 'It was the great netizens who alerted the police and gave them her details to arrest her.'
>
> (Fletcher, 2008, June 25)

Not only are officials of the state condoning the use of RRSS for the punishment of wrongdoing, but in this case, the police accepted the information collected by Chinese netizens and acted on it to punish the victim of the RRSS. Together with the judgment in the Human Search Trial later in 2008, this constitutes a clear approval of RRSS and the behaviour of Chinese 'cyber-mobs' by Chinese government officials and institutions. Different government institutions appear willing to allow ordinary citizens to address problems on their own, and to punish those that they think deserve punishment. Ordinary citizens are thus empowered to judge other ordinary citizens based on their behaviour and to mete out punishment, with the occasional support from government authorities.

## ... to protests against government officials

While Chinese government authorities have been willing to allow netizens to form online lynch mobs to punish other ordinary citizens, a number of RRSS have been used to attack government officials as well. The officials targeted by RRSS were accused of corruption, collusion with criminals, crimes, etc. and a number of them lost their positions or have even been arrested on the basis of evidence produced by RRSS.

One such official, Lin Jiaxiang, the Party secretary of the Shenzhen marine affairs office, attempted to molest an 11-year-old child in a restaurant while drunk (Fauna 2008, November 1). When the parents of the girl confronted him, he shouted at them, claiming to be a high-ranking official from Beijing, and demanded to be treated with respect. He admitted to molesting the child and offered to pay off the parents (Tang, 2008, November 8), who refused to be cowed and called the police. The police, however, did not address the accusations and allowed Lin Jiaxiang to leave the restaurant. Once everyone had left the restaurant, though, someone uploaded the video feed from the surveillance cameras inside the restaurant to the Internet, and it immediately spread across many websites. Several RRSS were started and the high-ranking official from Beijing was instead identified as the secretary of the Communist Party unit of the Shenzhen marine affairs office. His contact details, including his official address and telephone numbers and his personal mobile number, were published online, together with the details of how to contact the Marine Administrations Disciplinary Inspection Office (Fauna, 2008, November 1), and large numbers of netizens used the information to complain about Lin Jiaxiang. The central government took the incident very seriously, especially as it happened just after the Party had called on its members to work on improving its public image (Soong, 2008, November 2). The Party committee of the Ministry of Transport stepped in to sack him soon afterwards for causing embarrassment to the Party by his behaviour (Chen, 2008, November 4), although he was cleared of all criminal charges, due to a lack of conclusive evidence (Chen, 2008, November 6).

Another official, a housing department director from Nanjing, by the name of Zhou Jiugeng, came to the attention of China's cyberspace when he spoke out for higher property prices on the Chinese real-estate market in an interview (Soong, 2008, December 17). Angry netizens started an RRSS on him, and soon found pictures of Zhou Jiugeng smoking expensive cigarettes and wearing a very expensive watch, both unaffordable on his government salary. Netizens collected these pictures and forwarded them, together with other evidence, to the housing department. Shortly afterwards, Zhou Jiugeng was relieved of his duties (Mu, 2008, December 29) and the housing department issued a statement correcting his original comment about real-estate prices (Soong, 2008, December 29). Ten months later, Zhou Jiugeng was sentenced to eleven years in prison and his personal property was confiscated (Macartney, 2009, October 11).

The Chinese central government applauded the perseverance of the netizens involved in the RRSS and encouraged them to continue their efforts. Hao Mingjin, the Vice Minister of Supervision, whose office deals with government corruption, stated in an interview that his office took tips from the Internet very seriously, while the head of the General Administration of Press and Publication (GAPP), Liu Binjie, even supported RRSS as a crucial feature of democracy in China:

> Internet supervision is playing a very important role in promoting democracy and ensuring the people's right to know, which should be fully encouraged and supported.
>
> (Xinhua News Agency, 2009, October 12)

In a more serious case in 2009, a young woman called Deng Yujiao, who worked at a foot massage centre in a hotel in Hubei province, was sexually assaulted by a group of officials and defended herself with a knife. The officials tried to force her down on a sofa, ripped open her clothes, and attempted to rape her, while slapping her in the face with a wad of money, saying that would pay her well for her services. She lashed out with a knife, killed one of the officials, and wounded another one, at which point the others fled. Later she called the police and gave herself up, only to be charged with homicide, as the deceased was a Party member and the director of the local business promotion office. The story caught the attention of the worldwide press (e.g., Branigan, 2009, May 27; Canaves, 2009, June 17; Macartney, 2009, June 17) and even resulted in an article on Wikipedia (2009).

Netizens expressed anger and disbelief that this act of self-defence had been labelled homicide and started RRSS to identify all the people involved in the attempted rape. The online uproar soon forced the police to re-evaluate their charges and to conduct a proper investigation (Soong, 2009, May). Lawyers from Beijing agreed to defend Deng Yujiao pro bono publico, and began questioning the story spread by the police and the prosecution (Martinsen, 2009, May 24), while netizens followed and discussed every new facet of the case (Chen, 2009, May 17). In the end, Deng Yujiao was found guilty of using excessive force in defending herself but was released, based on the police's evaluation that she was mentally imbalanced (Martinsen, 2009, June 17). The verdict allowed the court to please public opinion by releasing her, while also declaring her guilty of the murder. The officials involved were subsequently punished as well. The county's Communist Party Discipline Inspection Committee sacked two of them from their positions and deprived one of them of his membership in the Communist Party before ordering his arrest for committing offences against the public order. Although Deng Yujiao had been declared guilty, and the officials had not been charged with rape, Chinese netizens celebrated the case as a huge victory for the Chinese Internet against corrupt and criminal officials.

Affecting more than just a few officials, a large disturbance in 2007 attracted worldwide media attention after starting in Chinese cyberspace (Watts, 2007; Associated Press, 2007). Desperate parents who had lost their children suspected that they had been kidnapped and were being forced to work as slaves in a number of small brick-making factories in Henan province. Local authorities were reluctant to help the parents in the search for their children and in several cases refused to help even when the parents had proof of their claims. In desperation, 400 fathers joined together and posted an open letter online, asking netizens to help them recover their children and to pressure authorities into taking action. Netizens responded in large numbers, and several RRSS succeeded in identifying factories that employed slaves and publishing the names of their owners, together with details of their financial backers, online. Through their support and action, as well as through Western media attention to the uproar online, the situation was brought to the attention of the Chinese central government, who decided to take direct action to crack down on brick-making factories in a large-scale series of police raids that ended up in freeing thousands of young Chinese who had been forced into slavery by business owners and colluding local officials.

Another case that targeted an entire national institution in China in January 2008, the 'so yellow, so violent' incident, caught the attention of much of Chinese cyberspace and created the first buzz-phrase of the year (Kennedy, 2008; Soong, 2008, January 7). During a report on the depravity of parts of the Chinese Internet, CCTV showed a brief interview clip of a Beijing elementary school student by the name of Zhang Shufan, who had been surfing the Internet when a web page popped up that she described as 'so yellow, so violent' (yellow meaning pornographic in Chinese). Once the phrase and a short video clip had been posted online, China's cyberspace exploded with comments from outraged netizens, who at first attacked the girl for lying on national TV. They claimed that violent pornographic material was not usually available on Chinese websites and that pornographic materials would only pop up on sites that were already pornographic, but not on 'normal' websites a young girl might surf to. After the publication online of a letter by the young girl's father, explaining that his daughter was an innocent victim and that the fault lay with the journalists involved, the attack began to include CCTV and its reporting standards, accusing it of having provided the girl with pre-scripted remarks to represent its own biased view of the Internet. Netizens began identifying the journalists responsible for the broadcast through RRSS and later broadened their attacks to condemn all reporting on CCTV as biased, propaganda based, or simply lies. Government officials, however, remained quiet throughout the uproar and did not interfere with the online debates, showing much restraint despite the widening attacks on one of the Communist Party's main policy propagation units.

In a similar case in 2009, the programme *Focus Interview* on CCTV reported on the easy availability of pornography on Google's Chinese search engine and interviewed a university student by the name of Gao Ye (Soong, 2009, June). Gao Ye was portrayed as a representative of Chinese netizens and talked about how one of his fellow students had been drawn deeper into an addiction to pornography because of Google. Netizens were outraged that Gao Ye presumed to speak for them, and RRSS were launched to find out who he was, which resulted in the online publication of his own and his girlfriend's details (Ye and Canaves, 2009, June 22). Soon it emerged that Gao Ye had been an intern working for *Focus Interview* at the time of the broadcast, which led many to believe that the interview had been scripted by the producers. Netizens began accusing CCTV of trying to blackmail Google, pointing out that Baidu, Google's biggest competitor in China, had sponsored the CCTV Spring Festival Gala with a large sum of money, and was therefore not criticized by CCTV, although its results produced as many pornographic images and links as those on Google (Soong, 2009, June, and Fauna, 2009, June 21).

The outcome of CCTV's attack on Google was a backlash against CCTV and much sympathy for Google in China. Google's traffic from China increased (BloggerInsight, 2009, June 25), while China's netizens began questioning whether there was more to the story than merely a blackmail attempt by CCTV. Instead, several netizens pointed out that the story could have provided the central government with arguments in support of the introduction of the Green Dam software system, which was supposed to censor all Internet usage in China but was dropped because of the outspoken protests of Chinese netizens (Lam, 2009, June 24). Google itself showed its sense of humour and searches for 'Gao Ye' on the Chinese Google site returned only the sentence: 'Your search results may involve content that violates laws, regulations, and policies, and cannot be displayed' (Martinsen, 2009, June 24).

In marked contrast to the personal vendettas and online lynch mobs discussed earlier, the participants in the RRSS against government officials and institutions focus more on the collection of evidence rather than the harassment of individual officials. They do not rebel against a corrupt or oppressive system, but instead support the system by alerting it to localized problems. Netizens use the Internet to circumvent local authorities and to make direct contact with higher levels in the hierarchies of power in China, thus providing a new form of checks and balances previously missing from Chinese politics.

## Conclusions and outlook

As the RRSS examples presented show, the Chinese Internet is a place somewhat outside the strict enforcement of the laws and regulations of the People's Republic of China. Netizens seem free to collect evidence against and to punish those who they agree need punishing. In this pursuit of 'justice', they generate a lot of noise and cause many innocents to suffer, yet the RRSS seem to occupy a growing role within the political system of the People's Republic of China. Both the Communist Party and the Central government seem willing to engage with netizens, and have acted on information produced by RRSS.

The reactions that instances of RRSS have produced in government offices demonstrate that RRSS are more than mere anecdotes of outrageous behaviour on the Chinese Internet. They are also more than a 'crowd-sourcing [of] "justice"' (RyanM, 2009, January 28) for individuals wanting revenge. Rather,

> the Internet is introducing a new measure of public accountability and civic action into China's [...] political system. [...] For the moment, the central government in Beijing appears to be allowing Internet protests to continue, and in some instances even encouraging them – as long as the campaigns are confined to local issues and target local officials.
>
> (Richburg, 2009, November 9)

As Steven Dong, a State Council adviser put it:

> The Internet has become the most powerful media in every government official's daily life [...]. Last year, we had over 84 government officials who were (affected by cyber-vigilantism) and one third of them lost their jobs.
>
> (Agence France Presse, 2009, August 11)

While critics continue to argue that the Chinese government is keeping a tight control over the Internet and censoring everything it does not like, this is only one side of the rather more complex relationship between the Chinese authorities and the Internet. This chapter does not want to pretend that such censorship does not happen, nor that the control of the Chinese government is non-existent. Quite the contrary. However, given the level of control that the Chinese government is capable of exercising over the Internet, it is even more noteworthy how much attention government officials are paying to the online 'chatter'. Chinese officials at all levels are expected and encouraged to keep in touch with Chinese cyberspace and with the netizens who populate it, and face punishment if they do not (Chen, 2009, August 12; Canaves, 2009, June 2).

The acceptance of RRSS by the Chinese government does not mean that China is on its way to becoming a European-style democracy, despite the rule of a 'mob' being one of the purest forms of democracy. It does mean, though, that there is a new, democratic element in Chinese politics, accepted and to some extent supported by the central government as a form of checks and balances for local and mid-level politicians and party members. For most of the past 5,000 years, China's rulers have been following the maxim: 'Heaven is high and the emperor is far away', leaving local officials to work with a high degree of autonomy. Central regulations and laws have always been hard to implement and to control, as supervision was difficult at best. As the past few years have shown, though, RRSS have (been given) the power and the willingness to provide feedback on local government corruption, crime, criminal liaisons, etc., thus offering a bridge between the central government and the people and, as Rebecca MacKinnon put it:

> If the Communist Party manages things well, they may stay in power longer if they use the Internet than they would if the Internet didn't exist.
>
> (Fletcher, 2009, March 6)

## References

admin. (2009, June 14). Zhege nuren xidu hai hai wo haizi de baba, you zhaopian [This woman does drugs and is harming the father of my child, with pictures]. Renrousousuowang. Retrieved November 28, 2009, from http://www.ren-rou.cn/html/faburenrousousuo/xunrenqishi/200906/14-7582.html

admin. (2009, November 23). Xunzhao shisan liang nian de didi qiuqiu dajia bangbang-mang [Please everybody, help me find my younger brother, who has been missing for two years]. Renrousousuowang. Retrieved November 28, 2009, from http://www.ren-rou.cn/html/faburenrousousuo/xunrenqishi/200911/23-9032.html

Agence France Presse. (2009, August 11). China's Internet a major concern to officials. *AsiaOne Digital*. Retrieved November 15, 2010, from http://digital.asiaone.com/ Digital/News/Story/A1Story20090811-160370.html

Ante. (2009, March 11). Ji zhao qizi [Urgently looking for my wife]. 51zhaoren. Retrieved November 28, 2009, from http://51zhaoren.com/renrou/renrousousuo/512.html

Associated Press. (2007, June 14). China reports rescue of 217 people forced to work as slaves at brick kilns. *San Diego.com*. Retrieved April 29, 2010, from http://legacy. signonsandiego.com/news/world/20070614-1308-china-slavery.html

Baidu Baike. (2009). Renrou Sousuo Yinqing (= Human Flesh Search Engine). Retrieved August 24, 2009, from http://baike.baidu.com/view/542894.htm

BloggerInsight. (2009, June 25). Chinese Web insights: CCTV's attacks increased Google's traffic. CNReviews.com. Retrieved December 1, 2009, from http://cnreviews. com/business/research-insights/chinese-web-insights-cctv-attacks-increased-google-traffic_20090625.html

Branigan, T. (2009, May 27). Chinese police bail Deng Yujiao over stabbing after online outcry. *Guardian*. Retrieved December 1, 2009, from http://www.guardian.co.uk/ world/2009/may/27/china-bails-deng-yujiao

Buxi, T. (2008, July 10). Classmate Yang goes online: Chinese officials engage netizens. Fool's Mountain: Blogging for China. Retrieved December 4, 2009, from http://blog. foolsmountain.com/2008/07/10/classmate-yang-online-officials-engage-netizens/

Buxi, T. (2008, July 19). Senior judges discuss 'human search engine'. Fool's Mountain: Blogging for China. Retrieved August 26, 2009, from http://blog.foolsmountain. com/2008/07/19/senior-judges-discuss-human-search-engine/

Canaves, S. (2009, June 2). Local officials urged to get savvy on Internet PR. *Wall Street Journal*. Retrieved December 3, 2009, from http://blogs.wsj.com/ chinarealtime/2009/06/02/local-officials-urged-to-get-savvy-on-internet-pr/

Canaves, S. (2009, June 17). China's court of public opinion. *Wall Street Journal*. Retrieved December 1, 2009, from http://blogs.wsj.com/chinarealtime/2009/06/17/ chinas-court-of-public-opinion/

CCTV 2. (2007, May 31). Haiyi shijian [The Haidian Arts School Case]. Diyi Shijian Du Bao [Reading the papers for the first time]. Retrieved March 20, 2010, from http:// www.tudou.com/programs/view/MOuU5eI8–4w/

CCTV News. (2007, June 1). Haiyi Shijian [The Haidian Arts School Case]. Shehui Jilu [A record of society]. Retrieved March 20, 2010, from http://www.tudou.com/programs/ view/a1dH1Z-pKiE/

Chase, M., & Mulvenon, J. C. (2002). *You've got dissent! Chinese dissident use of the Internet and Beijing's counter-strategies*. Santa Monica, CA: Rand Corporation.

Chen, B. (2009, May 17). China: Netizens stand with the waitress who killed an official. Global Voices Online. Retrieved December 1, 2009, from http://globalvoicesonline. org/2009/05/17/china-netizens-stand-with-the-waitress-who-killed-an-official/

Chen, H. (2008, November 4). Shenzhen marine official sacked for molesting child. *China Daily*. Retrieved November 30, 2009, from http://www.chinadaily.com.cn/china/2008-11/04/content_7169949.htm

Chen, H. (2008, November 6). Shenzhen official cleared of child molestation charge. *China Daily*. Retrieved November 30, 2009, from http://www.chinadaily.com.cn/china/2008-11/06/content_7178318.htm

Chen, J. (2009, August 12). Officials told to face online critics or suffer criticism. *China Daily*. Retrieved December 3, 2009, from http://www.chinadaily.com.cn/china/2009-08/12/content_8560569.htm

Chen, P. (2006, August 31). Shanghai + Sex + Blog + Controversy = Book Deal? *Shanghaiist*. Retrieved November 15, 2010, from http://shanghaiist.com/2006/08/31/we_gonna_go_to.php

China Daily. (2006, November 16). Driver sorry for throwing foreign woman's bike. *China Daily*. Retrieved March 20, 2010, from http://www.chinadaily.com.cn/china/2006-11/16/content_734463.htm

Chinabounder. (n.d.). *Sex and Shanghai*. Retrieved November 15, 2010, from http://china-bounder.blogspot.com/

Chinaview.cn. (2008, December 18). Web site ordered to pay damages to China's first 'virtual lynching' victim. Xinhua News Agency. Retrieved August 26, 2009, from http://news.xinhuanet.com/english/2008-12/18/content_10525436.htm.

Daily Telegraph. (2006, March 4). Who is the glamorous kitten killer of Hangzhou. Retrieved August 26, 2009, from http://www.chinadaily.com.cn/english/doc/2006–03/04/content_526563.htm

Daily Telegraph. (2009, August 14). US tests system to beat web censorship in China and Iran. Telegraph.co.uk. Retrieved March 20, 2010, from http://www.telegraph.co.uk/news/worldnews/asia/china/6026538/US-tests-system-to-beat-web-censorship-in-China-and-Iran.html

Damm, J., & Thomas, S. (Eds.). (2006). *Chinese cyberspaces: Technological changes and political effects*. Abingdon and New York: Routledge.

Fauna. (2008, November 1). Government official attacks 11-year-old girl. Chinasmack. Retrieved November 30, 2009, from http://www.chinasmack.com/videos/government-official-attacks-11-year-old-girl/

Fauna. (2009, February 8). Xidan girl sings 'Angel's Wings', becomes famous. Chinasmack. Retrieved November 28, 2009, from http://www.chinasmack.com/videos/xidan-girl-sings-angels-wings-becomes-famous/

Fauna. (2009, June 21). Chinese netizen reactions to CCTV attacking Google. Chinasmack. Retrieved December 1, 2009, from http://www.chinasmack.com/stories/chinese-netizen-reactions-cctv-attacking-google/

Fletcher, H. (2008, June 25). Human flesh search engines: Chinese vigilantes that hunt victims on the web. Times Online. Retrieved November 28, 2009, from http://technology.timesonline.co.uk/tol/news/tech_and_web/article4213681.ece

Fletcher, O. (2009, March 6). China officials seek image boost via public Internet chats. MIS-Asia. Retrieved December 3, 2009, from http://www.mis-asia.com/news/articles/china-officials-seek-image-boost-via-public-internet-chats

French, H. (2006, June 3). Online throngs impose a stern morality in China. *New York Times*. Retrieved December 4, 2009, from http://www.nytimes.com/2006/06/03/world/asia/03china.html?_r=1

Giese, K. (2006). *Challenging party hegemony: Identity work in China's emerging virreal places*. Hamburg: German Overseas Institute.

Goldsmith, J., & Wu, T. (2006). *Who controls the Internet? Illusions of a borderless world*. Oxford, New York: Oxford University Press.

Google China. (2009). Renrou Sousuo (= Human Flesh Search Engine). Retrieved July 17, 2009, from http://www.google.cn/intl/zh-CN/renrou/index.html

Hachigian, N. (2001). China's cyber-strategy. *Foreign Affairs, 80*(2), 118–133.

Hartford, K. (2005). Dear Mayor: Online communications with local governments in Hangzhou and Nanjing. *China Information, 19*(2), 217.

Kahn, J. (2007, May 19). China places 2 activists under house arrest. *New York Times*. Retrieved December 4, 2009, from http://www.nytimes.com/2007/05/19/world/asia/19iht-china.1.5780336.html

Kennedy, J. (2008, January 8). So yellow, so violent. Global Voices. Retrieved March 20, 2010, from http://globalvoicesonline.org/2008/01/08/china-so-yellow-so-violent/

Lagerkvist, J. (2005). The techno-cadre's dream: Administrative reform by electronic governance in China today? *China Information, 19*(2), 189.

Lam, O. (2009, June 19). CCTV's propaganda campaign against Google.cn. Global Voices Online. Retrieved December 1, 2009, from http://globalvoicesonline.org/2009/06/19/cctvs-propaganda-campaign-against-googlecn/

Macartney, J. (2009, June 17). Waitress Deng Yujiao who stabbed to death communist official walks free. Times Online. Retrieved December 1, 2009, from http://www.timesonline.co.uk/tol/news/world/asia/article6513750.ece

Macartney, J. (2009, October 11). China jails corrupt government official Zhou Jiugeng. Times Online. Retrieved November 30, 2009, from http://www.timesonline.co.uk/tol/news/world/asia/article6869806.ece

MacKinnon, R. (2008). Flatter world and thicker walls? Blogs, censorship and civic discourse in China. *Public Choice, 134,* 31–46.

MacKinnon, R. (2009). China's Censorship 2.0: How companies censor bloggers. *First Monday* [Online], *14*(2).

Martinsen, J. (2009, May 24). Dueling statements in the Deng Yujiao murder case. Danwei. Retrieved December 1, 2009, from http://www.danwei.org/law/dueling_statements_in_the_deng.php

Martinsen, J. (2009, June 17). Deng Yujiao leaves court a free woman. Danwei. Retrieved December 1, 2009, from http://www.danwei.org/front_page_of_the_day/deng_yujiao_convicted_set_free.php

Martinsen, J. (2009, June 24). Google says 'Gao Ye' is a sensitive word in any form. Danwei. Retrieved December 1, 2009, from http://www.danwei.org/net_nanny_follies/google_gao_ye_sensitive_words.php

Mop.com. (2009a). Renrou Sousuo (= Human Flesh Search Engine). Retrieved July 17, 2009, from http://dzh2.mop.com/

Mop.com. (2009b). Mop Renrou Sousuo (= Mop Human Flesh Search Engine). Retrieved August 24, 2009, from http://dzh.mop.com/c/16.html

Mu, E. (2008, December 29). Official fired over pricey cigarettes. Danwei. Retrieved November 30, 2009, from http://www.danwei.org/front_page_of_the_day/zhou_jiugeng.php

Mu, E. (2008, June 20). Online chat with Hu Jintao. Danwei. Retrieved July 15, 2009, from http://www.danwei.org/internet/president_hu_jintao_talks_to_n.php

Richburg, K. (2009, November 9). China's 'netizens' holding officials accountable. *Washington Post.* Retrieved December 3, 2009, from http://www.washingtonpost.com/wp-dyn/content/article/2009/11/08/AR2009110818166.html

RyanM. (2009, January 28). Human flesh search engines – crowd-sourcing 'justice'. CNET Asia. Retrieved December 3, 2009, from http://asia.cnet.com/member/RyanM/blog/?v=post&id=63008617

Shanghai Daily. (2006, March 16). High-heeled kitten killer apologizes. Retrieved August 26, 2009, from http://www.chinadaily.com.cn/english/doc/2006–03/16/content_540375.htm

Shaohua. (2008, September 25). Peasant girl: My life is miserable because I am poor. Chinasmack. Retrieved November 28, 2009, from http://www.chinasmack.com/stories/peasant-girl-my-life-is-miserable-because-i-am-poor/

Shaohua. (2008, October 25). CCTV investigates peasant girl's BBS forum post. Chinasmack. Retrieved November 28, 2009, from http://www.chinasmack.com/videos/cctv-investigates-peasant-girls-bbs-forum-post/

Shie, T. R. (2004). The tangled web: does the internet offer promise or peril for the Chinese Communist Party? *Journal of Contemporary China, 13*(40), 523–540.

Soong, R. (2006, April 17). The most famous pervert in China. EastSouthWestNorth. Retrieved March 20, 2010, from http://www.zonaeuropa.com/20060417_1.htm

Soong, R. (2006, August 28). The Immoral Foreign Blogger. *EastSouthWestNorth*. Retrieved November 15, 2010, from http://www.zonaeuropa.com/20060828_1.htm

Soong, R. (2006, October 27). A foreign lady in Beijing. *EastSouthWestNorth*. Retrieved March 20, 2010, from http://www.zonaeuropa.com/20061027_1.htm

Soong, R. (2007). The Haidian 'Teacher Abuse Gate' special. *EastSouthWestNorth*. Retrieved March 20, 2010, from http://www.zonaeuropa.com/2007011_1.htm

Soong, R. (2008, January 7). Very yellow, very violent. *EastSouthWestNorth*. Retrieved March 20, 2010, from http://www.zonaeuropa.com/20080107_1.htm

Soong, R. (2008a). Suicide MM's blog. *EastSouthWestNorth*. Retrieved August 26, 2009, from http://www.zonaeuropa.com/20080120_1.htm

Soong, R. (2008b). The first 'human flesh search' trial. *EastSouthWestNorth*. Retrieved August 26, 2009, from http://www.zonaeuropa.com/20080802_1.htm

Soong, R. (2008, November 2). EastSouthWestNorth: Daily brief comments, November 01–10, 2008. Retrieved November 30, 2009, from http://www.zonaeuropa.com/200811a.brief.htm#009

Soong, R. (2008, December 17). EastSouthWestNorth: Daily brief comments, December 11–20, 2008. EastSouthWestNorth. Retrieved November 30, 2009, from http://www.zonaeuropa.com/200812b.brief.htm

Soong, R. (2008, December 29). EastSouthWestNorth: Daily brief comments, December 11–20, 2008. EastSouthWestNorth. Retrieved November 30, 2009, from http://www.zonaeuropa.com/200812c.brief.htm

Soong, R. (2009, May). EastSouthWestNorth: Daily brief comments, May 21–31, 2009. Retrieved December 1, 2009, from http://www.zonaeuropa.com/200905c.brief.htm

Soong, R. (2009, June). EastSouthWestNorth: Daily brief comments, June 11–20, 2009. Retrieved December 1, 2009, from http://www.zonaeuropa.com/200906b.brief.htm

Tan, K. (2008, May 22). Online lynch mobs find second post-quake target; Liaoning girl detained by the police. Shanghaiist. Retrieved August 27, 2009, from http://shanghaiist.com/2008/05/22/online_lynch_mo.php

Tang, B. (2008, May 21). Internet mob rides again – Liaoning bitch-girl. Fool's Mountain: Blogging for China. Retrieved August 27, 2009, from http://blog.foolsmountain.com/2008/05/21/internet-mob-strikes-again-liaoning-bitch-girl/

Tang, S. (2008, November 8). China: Should Lin Jiaxiang be charged of assaults? Global Voices Online. Retrieved November 30, 2009, from http://globalvoicesonline.org/2008/11/08/china-wheres-the-sense-of-shame-of-high-official/

Washington Times. (2009, January 21). Obama's address censored in China. *Washington Times*. Retrieved December 4, 2009, from http://www.washingtontimes.com/news/2009/jan/21/obamas-inaugural-address-censored-china/

Watts, J. (2007, June 16). Enslaved, burned and beaten: Police free 450 from Chinese brick factories. *Guardian*. Retrieved November 15, 2010, from http://www.guardian.co.uk/world/2007/jun/16/china.jonathanwatts

Wikipedia. (2009). Deng Yujiao incident. Wikipedia. Retrieved December 1, 2009, from http://en.wikipedia.org/wiki/Deng_Yujiao_incident

Xiao, Q. (2009, June 26). Mass incident in Gangkou Town, Zhongshan City, Guangdong. China Digital Times. Retrieved December 4, 2009, from http://chinadigitaltimes.net/2009/06/mass-incident-in-gangkou-town-zhongshan-city-guangdong-with-photos/

Xinhua News Agency. (2005, June 27). Building harmonious society crucial for China's progress: Hu. People's Daily Online. Retrieved July 15, 2009, from http://english. peopledaily.com.cn/200506/27/eng20050627_192495.html

Xinhua News Agency. (2009, October 12). Official outed by netizens gets 11 years. *China Daily*. Retrieved November 30, 2009, from http://www.chinadaily.com.cn/china/2009– 10/12/content_8777619.htm

Yang, G. (2008). Contention in cyberspace. In K. J. O'Brien (Ed.), *Popular protest in China* (pp. 126–143). Cambridge, MA: Harvard University Press.

Yang, G. (2009). *The power of the Internet in China: Citizen activism online*. New York: Columbia University Press.

Ye, J., & Canaves, S. (2009, June 22). In flap over Google in China, an accuser is accused. *Wall Street Journal*. Retrieved December 1, 2009, from http://blogs.wsj.com/ chinarealtime/2009/06/22/in-flap-over-google-in-china-an-accuser-is-accused/

Yunluo. (2008, December 17). Xunzhao bangzhuguo wo de ren [Looking for the man who helped me]. 51zhaoren. Retrieved November 28, 2009, from http://51zhaoren.com/ renrou/renrousousuo/16.html

Zhang, X. (2007, May 30). Students' Internet video provokes rage. *China Daily*. Retrieved March 20, 2010, from http://www.chinadaily.com.cn/china/2007–05/30/ content_883399.htm

Zhouhaichuan0. (2008, May 22). Juran hai you zhei zhong ren ah – (Zhao ma de Liaoning Nuhail) Gao Qianhui [That such people still exist (Looking for the swearing Liaoning Girl) Gao Qianhui]. YouTube. Retrieved November 28, 2009, from http://www.youtube. com/watch?v=PmISXtnRKrM

# 8 In search of motivations

## Exploring a Chinese Linux User Group

*Matteo Tarantino*

## Introduction

This chapter presents insights on the contemporary panorama of Free and Open Source Software (FOSS) development in China, mostly from the perspective of cultural analysis. As such, it tries to distance itself from other analyses more concerned with economic or political factors: more than assessing the current situation of FOSS in numerical terms, it will attempt to explore the way Chinese ICT professionals gravitating, for various reasons, around FOSS think and act with respect to FOSS itself. The empirical work underpinning this chapter was carried out in 2007 in a Linux User Group located in a major Chinese metropolitan area. Along with performing participant observation at online and offline activities of the club, a total of 12 in-depth interviews were conducted with Chinese members of the club. Ten of the informants worked as computer programmers, and four doubled as journalists for IT magazines. Two were computer science students. The average age of the informants was 30, on a par with that of the club; all of them were male, although a small but growing number of female members have been active in the club and, between 2007 and 2009, managed to reach directive positions. Informal conversations were held with the Western members of the club, although none was subject to in-depth interviewing.

For the purposes of this paper, a broad definition of FOSS will be adopted, as software distributed to the public domain along with the relative source code, which can be freely modified and redistributed (be it for a price or not) (for references and other definitions, see Raymond, 2001). Originated from the encounter between academic culture and hacker culture, this software development model became in time the cornerstone of a loose and decentralized international movement which advocates an increase in the recourse to FOSS, which we will henceforth refer to as the 'FOSS movement'. FOSS production models originated many successful projects, among others the Firefox Web Browser, the Apache Server, and the Linux Operating System (Raymond, 2001).

## FOSS in China

The history of FOSS/Linux in China is relatively recent. While studying at the Helsinki University of Technology in 1990, doctoral candidate Gong Min encountered Linux (which, as widely known, was originally a product of Finnish engineer

Linus Torvalds) and, in 1996, brought it back to China on 20 floppy disks. One year later, the first Linux server was set up in Changzhou with the domain name cLinux.ml.org. In the same year, the first Linux User Group was established in Shanghai (Puhakka, 2007).

Since then, the relationship between China and FOSS has been a dynamic one, due to an ambiguous relationship with Chinese politics. On the one hand, the Chinese government appears (or at least declares) to understand and nurture the potential of FOSS software for the development of an indigenous software industry. The 5th National Five-year Plan (2000–2005) contained the 'Software Key Project of the National High Tech Research and Development Program' (also known as the 863 Program), which supported Linux and FOSS software development. The government's sponsorship of FOSS initially assumed the form of direct investment into public companies, then transformed into more indirect financial support to specific projects (such as Red Flag Linux, a Chinese-specific Linux distribution) and finally to FOSS-promoting associations, mostly of academic origin (Yang, 2005). This strategy created privileged semi-public enterprises, to the discontent of private firms who did not get equal support (Yang, 2005). These semi-public realities, each tied and supported by a particular power centre (such as municipalities or ministries) could not organically cohere into a proper 'Chinese FOSS movement' and appeared to some commentators to be more focused on the pursuit of particular goals. The problematic nature of government-sponsored FOSS institutions was also remarked upon by some of our informants, who perceived government subsidies to be unfairly assigned and applied. One of them (programmer/journalist Zhang, 25 years old) thought that

> Many famous people, professors and scientists, say the Open Source is good. They get a lot of money from the government to do Open Source; however, they don't use this money to develop … to do Open Source. They use it to do other things, to do business.

Moreover, as a *People's Daily* article acknowledged, a large amount of the FOSS-related output by these organizations has been accused of being copied from foreign FOSS products (People's Daily Online, 2006). Red Flag Linux recently faced similar accusations of plagiarizing the Red Hat distribution (Fletcher, 2009) without making any significant improvement or changes.

On the other hand, the Chinese software market (including the public administration software) has historically been dominated by Microsoft products, a monopoly in which widespread software piracy played a significant role. In the literature on the subject, piracy is amongst the most-cited explanations for the problematic state of FOSS in China (Ju & Shanghai, 2001; Kshetri, 2005; Li & Zheng, 2004; Noronha, 1999; Puhakka, 2007; Shen, 2004; Yang, Ghauri, & Sonmez, 2005). The dominating argument is that piracy effectively renders commercial software free, thus hindering the prospect of saving on licensing fees as a driver for FOSS adoption in companies, especially large-scale ones. Explicit government sponsorship of FOSS software such as Red Flag Linux has not sufficed to make it a true competitor to Microsoft products, which have always been available on the pirate market for the equivalent of a few US dollars. Until broadband connections became widespread in the mid-2000s, piracy ensured the continued predominance of proprietary software, which was competing with FOSS products on the same markets for the same price but with higher brand recognition and a stronger install base. Moreover, the economic model of most FOSS-related companies, centred on giving away the software itself for free and selling related services (such as assistance), is further complicated in China by the still relatively low average wages, which make internal IT departments more convenient than outsourcing to companies such as Red Hat. Because of this, FOSS software has yet to success-fully penetrate the Chinese market and, therefore, ensure profitability to compa-nies and offer desirable careers to young programmers.

## The Microsoft opium: a problematic founding myth for Chinese FOSS

Apart from declared intentions, it appears hard to disentangle how much the governmental support to FOSS/Linux development was aimed at developing an open source-oriented software industry, and how much towards the (eventually successful) achievement of a stronger bargaining position with Microsoft. When the conflict was at its peak, during the second half of the 1990s, Linux became a cornerstone of what we may define as the Chinese 'techno-nationalistic imagery': that is, it was presented as a key element for the whole of China's national develop-ment (see Edgerton, 2007 for a discussion of the concept of 'techno-nationalism'). Newspaper articles made explicit references to Chinese mythology by comparing the Windows monopoly to the tyranny of Qin rule and Linux to the mythical rebel generals Chen and Wu, who rallied the population against unjust oppression:

> The rise of Linux is legendary, a little like the peasant uprising of Chen Sheng and Wu Guang. In a world of hegemony long suppressed, many feel oppressed but the majority doesn't know where their suffering originates. Once someone stands up, he will have followers like clouds.
>
> (China Youth Daily as quoted in Leonard, 1999)

A rebellion against external oppression and aggression has been the backbone of traditional Chinese nationalist discourse since the nineteenth century, and remains a powerful image to this day (Gries, 2004). The idea of a Chinese soft-ware industry somehow 'oppressed' by a foreign power was further strengthened by the parallel between Microsoft software and opium (one of the key subjugating factors in traditional nationalist discourse), quite popular in late-1990s Chinese computer culture, which stated that piracy in China was actually supported by Microsoft as a way to get users 'addicted' to Microsoft software, thus surrepti-tiously establishing a de facto monopoly. The following is one of many quotations retelling this narrative, taken from a blog post:

> Microsoft's present situation has a special agenda. As early as 1998, during an interview with Fortune magazine, Bill Gates said the following: 'Let them steal our stuff if they really would like to steal. They will get hooked on the

acts, then we are going to figure out ways to ask them to pay it back in the next ten years or so.' From Bill Gates' words, we can see that Microsoft's laissez faire policy is deliberately intended, which is comparable to a calculated 'Opium War.' During those ten years Microsoft first let the people have free products that lead to an addiction. Then they collect the fishing net at just the right time and you cannot escape and fight back!

(Northway, 2008)

In the case of FOSS, however, the mobilizing power of nationalist discourse appeared quite weak, as a gulf between discourse and action appeared relevant at both political and individual levels. This gulf was explicitly acknowledged by some of our informants. From their words, it appears that the political significance of Linux as a factor for the development of China belongs to an outdated imagery, and as such is looked down upon almost with contempt:

I remember around 2000 or 2001, I knew a lot of programmers publicly saying to be against Microsoft. Some parts of the government and some local governments took on backing Linux, we backed Linux strongly. Of course, we said so but we all had Windows at home [laughs] and at work, because anyway nobody, no user, used Linux. But I remember considering seriously installing Linux at home, and even contributing to some projects. [...] It was a long time ago, I don't remember why I didn't do it ... I probably simply had no time ...

(Li, 30, programmer)

At both micro and macro levels (that is, individual user/developers and government), mundane needs appear to have played a much stronger role in shaping Chinese FOSS than any shared mobilizing narrative or myth (if any shared narratives are present, they are justifying non-involvement in FOSS). We will discuss the implications of this at the micro level in the following paragraphs. Concerning the political/regulatory level, Hiner (2007) showed that when the anti-Microsoft sentiment in politics waned in 2004, due to a change in Microsoft's policy towards China (from 2003 it responded to the government's main objections by cutting the price of its Windows licences to $7–$10 and allowing modification to Windows source code to accommodate encryption technology), the central government returned to Windows for its IT needs. While FOSS projects such as Red Flag Linux did not lose their financial support, the precious symbolic sponsorship of the Chinese government and the media almost disappeared. The nationalist FOSS discourse resurfaces from time to time, though significantly diminished. Appeals to China's need for autonomy from Western software appear in the writings of Professor Ni Guangnan, a high-profile IT personality (the inventor of the Hanzi card, a former LENOVO scientific director and a fellow at the Chinese Academy of Sciences), who is presently one of the most famous and outspoken advocates of Linux in China.

It appears that all the (symbolic or financial) support that FOSS enjoyed between 1999 and 2004 could not prompt the creation of a grassroots movement, which is a key factor in nurturing a FOSS 'scene', apart from (more or less privileged) semi-public efforts. In this chapter we will concentrate on the question: is there a Chinese FOSS culture? To try to answer this question we have adopted as a case study one of the most representative spaces dedicated to FOSS, where this culture should have been readily observable as a prime motivating factor: a Linux User Group.

## Exploring a Chinese LUG

Linux User Groups (LUG; also sometimes referred to as Linux User Clubs) are informal associations of open source supporters, mostly developers, who gather online on a dedicated website or mailing list and periodically meet in person. LUGs are present in most countries reached by the Internet (see http://www.linux.org/groups/) and can be considered as the local 'chapters' of the international FOSS movement, providing that the loose and decentralized nature of the movement is kept in mind. The 'Linux User Club HOWTO' available online (formally assembled by Moen but co-produced by many others) works as an important reference point for such organizations. It describes the core four objectives of a club as 'advocacy, education, support and socializing' (Moen, 2010). As such, a properly functioning Linux club would act as an agent for the popularization of the movement's ideals and product, such as Linux, Apache and OpenOffice. The core mission of the association appears to be advocacy, that is, the propagation of FOSS ideals:

> The urge to advocate the use of GNU/Linux is widely felt. When you find something that works well, you want to tell as many people as you can. LUGs' role in advocacy cannot be overestimated, especially since wide-scale commercial acceptance is only newly underway.
>
> (Moen, 2010)

The Chinese LUG we observed had been founded in the late 1990s by Westerners residing in China who operated FOSS-related businesses, such as consulting firms and development studios. With respect to coding activity, most of the founding members had been software coders, and some continued this activity along with (or as a part of) their entrepreneurial efforts. None of the Western members was, at the time, working for Chinese-owned firms. At the time of our observation, Westerners were by far the most prominent and active members of the club. The president was a young European man, and Scandinavian and American members constituted the core directorate of the association (albeit seldom acknowledged as such).

Around this nucleus a growing number of Chinese members gravitated, attending weekly meetings and intervening on the club's online boards. Chinese members largely appeared to be computer programmers, mostly employed by Chinese firms. English was the language of choice of the club, both in the meetings and on the website (a factor that, as we shall see, was of a certain importance). The average age was around 30, with the youngest members being around the age of 22 and the oldest member around 50. While the club agenda included online activities (i.e. members operated individual blogs which were linked to on the club's website and message boards were relatively populated), in-presence, live activities appeared much more lively and important. More than an autonomous virtual space, the LUG's website appeared as a mere portal to the club, and was largely used as a message board for in-presence activities. In general, new members came into contact with the LUG through the website, introduced themselves on the forums, and were instantly invited to join in-presence activities. The local and physical dimension appeared to be much more central to the club than the virtual one. In-presence meetings were frequent (at least once a week) and systematic, and the joining policy of the club deemed participation as mandatory for maintaining membership.

Weekly meetings were held in restaurants in the business and diplomatic district of the city. While such meetings always included informal dinners, most of the meetings had specific focuses such as speeches by external guests about FOSS-related topics or the demoing of FOSS applications. At times, the company of one of the Western members lent its office space for meetings and celebrations, such as club anniversaries. Apart from the weekly meetings, the club also organized so-called 'install-fests', playful events (often referred to as 'initiation rituals') where Linux novices are helped by experienced users to install distributions on their laptops; moreover, girls-only 'tech nights' were also organized by the female members. The centrality of the in-person activities was functional to the exchange of ideas, expertise and contacts (all prominent activities during the meetings) and also to what the LUG-HOWTO documents call 'advocacy': the diffusion of FOSS ideals.

## Dividing lines

At the time of our observation, Chinese and Western members were almost equal in numbers. While the general tone and interaction between the two groups appeared friendly and smooth, upon closer observation, a certain number of dividing factors appeared: language, attitude towards programming and attitude towards FOSS contributed to a gap between Chinese and Western members of the club, proportional to the symbolic investment required.

### *Language*

The first, and immediately perceivable, dividing line was a linguistic one, English being the language of choice for all club activities. This constituted an issue for some of the Chinese members, who could all understand English fairly well but did not possess equal speaking fluency. The same applied for most Western members with respect to Mandarin. As Li, one of our Chinese-speaking (but Malaysian-born) informants stated, these linguistic dividing lines induced a certain degree of linguistic homogeneity within each of the two groups:

> I can understand 90, 95 percent of what is being said during the club sessions, but I seldom speak first because my English is not so good [laughs] ... I speak with other Chinese members in Mandarin [...] and I can make some

conversation with Western members when they speak to me; but I never speak first in English.

(Li, 22, programmer and student)

However, as Li acknowledged, this linguistic discrepancy also worked as a driver for Chinese participation in the club. Attendance appeared to offer our Chinese informants a chance to practise English, a precious skill in contemporary China – even more so in the IT sector – which they apparently had little chance of cultivating after university:

In the club I can speak and listen to English … A lot of computer-related words and expressions there every night. This is very convenient to me, because I don't speak English at work and seriously need to practise it [laughs] [...] In truth, I quit speaking English since I finished high school!

(Li, 22, programmer and student)

### Attitudes toward programming

Another relevant dividing line between the Chinese and Western members was relative to the overall attitude towards programming. In discussing the motivations driving Open Source developers, Hars and Qu speak of 'the joy for programming', as epitomized by one of their respondents who spoke of an 'innate desire to code and code until the day I die' (2002: 28). Such sentiments are common in computer circles in Western cities, and especially in LUGs, whose members can often be rightfully called 'enthusiasts'. However, most of our in-depth interviews indicated that such a sentiment was lacking in Chinese members. All of our informants (both students and professionals) explained their (and other members') career choice as software developers, as well as their approach to programming, in mostly pragmatic terms. For example, Min, a computer programmer born in 1978, explained that computers didn't enter his field of interest until he was required to choose a college path. And even then, IT never 'passioned' him: Min merely chose what appeared to be the most lucrative career.

I had never touched a computer before going to college. We did not have computers in my high school … No, wait, we had some, but they were very few and very old, and we had to take turns to use them. I chose computer science as a career after high school because it looked like one of the most lucrative ones [...] I think computer programmer is still one of the best-paid jobs in China.

(Min, 29, programmer)

Interestingly, Min suggested that computer technology might have had a higher symbolic value for his parents, although they could not grasp the technology. This may have been because his parents were more exposed than the young Min to the Deng Xiaoping-sponsored hype on microcomputer technology which invested Chinese public discourse in the early 1980s.

My parents did not know anything about computers, but they supported me. [Laughs] They did not know anything about it but they remembered Deng Xiaoping appearing on television and declaring that computers were the single most important technology for China ... and that China had to develop them. So they were happy.

(Min, 29, programmer)

Min reflexively understands that he is somehow 'distant' from the ideal LUG member, as defined by the documents available online.

I like my work, but no, I cannot say I have a 'passion' for programming ... I would never do it in my free time. It's my job. Just my job.

(Min, 29, programmer)

We are quite far away from the 'innate desire to code and code and code until the day I die' declared by Hars and Qu's informants, or from the 'ludic payoff' to programming delineated by Bitzer, Schrettl, and Schröder (2007). In other words, none of our informants spoke of programming as a 'hobby' taken up for leisure and later evolved into an occupation. Instead, it appeared as one path among many equals, chosen after purely economic considerations. While survey-based studies on motivations towards FOSS tend to underestimate the importance of intrinsic drives in favour of external rewards (which can be more easily computed), we think that the lack of a ludic or aesthetic frame for programming is a central element in shaping our informants' attitude towards FOSS.

Contemporary Chinese culture seems to be lacking such a frame and, at least from our interviews, the programmer appeared as a de-romanticized figure. The roots of this different attitude towards programming can be traced to the general pragmatic attitude of modern Chinese culture towards human activities (Pye, 1986), in which material preoccupations and drives tend to outweigh emotional factors. Looking more specifically at computer culture, it appears that Chinese cultural framing of computer technology substitutes the Western notion of 'radical empowerment of the individual through technology' ('technology will make you super') with the narrative of collective rebirth from a state of collective subjugation to Western powers and technology ('technology will make us rise again') (see Tarantino, forthcoming). As a result, the image of the 'programmer-wizards' with unlimited power literally at their fingertips, so common in Western popular culture, appears less in Chinese technological imagery. As a result, computer 'power' may have appeared less seductive to the current generation of Chinese programmers than to their Western counterparts. Western members spoke in informal conversation of their careers in computer programming as being motivated by an interest which mostly originated in their teenage years. Two of the northern European members once engaged in evoking fond memories of after-school afternoons during the 1980s spent writing programs in BASIC language on the Commodore 64 home computer.

While we are obviously not ruling out the existence of a 'passion for programming' in all Chinese programmers, we need to note that an important dividing line in this respect could be perceived in the LUG. However, the overall situation may change for the current generation of young programmers (born after 1985), who grew up with the image of 'nationalist hackers' as heroes. The wide circulation of narratives about Chinese nationalist hackers (including, but not limited to, the well-known Honker movement) fighting cyber-wars against Western powers in defence of the Chinese Internet may lead to a romanticizing of programming in China (Henderson, 2007). In 2005, a survey showed (concernedly) that Chinese hackers are considered heroes by elementary school children (Shanghai Daily, 2005).

While a full discussion of the issue goes far beyond the scope of this chapter, it is worth underlining that Chinese hackers appear to belong to a completely different 'techno-culture' than their Western counterparts. In their ideal form, as emerging from the collective imagery, Western hackers are individualistic, anti-system 'wizards' whose ultimate goal is to 'free computer power' from the shackles of the corporate/capitalist system, thus setting themselves up as anti-system rebels. Castells (2003) locates the root of this position in the influence of late-1960s counterculture on the birth of the hacker movement. According to Raymond (2001), the FOSS model itself is a product of hacker ethics applied to software development. Due to this legacy, FOSS is often presented as being innately 'anti-system' (a position which actors like Microsoft try to present as 'anti-American' – see Leonard, 2001). By contrast, Chinese hackers are publicly supporting the status quo with their activities, as both Schneier (2008) and Henderson (2007) indicated, without being necessarily employed by the political system, and quite often being publicly condemned by it, serving the ideology of 'Greater China' against such threats as US global influence, Tibetan independence and Taiwan autonomy (Henderson, 2007). Although, as we have seen, FOSS co-optation into neo-nationalist discourse has been an unsuccessful (at least as of 2009) top-down process, the romanticizing of hackers, as a bottom-up process, might be more successful. From their position as 'defenders' (which fits into Chinese imagery more than that of 'aggressors'), they exert a considerable cultural seductiveness on Chinese youth, and may play an important symbolic role in the evolution of Chinese computer culture.

### Attitude towards FOSS

The broadest gap between Chinese and Western members of the club appeared to concern their attitudes towards FOSS itself. The degree of emotional involvement with FOSS philosophy appeared to be very dissimilar between Western and Chinese members of the club. Zhang, a 45-year-old computer journalist and former software developer who studied for his PhD in the United States, was by far the most reflexive and historically conscious among our informants. Zhang divided the club members into two groups: 'religious' people, who 'truly believed' in FOSS ethics and tenets, and what we might term 'agnostics', members who attended to the club activities without adhering to the ideal system, pursuing mostly pragmatic objectives.

> I know a few of them, very ... religious persons, who really believe in the
> Open Source ideal ... But the majority of Chinese do not believe in it, they

only see it as an opportunity. [...] No, none of religious persons I know is part of the club here.

(Zhang, 45, programmer and journalist)

It is important to underscore that Zhang showed no contempt for agnostics: despite his US education and his high degree of knowledge of FOSS philosophy, he put himself 'as a Chinese' somewhere in the middle between the two poles. FOSS's goals appeared, if to some extent shareable, a little too 'high' for an apparent innate core pragmatism which (confirming Pye) could be found in all our interviewees, who often introduced their distance from FOSS philosophy as being a result of their cultural roots ('since I am a Chinese ...'). If any contempt was shown by Zhang, it was directed towards the perceived hypocrisy of Chinese FOSS 'idealists', whose public apparent attachment to the cause hid, in Zhang's opinion, ulterior, more pragmatic motives – in this case, the gaining of reputation and visibility in the programmers' community:

I kept asking them ['religious' developers] the same question: 'why do you keep devoting so much to Open Source developing, they can't really ... I mean, they could list many reasons ... but the most important one is: reputation. It would help them to get more prestige ... [...] it is completely devoid of any ideology.

(Zhang, 45, programmer and journalist)

The central claim here, that material drivers outweigh emotional ones in determining a programmer's resolution, is backed up by other informants, with more specific reference to attendance to the club. For example, Luo, another programmer/journalist, added to the motivation of English practice that of practical knowledge and contacts:

[Most Chinese members] hang out at the club for getting connections and learning new tricks. There are many experienced programmers there, and some of them work in big companies. It is quite useful.

(Luo, 24, programmer and journalist)

Luo attributed the fundamental difference between Western and Chinese members of the club to a broad cultural misunderstanding of FOSS ethics:

[...] Chinese do not 'believe' in Open Source – most of them do not even understand well the concept.

(Luo, 24, programmer and journalist)

While acknowledging the 'misunderstanding', Luo, like Zhang, did not look down on agnostics. Also like Zhang, Luo located himself in the middle between the two poles, leaning towards the agnostic position. The argument of a radical incompatibility between FOSS and Chinese culture returned several times during our interviews.

I think Open Source does not fit with the Chinese mind-set. It is really a Western concept, and it just ... doesn't fit.

(Meng, 28, programmer)

Open Source has one big issue in China – that Chinese do not get it, they see it as stupid and senseless.

(Zhang, 45, programmer and journalist)

## Factors for incompatibility

It could be said that, in the absence of immediate prospects of financial reward, or any emotional attachment to programming, or of a shared and solid supporting narrative (of a 'founding myth'), FOSS appears to be largely perceived by our informants (and, from their statements, by many of their peers) as a clunky, alien object. Without an effort of cultural adaptation, many of its tenets are perceived (by our interviewees and possibly by larger audiences) as incompatible with the Chinese context. Our research highlighted three main factors (others could be found, with further empirical work): two are contingent (visibility/education and market) and one appears more structural (hierarchy). All of them appear closely intertwined, reinforcing and supporting each other.

### *Hierarchy*

Our Chinese informants perceived the FOSS production model as being too loose and de-structured to be compatible with Chinese work modalities. Our Chinese programmers confessed having to more difficulties than their Western counter-parts in dealing with the horizontal communicative practices required by Open Source. The hierarchical structure prevalent in Chinese work relationships stood in conflict with the requirements of FOSS production models, in which anyone can take the product of long hours of coding and freely criticize and modify it. Far from being perceived as a 'liberating' model (by maximizing recognition of merits and minimizing individual responsibility for weaknesses, as in the original formulation), FOSS appeared to threaten our Chinese informants with consid-erable emotional distress. For example, Min described the potentially insulting nature of the act of revision:

Open Source requires that someone else who is your equal takes your code and modifies it. This is not ... so acceptable to Chinese as it is to a Westerner. We can take that kind of ... brute ... correction from superi-ors, not from equals. Your code is taken and changed, without telling you anything ... Or your contribution is simply deleted and replaced without a word to you. A Chinese will probably take this as an insult, and drop out of the project. This is a serious, a very serious problem for Open Source in China.

(Min, 29, programmer)

Hierarchy is seen as a necessary element for any endeavour to work in the Chinese context. Zhang describes a Chinese FOSS project as being relatively successful precisely because of hierarchy.

> One of the open source projects I know in China is led by a Microsoft guy ... when he left Microsoft he managed to persuade two colleagues to join his project and these three constitute the core of the project ... apparently it is a very structured, hierarchical structure in the core of the project community, and then many others ran there and contribute.
>
> (Zheng, 45, programmer and journalist)

However, this particular endeavour appears quite peculiar in the way it deals with FOSS ethics. Zhang admits that contributors were largely attracted by the prestige of core members and the chance of establishing close relationships with them through their contribution to the project. Corporate software production models (theoretically the opposite of FOSS), with clear command and accountability chains, are described by Zhang as being a necessary factor in China.

> Without this structured hierarchical core I don't think it would have been successful. You need structure ... they come from the same company so it was very easy for them to get structured. [...] You have to understand that in the West everything is voluntary, in China it is better if you have a structure, a hierarchy.
>
> (Zhang, 28, programmer and journalist)

For Zhang, therefore, a successful FOSS project in China would look like a standard software development enterprise (actually, the closer the resemblance, the better), only rewarding contributors with relational and knowledge rewards instead of financial ones.

### *Visibility/education*

To most of our informants, one of the foremost problems of FOSS in China appears to be education, especially regarding two aspects: education to open source and education for open source. First of all, Chinese users are described as not being educated in the use of FOSS software (and of recognizing as such the software they might be using – given the above-described market situation in which any software is practically free of charge), which hinders its popularity and therefore the base of potential contributors:

> Open Source software is more complicated than Microsoft, and education ... Students have no chance of using Open Source software in college, [let alone] develop it. And when you buy a computer, the operating system is Windows, not Ubuntu, not Linux. What chance do you have? Most people do not even know about Open Source software.
>
> (Luo, 24, programmer and journalist)

The other form of education described as missing is education for open source, that is, the acquisition of the necessary programming skills to contribute to FOSS projects. In this respect, the blame is put totally on the university system itself, in terms of the quality of computer science education. As FOSS requires its contributors to create software on a par with commercial software, it requires its practitioners to know and practise cutting-edge coding techniques. However, universities are largely described as being focused on teaching outdated 'basic' skills, and thus not preparing their graduates for the needs of FOSS. This point is also acknowledged by external commentators: as Michael Iannini, an OSS entrepreneur in China and columnist, stated in an op-ed about FOSS in China:

> If you are looking for a C++ developer, you are in luck, China's got plenty; the bad news is Microsoft and Google have done a pretty darn good job snatching up every decent programmer in the market. When it comes to PHP, Perl, Python, Joomla or any other development language outside of C++, and Java, your best option is to look outside the mainland.
>
> (Iannini, 2006)

In discussing this topic, our informants always expressed an unfavourable comparison with Western programmers:

> Universities in China teach old things, mostly C when I was there. Now maybe they do some Java. What we learned was absolutely not comparable with Western programmers. I remember being taught ... Old things by old teachers ...
>
> (Luo, 24, programmer and journalist)

This argument appears strongly correlated with the questions of 'face' and 'reputation' central in Chinese relational ethics. The group effort required by FOSS appears to threaten (perhaps unreasonably so) to expose Chinese programmers to the risk of shaming; as we have seen, their contribution might be deemed unworthy, and discarded. As such, in the absence of other drivers, Chinese programmers do not see any reason to undertake such an endeavour. Zhang, who experienced American education, spoke explicitly of an 'inferiority complex' which, while clearly not applicable to all Chinese programmers, might play an important role in their distancing from FOSS development:

> Young Chinese programmers don't want to feel embarrassed when their contribution to a project is unfavourably compared with that of others ... But our universities still focus on old programming techniques, so American and Australian young programmers are much better than Chinese. It's ... not good enough ...
>
> (Zhang, 45, programmer and journalist)

In this respect, our research recorded a significant awareness of the fact that the Linux kernel supposedly featured no Chinese contributions at the time of observation. A whole Internet page (http://www.remword.com/kps_result/china. php) is devoted to keeping track of the 'Chinese contribution' to the Linux kernel. However, the page employs the questionable technique of attributing Chinese nationality from the analysis of the contributor's email address. Furthermore, as the page itself acknowledges, '"Chinese" means who ethnically belongs to Chinese descent and many different nationalities are represented'.

The only Chinese contributor, none other than the 'father of Linux' Gong Min, had his contribution ultimately rejected by the community. The relevance of this episode illustrates the difficulties encountered in dealing with the depersonalization requirements of FOSS production models. As Li, the youngest among our informants, said:

> Nobody wants to be the next Mr Gong.
>
> (Li, 22, programmer and student)

It might be inferred (although not much evidence for this appears in our interviews) that an important role is played in this context by the lack of emotional attachment to programming. In the West, programming knowledge has historically been largely self-taught by young enthusiasts (as the programming subculture offered plenty of learning materials even before the advent of the Internet) who often reach universities – structurally oriented towards teaching core, and therefore often outdated, skills – with far more knowledge of the matter than what their curricula require.

The author of this chapter is himself an amateur programmer whose career started in middle school. In Italy, certainly not the most tech-savvy country in the West, programmer manuals could be found in every library, computer clubs produced plenty of 'programmer fanzines', and a certain number of amateur programmers could be found even in rural high schools. In these circles, a good knowledge of object-oriented programming, especially C++, and even assembly language, was commonly attained before entering college. Fascination for computers and programming was the main factor sustaining the gathering, practising and sharing of such knowledge. But in the absence (at least in their biography) of any motivation to self-teaching, our Chinese informants appear to expect that universities, as the top education institutions, will supply enough programming knowledge to put them on a par with their Western counterparts.

### *The money/time relationship*

The Chinese programmer's life is described by our informants as being a hard one. Without a market able to transform FOSS into a career, participation has to be motivated by a purely internal drive and has to take place during the programmer's free time. While programming jobs were reported by our informants as being desirable positions in terms of salary, the rising cost of living in Chinese metropolitan areas was putting an extreme strain on them, resulting in overwork and lack of free time. The result was a perceived impossibility to devote any time to FOSS:

> I …we … cannot devote much time to Open Source development, I mean, we haven't much free time. We have to work hard to support our families; and when I get home, the last thing I want is to sit down and write some more code. I want to stay with my wife.
>
> (Min, 29, programmer)

Professional Open Source development during working hours (i.e. being employed by a FOSS firm) does not fare any better, either. Our respondents all deem the Chinese FOSS market to be simply not big enough to support such an activity. As the market context appears unable to support FOSS, programmers such as Luo do not see any valid reason to take the burden upon themselves:

> The only way for a Chinese programmer to contribute to Open Source is being employed in an Open Source firm, and Open Source is presently not popular enough in China for someone to invest in it. We all need to make money.
>
> (Luo, 24, programmer and journalist)

Again, the lack of immediate financial rewards, emotional drivers and shared supporting narratives appear to be mutually reinforcing. Stripped of these elements, FOSS is reduced to the bare notion of 'working for free', and as such it 'cannot be understood' – not in terms of the comprehension of its articles (which are very clear to all of our informants), but in terms of how they can be incorporated into the Chinese context – of how they can be interiorized:

> Chinese do not understand well the concept of Open Source. They do not understand why they should work for free. They consider 'free software' as in 'free of charge', but do not understand the logic of contribution and participation. Myself, I have never contributed to any FOSS project.
>
> (Luo, 24, programmer and journalist)

Luo returned to the concept in even more explicit terms by questioning the reasons why a Chinese programmer should 'give away' code that could be used to get financial benefit. Should Luo perceive weaknesses in an existing FOSS product, this would not drive him towards contributing to ameliorate it; instead, ideally, he would exploit this weaknesses to start a new, better and, what's more, proprietary project.

> I can speak for myself: when I use the Open Source software it is OK. I could even write some additional code for it, make it better. But I want to use the code to get some money. So I would probably start another, better project to put on the market.
>
> (Luo, 24, programmer and journalist)

The idea of a presently (but not necessarily forever) broken feedback circle between China and FOSS returns time and again in our interviews. The Chinese context is described as being presently unable to 'give back' what it 'takes' from FOSS (code, ideas and final products): however, the situation might change in the future, once immediate rewards become more clear, tangible and desirable.

> So in China I think that they like Open Source software. They use it. But they don't give back to Open Source. They do not like to program Open Source.
>
> (Zhang, 45, programmer and journalist)

> Maybe in the future, if we have more money we can give back, but for now ...
>
> (Luo, 24, programmer and journalist)

## Negotiating positions

The above analysis outlines a number of factors jeopardizing and possibly reducing the degree of commitment to the FOSS cultural project by Chinese programmers, who find (or depict) a number of obstacles in incorporating it into their lives. Therefore, their proximity to FOSS-related activities such as the club appears to be prominently driven by pragmatic concerns, such as the acquisition of linguistic, relational and knowledge capital. In this respect, Iannini's final judgement appears very harsh:

> Most Chinese IT professionals are not interested in the culture of FOSS, they are interested in what experience will help them get the best job in the best company, and earn the best wage.
>
> (Iannini, 2006)

In our Chinese LUG, this dividing line between 'religious' and 'agnostic' members appeared to be strongly related to nationality. European and American members appeared to lean more towards the 'religious' side, and Chinese members to the 'agnostic' one, and the majority of Chinese 'religious' members encountered in this research had obtained their academic degrees in the United States. 'Religious' members appeared to have none of the geeky and fanatical attitude sometimes found in popular depictions of FOSS activists. However, from time to time they did show signs of a militant, anti-capitalist attitude. When a piece of club hardware ended up broken, the club started a fundraising campaign on the website to buy a new one. A manager employed in a big, closed-source commercial software company, who had been expressing interest in the club both online and offline, offered on the group's BBS a significant financial contribution. However, during one of the meetings, the club president announced that the association was going to refuse the offer, for it 'sounded like a bribe': 'we' stated the president during the meeting 'will not be bought by big companies'. However, the statement did not raise particular enthusiasm in the audience, it was not reported on the forums, and the issue was not discussed again.

Some of the 'religious' members were actively involved in offline advocacy through presentations and interventions in conferences and seminars. Moreover, they took part in organizing or sponsoring a number of China-based FOSS-related events (which have been on the rise during the last few years, under the active sponsorship of Western individuals or corporations). For example, in 2007 the first Chinese BARCAMP event (bottom-up conferences originated in hacker culture) was held in Beijing (with the attendance of most 'religious members'). Since then, events like the Open Office conference (2008) have drawn considerable attention among the international FOSS community. In the organization of some of these events, such as Linux World conferences, 'religious' members have taken an active part.

Online advocacy has also been used, although on a less-impressive scale. Some of the 'religious' club members (both of Chinese and Western origin) doubled as columnists on web-based periodicals about ICTs. From this position, they advocated the recourse to FOSS and discussed the issues of FOSS in China. Moreover, many of the activists had personal blogs (only in English for Western members, mostly in English for the Chinese) in which they also discussed FOSS-related questions and issues.

However, within the group, advocacy had to be negotiated with the agnostic position, which, although silent in public, was not a minority. In this context, militant attitudes appeared against the activists themselves: one of the Western members confessed during an informal conversation that he felt that insisting on the idealistic aspects (including the good vs. evil, Linux vs. Windows, Open vs. Closed dichotomies) 'makes some of them [agnostics, albeit never referred to as such)]feel they are being criticized for not ... how to say ... "believing" the same way' and, as such, 'eventually pushes them away'.

While such a notion never emerged during our in-depth interviews with 'agnostics' (who never perceived themselves as being looked down upon, and never discussed distancing themselves from the club), it appeared to subconsciously drive the strategies of 'religious' members, which mostly relied on consolidation through socialization, support and education. Paradoxically, it was not the 'idealistic' part but instead the emphasis on in-presence activities which was perceived as problematic by our Chinese informants. As Zhang phrased it: '[the LUG] is a little ... strict. If you don't attend to all their activities, they start treating you differently, like we are not friends ... no, like you're not one of us.'

In terms of motivation, our Chinese LUG offered a place for community identification and self-promotion without insisting too much on intrinsic motivations. While quite distant from the ideal LUG described in the LUG-HOWTO documents (especially in terms of internal cohesion), the club did play an active role in trying to establish FOSS in China, and could not be described merely as a themed expatriate club, albeit many resemblances could be found and that might have been one of its original, undeclared functions.

To remain inside the 'religious' framework (and maybe stretching it a bit), FOSS activists could be considered (and sometimes presented themselves as) akin to missionaries trying to establish a foreign credo in another culture. However, their efforts must also be seen in the proper context. As we have already mentioned, most Western 'religious' members were FOSS entrepreneurs who had more than a vested interest in the growth of the movement and were actively taking advantage of the wage rate in China. By contrast, the majority of 'agnostics' were young hired programmers, mostly working for Chinese firms. Although the importance of class divisions in the LUG should not be exaggerated, the elitist nature of the FOSS movement in China had already been underscored by Greenberg (2000), who aptly titled a paragraph of his news report 'Linux and Mango Frappuccinos: for elite only'.

## Conclusions, limitations and perspectives

We are now in a better position to address again the opening question. It appears that, because of a number of internal and external factors, a specifically Chinese FOSS culture able to motivate individuals is presently very weak or absent. At the same time, the 'global' FOSS culture appears to encounter a number of difficulties when being incorporated into the Chinese context. However, our exploration barely scratched the surface of the issues involved in the problematic relationship between China and FOSS. While a symbolic/emotional drive (or specifically, the lack thereof) appears to be the central agent in defining the situation of FOSS in China at the time of our observation, the number of factors involved in this absence and their complex entanglements (sometimes in deep-seated cultural features, sometimes in contingent phenomena related to modernization) appear too complex to disentangle within a short chapter.

The factors we isolated (lack of a shared supporting narrative because of political mutability; lack of immediate rewards, due to the market situation; and structural issues related to the communication modalities required by FOSS) might be broken into a myriad of sub-problems, each worth a separate analysis. Moreover, it cannot be stressed enough that our findings should not be generalized for the whole Chinese software development scene but must be taken in their context. It appears more than probable that passionate programmers do exist in China, and that some of them might even be contributors to FOSS projects. Further research appears to be very much needed to explore their representation of themselves, of Chinese modernization and of how FOSS can be incorporated into the Chinese context.

## References

Bitzer, J., Schrettl, W., & Schröder, P. J. H. (2007). Intrinsic motivation in open source software development. *Journal of Comparative Economics, 35*(1), 160–169.

Castells, M. (2003). *The Internet galaxy: Reflections on the Internet, business, and society.* Oxford: Oxford University Press.

Edgerton, D. E. H. (2007). The contradictions of techno-nationalism and techno-globalism: A historical perspective. *New Global Studies, 1*(1), 1–32.

Fletcher, O. (2009, July 15). Open-source adoption faces extra obstacles in China. *PC World.* Retrieved July 16, 2010, from http://www.pcworld.com/article/168455/open-source_adoption_faces_extra_obstacles_in_china.html

Greenberg, J. (2000, August 9). Linux in China: Not ready for prime time. *Salon.* Retrieved July 16, 2010, from http://www.salon.com/technology/feature/2000/08/09/linux_china/

Gries, P. H. (2004). *China's new nationalism: Pride, politics, and diplomacy.* Berkeley: University of California Press.

Hars, A., & Qu, S. (2002). Working for free? Motivations for participating in open-source projects. *International Journal of Electronic Commerce, 6*(3), 25–39.

Henderson, S. J. (2007). *The dark visitor: Inside the world of Chinese hackers*. Raleigh: Lulu.

Hiner, J. (2007, July 27). Sanity check: How Microsoft beat Linux in China and what it means for freedom, justice, and the price of software. *Tech Republic*. Retrieved July 16, 2010, from http://blogs.techrepublic.com.com/hiner/?p=525

Iannini, M. (2006, September 18). Recruitment woes. *ZDNet*. Retrieved July 16, 2010, from http://www.zdnetasia.com/blogs/recruitment-woes_bp-61953551.htm

Ju, D., & Shanghai, A. (2001). China's budding software industry. *IEEE Software, 18*(3), 92–95.

Kshetri, N. (2005). Structural shifts in the Chinese software industry. *IEEE Software, 22*(4), 86–93.

Leonard, A. (1999, July 6). Linux is like a Chinese peasant uprising. *Salon*. Retrieved July 16, 2010, from http://www.salon.com/technology/log/1999/07/06/linux_china

Leonard, A. (2001, February 15). Life, liberty and the pursuit of free software. *Salon*. Retrieved July 16, 2010, from http://dir.salon.com/tech/log/2001/02/15/unamerican/

Li, M., & Zheng, J. (2004). Open source software movement: A challenging opportunity for the development of China's software industry. *Journal of Electronic Science and Technology of China, 2*(3), 47–52.

Moen, R. (2010, June 17). Linux user group HOWTO. *TLDP.org*. Retrieved July 16, 2010, from http://www.tldp.org/HOWTO/User-Group-HOWTO.html

Noronha, F. (1999). Linux: Open source software for South Asia. *Economic and Political Weekly, 34*(46), 3273–3275.

Northway. (2008, October 16). Weiruan heibing, shi xin shidai de yapian zhanzheng. *Sina Blogs*. Retrieved July 16, 2010, from http://blog.sina.com.cn/s/blog_487e34b80100b0gt.html

People's Daily Online. (2006, June 17). Gloomy prospects for domestic Linux industry. *Renmin Wang*. Retrieved July 16, 2010, from http://english.peopledaily.com.cn/200606/17/eng20060617_275003.html

Puhakka, M. (2007, August 27). Part II – Emergence of open source within Chinese software industry. *Opensource Blogi*. Retrieved July 16, 2010, from http://blogit.digitoday.fi/opensource/part-ii-emergence-of-open-source-within-chinese-software-industry

Pye, L. W. (1986). On Chinese pragmatism in the 1980s. *The China Quarterly*, (106), 207–234.

Raymond, E. (2001). *The cathedral and the bazaar: Musings on Linux and open source by an accidental revolutionary*. Sebastopol, CA: O'Reilly & Associates.

Schneier, B. (2008, June 19). The truth about Chinese hackers. *Schneier on Security*. Retrieved July 16, 2010, from http://www.schneier.com/essay-223.html

Shanghai Daily. (2005, December 12). Morals lost online as kids make hackers idols. *China Daily*. Retrieved July 16, 2010, from http://www.chinadaily.com.cn/english/doc/2005-12/12/content_502624.htm

Shen, X. (2004). Developing country perspectives on software: Intellectual property and open source. A case study of Microsoft and Linux in China. *International Journal of IT Standards & Standardization Research, 3*(1), 21–43.

Tarantino, M. (forthcoming). Is there a Chinese digital sublime? Some reflections on the cultural representations of technology. In P.-L. Law (Ed.), *New connectivities in China: Virtual, actual, and local interactions*.

Yang, C. N. (2005, December 23). China changes Linux tactics. *Linux.com*. Retrieved July 16, 2010, from http://www.linux.com/archive/articles/50468

Yang, D., Ghauri, P., & Sonmez, M. (2005). Competitive analysis of the software industry in China. *International Journal of Technology Management, 29*(1), 64–91.

# 9 Identity vs. anonymity

## Chinese netizens and questions of identifiability

*Kenneth Farrall and David Kurt Herold*

## Introduction

In the spring of 2007, citizens of Xiamen became concerned over a new 11 billion Yuan (USD$1.4 billion) chemical plant to be built in the city's Haicang district. Although the project had overwhelming support from the city government, citizens in Xiamen were able to make use of Internet bulletin boards, emails and short messaging services to organize a public protest of more than 10,000 people at the city centre on 1 and 2 June, leading to the temporary abandonment and eventual halting of the project.

A few months after the protest, the city government announced draft rules banning anonymous Web postings by city residents (Dickie, 2007). The move caused considerable controversy and was widely debated in Chinese cyberspace, but appears to have been a unilateral action by the city government of Xiamen. Guangzhou city's *South Metropolis News* quoted He Bing of the China University of Political Science and Law in Beijing as saying, 'Only the National People's Congress has the right to legislate on this issue' (China Daily, 2007).

The Xiamen government saw anonymous discourse online as a clear threat to its power. Individual, anonymous actions online led to a massive, offline protest, forcing government officials to abandon plans for what would have been a highly lucrative industrial project.

Online anonymity allowed citizens to escape the imagined, ever-present gaze of the panopticon (Foucault, 1995). They were able to elude the system of government controls and the self-enforced compliance of citizens attendant with their general online visibility. Anonymity, in this case, prevented (or at least complicated) the identification of specific individuals seen as having incited the masses of citizens in Xiamen to rebel against the legal authority of local government officials.

The netizens (Internet + citizens) who started the online protest remained protected by their anonymity. Contrary to Euro-American Internet behaviour, though, their anonymity is not an assumed one, hiding an individual's identity to avoid the consequences of one's actions. Instead, this chapter argues that the Chinese practice of anonymity online is fundamentally different from Euro-American practice. Specifically, it is based on different defaults, around the absence of a link between an online identity and the offline user, rather than the hiding of such a link in specific contexts.

After providing some preliminary definitions of anonymity and of the terms connected to it, this chapter considers the cultural underpinnings of Chinese approaches to anonymity, as well as its present online forms and consequences. The chapter will close with some speculation on how the Chinese concept and related practices might evolve and influence the non-Chinese Internet.

## Anonymity and identity

The core definition of anonymity in the online context is understood and agreed upon by the general public with little variation. Anonymity is freedom from being identified, freedom from the personal accountability that identification affords. Within the general field of anonymous communication, individuals may create and experiment with multiple independent (single and group) identities, linked to pseudonyms, within specific social and professional contexts. Anonymity, on its own, is value neutral. It protects vital outlets of truly creative, democratic discourse (Akdeniz, 2002) while at the same time affording abuses of human body and spirit, such as those from lone, unaccountable bullies engaged in flaming (Alonzo, 2004) or the nameless, vengeful on- and offline crowds of Human Flesh Search Engines, which we will discuss in more detail below.

In recent years, the disappearance of online anonymity and its attendant positive or negative consequences for offline individuals has been raised as an issue in increasing numbers of discussions (O'Harrow, 2006; Solove, 2004 and 2007). At one level, anonymity is simply a perceived state. A Chinese citizen who perceives him or herself to be anonymous has some confidence that their actions within this space will not be traceable to their physical person, to their persistent, offline, indexical identity (Phillips, 2004). Free from the fear of consequence, the citizen may then be more likely to make statements that they otherwise might not make for fear of prosecution.

Of course, if the perception regarding the relative risks of free expression is false, and this supposedly anonymous activity can be easily identified by the government, these enthusiastic netizens could be in for a rude awakening. Whether or not a given communication or file is truly 'anonymous' turns out to be much more difficult to determine even at the abstract level of mathematics (Sweeney, 2002; Li, Li & Venkatasubramanian, 2007; Machanavajjhala et al., 2007; Schneier, 2007). At the practical level, records judged to be 'anonymized' often are not, especially when associated with records covering the same population (Ohm, 2009). Judging from the Chinese government's own policy actions in the past few years, such as the ongoing real-name initiative and the clear frustration of the Xiamen city government with the affordances of anonymous BBSs and blogs, however, it is clear that 'anonymity holes' remain in Chinese cyberspace.

For the purposes of this paper, we deal less with the formal definition or technical possibility of anonymity and more with the cultural assumptions that shape social practice. For example, we can imagine that cultures might differ in the importance of anonymity as compared to other social tools and values and its role in protecting those values. Cultures within different nation-states or regions may also differ on how anonymity and identifiability fit into the default rules for online communication and sociality.

The association of online identities with specific offline individuals has become the default position in human interactions with computers in Europe and North America. After the purchase of a new computer, users of Mac OS X as well as of newer versions of Microsoft Windows are strongly encouraged to link the login for their personal machine to an online identity via Apple's Mobile Me and Microsoft's .Net offerings (e.g. Microsoft, 2009). Universities, companies, NGOs, etc. usually require a user to log in to their workstations with personalized IDs and passwords so that a specific offline individual can be held responsible for the online behaviour logged on any of their machines. Online services from news providers to social networking sites, from gaming portals to blogging sites, offer individuals multiple possibilities for links between the different services they use with the promise of tailor-made content based on an individual's preferences. The currently prevailing opinion is that such a network of links between online services and the identity of an offline individual is essential for the future of the Internet, as it simplifies the use of the Internet by its users through the connection of information stored online about each user and linked to their offline identities (Chartier, 2008; Davis, 2009; Fogie, 2008; Gonsalves, 2008; Oltsik, 2010; Open ID Foundation, 2010; Perez, 2008). An individual obtains an email account linked to his/her offline identity, e.g. through his/her employment or studies, or through buying online access from an Internet Service Provider (ISP), then uses this email address to register for online banking services, business websites, social networking sites, etc., thus becoming identifiable in all his/her online activities. If this individual wants to engage in anonymous activities, he/she has to actively hide his/her identity, e.g. through the use of Internet proxies, anonymous email accounts, private web surfing, etc. (e.g., Anonymouse, 2009).

In China, however, an individual's initial engagement with computers and the Internet is fundamentally different and avoids the establishment of such a link between the offline individual and an online identity, even though, as will be shown later in this chapter, government authorities are actively attempting to narrow or even close this anonymity gap. Most users access the Internet from anonymous, so-called 'black' Internet cafés, which are unregistered and are therefore themselves not interested in registering their clientele (Chang and Chu, 2009; Ding, 2009; Hong and Huang, 2005: 378–380; Liang and Lu, 2010: 113; Liu, 2009). As the second author's experience of working in China for over eight years showed, even companies, universities, NGOs, etc. rarely require their staff to log in to their work stations with a personalized ID. The provision of university or company emails is also very rare, and the first step for many Chinese Internet users is not the creation of a personalized email, but rather the acquisition of an anonymous QQ number. QQ, which started out as a Chinese form of an online chat service comparable to ICQ or MSN, assigns its subscribers a random number as their identity, which then serves as reference point that can be used to sign up for personal blogs, forum identities, online banking, etc. The information required during the registration process for a QQ number does not establish a link back to an offline individual, as QQ does not check the veracity of the user's data, and requires only a minimum of information for the registration (User Display Name, birthday, gender, place of residence – see Tencent, 2010a). As a result, the online persona of a user cannot easily be linked to an offline individual. The IP address of the computer from which a specific Internet posting was made would have to be followed back to the physical location of the computer, and the individual user who accessed the computer at the time of the posting would have to be tracked down offline, which is possible, but cumbersome. Using the two Chinese terms for 'anonymity', it can be said that, in a very real sense, Chinese netizens are *wuming*, i.e. 'without a name', rather than *niming*, i.e. 'hiding a name', unless they actively establish a link between their online activities and their offline identity. There is also some evidence to suggest that Chinese netizens like this form of anonymity and feel uncomfortable when required to produce information about their offline identity, to the point that some deem 'disclosure of personal privacy the most disgusting online experience' (Kong, 2007: 159 – see also the discussion in Wang, 2002: 559–563 and Yao-Huai, 2005).

The QQ group of products was developed and is marketed by Tencent (2010b). QQ started as a chat program similar to ICQ or MSN, but quickly grew in functionality, range, and scope. Outside the main 'chat' program, the QQ website (http://www.qq.com/) now acts as an Internet portal offering everything from shopping to email services, to information, entertainment, and news. The chat program itself is currently actively used by over 350 million people (Wang, 2009, 12 January) who not only use it to chat with other users, but also to meet in groups that discuss events, chat as a group, play online games inside the QQ chat client, etc.

The QQ chat lies at the core of how Chinese Internet users establish their identity online. Signing up for QQ, the user is assigned a QQ number, which becomes their name and address online. Users can then add a 'screen name', which is, however, not a requirement. The screen name can be changed at will by the user, and many Internet users change their screen name regularly in order to express their opinions or to support or protest events in real life. For example, to express their support for the Chinese government, many QQ users changed their names in March and April 2008 to include the phrase 'I heart China'. A person's offline identity never appears within QQ unless the user wants it known, thus maintaining a high level of anonymity, while engaging in numerous activities online.

Another facet of this online anonymity can be found in China's most popular online payment service, called Alipay, or Zhifubao in Chinese, which was started to support the auction site Taobao (http://www.taobao.com/) but has since spread to other sites taking online payment. Alipay provides its payment service through cooperation between a growing number of banks, which were recently joined by the Visa credit card company, who handle the transfer of funds offline. In marked difference from the US company Paypal (http://www.paypal.com/), the payment of funds is not tied to an online identity or a specific address. Instead, customers of any of the participating banks arrange the 'online' transaction either from their own bank's Internet banking (if available), or from any branch in the real world. While it remains possible to connect the specific online bidder to the offline money transfer and the offline person setting it up, there still remains a gap between them, requiring offline investigation to link the two. Two additional payment methods were recently introduced that disassociated the online identity of a buyer even further from the offline user issuing the payment, as Internet users are now able to use Alipay-branded bank or store cards to spend money online that has first been paid into the card account. Additionally, Alipay users can now visit special payment offices or ATM-like machines set up in many supermarkets (e.g., Carrefour and Walmart) to pay for their online expenditures with cash payments, again making the linking of an offline user to an online identity very difficult (for different payment options, see Alipay, 2010).

Armed with an anonymous identity online, and an anonymous method of payment, Chinese Internet users are then able to enjoy Chinese cyberspace with less worry of endangering their offline lives, unless they actively create a link between their online identity and their offline persona.

## Anonymity and online carnival

### Anonymous groupings instead of individual actions

In contrast to the American or European Internet, much of the activity in Chinese cyberspace takes place on bulletin board services (BBS) or online forums, as well as on blogging sites. In Europe and America, both of these types of sites have been supplanted by new types of websites with the advent of the Web 2.0 'Internet revolution'. In China, the Web 2.0 types of websites have so far failed to gain much ground, and Internet users still prefer the older and more anonymous forms of Internet interaction represented by BBS and blogs.

There are a number of popular BBS providers in China, on whose boards Chinese Internet users can express their opinions, seek advice, or discuss topics of interest to them, e.g. QQ (http://bbs.qq.com/), Tianya (http://www.tianya.cn/), KDS (http://www.kdslife.com/), Netease (http://bbs.163.com), Sina (http://bbs.sina.cn/), Sohu (http://club.sohu.com/), Liba (http://bbs.sh.liba.com/), and many more. To sign up with any of them, all that is required is the choice of a nickname and the provision of an email address to be able to activate the user's account on the BBS. Similar to QQ, the different BBS do not allow for an easy linking of the user's chosen online identity to his or her offline persona, thus providing a very high level of anonymity of the users, although IP tracking and an offline follow-up investigation can still establish a link.

The names Internet users choose for their BBS postings have little to do with real 'names' and are instead chosen as a reflection of the topic the Internet user wants to comment on. The names are meant as a joke, or a clever remark, etc. In one recent discussion on Netease based on an article about the state of hospitals in China (Netease News, 2009), the different commentators changed their names to indicate where they were from. The commentators chose names like 'Netease Internet User from Hangzhou', 'Netease Internet User from Beijing', 'Netease Internet User from China', 'Netease Internet User from Mars', etc.

Personal blogging, another popular online activity in China, fulfils a very different function in China than it does in Europe or the USA. Blogs are not so much an individual's expression of his or her thoughts, in the form of an online diary, but instead a part of exchanges taking place in a large online community.

The homepages of popular blogging sites in China look less like the websites of providers of blogging services, and more like online news and entertainment portals, for example, compare Sina (http://blog.sina.com.cn/), Tianya (http://blog. tianya.cn/), or Sohu (blog.sohu.com/) to US offerings like Blogger (http://www. blogger.com/) or Livejournal (http://www.livejournal.com/).

European and American blogging sites offer to link an individual's blog to other facets of a user's online activities and are geared towards 'production' of content. Chinese blogging sites instead offer an anonymous sign-up (see, e.g., Sina (2010b)) and emphasize the 'consumption' of content. A blogger has to decide to link his or her identity on the blog to his or her identity offline and then take steps to make him- or herself identifiable online. Without an effort by the individual blogger, he or she remains anonymous online, as the online presence is not linked to the offline user. The online presence remains without a clear identity (or name = *wuming*), unless the individual user provides a link to his or her offline identity.

The emphasis on 'consumption' of content is evident both on the front page of the blogging services, where different blog posts are referenced in categorized lists of contents, and in special ranking lists of the most-read blogs. For Sina (2010a), the ranking shows that the top 20 blogs have received over 100 million hits each, demonstrating the level of consumption of blog contents and of connectivity that blogging involves in China even for anonymous blogs (see also Tianya (2010), where the top 10 bloggers easily receive over 40,000 hits within one week).

By contrast, social networking sites, which are currently very popular in America and Europe (e.g., Facebook), are comparatively unimportant. In 2008, several Chinese companies attempted to import the concept of social networking sites into China with Chinese versions of Facebook, and began to advertise their services widely. The main contenders at the moment are the education-based XiaoNei ('At School', http://www.xiaonei.com/) and the more open Kaixinwang ('Fun Internet', http://www.kaixinwang.com/). It is too early to gauge the likelihood of their success, although early reports indicate that those sites that offer social networking as a part of their wider portfolio – QQ.com, 51.com, and Baidu – rather than as a special niche, are dominating this form of online content (Godula, Li, and Yu, 2009).

### Fame and the lack of heroes

There are very few Chinese Internet users who have and care about an identifiable online presence, most of whom are using their notoriety for financial purposes.

The most famous duo on the Chinese Internet are two young men who go by the name of Backdorm Boys (= *Houshe nanhair*). The duo became famous while still at university for their lip-synching to pop songs. They had originally intended their first video as harmless fun, but friends of theirs uploaded the video to several video-sharing sites both inside China, as well as to YouTube, where the video became hugely popular. The two students followed this up with a number of additional videos and have since signed a record contract, gave several live concerts, and have achieved stardom, despite not being able to sing very well. They are marketing their image through their videos, blogs in English and Chinese, and other online and offline channels (see Dormitory Boys, 2008; 2009a; 2009b; 2010). What is truly surprising, though, is that they have so far not been imitated by anybody else. Although they have been very successful, their example has not been followed by other Chinese Internet users. While the video of the 'Numa Numa guy' Gary Brolsma started a flood of ever-new versions on YouTube of the 'Numa, Numa' song from people around the world, the Backdorm Boys have not been copied.

Similarly, another Chinese Internet celebrity, by the name of Furong Jiejie (Sister Lotus), who also achieved almost universal recognition in Chinese cyberspace without even having any real talent, stands out as never having been imitated by others. Furong Jiejie became famous because she posted videos and pictures herself online (Sister Lotus, 2006), expressing the firm belief that she was irresistibly sexy, beautiful, and a very talented singer and dancer. Her one attempt at a live show failed, due to a lack of interest (Pennay and Liu, 2008), but she did manage to win advertising contracts and minor roles in movies (Sapiens Brian, 2005), and proudly states that she is living her dreams.

A third person that should be mentioned here is Hu Ge (2010), a young man who became instantly famous in 2005 when he created a 20-minute satirical parody with the title 'The Blood Case of the Bun' (Falanke, 2006) with clips from Chen Kaige's movie *The Promise (Wuji)*. The movie itself had disappointed Chinese movie goers, and Hu Ge's parody was seen as a criticism both of the film, and of Chinese current affairs. When Chen Kaige tried to sue Hu Ge for stealing portions of his movie, Chinese Internet users started talking about the issue across most BBS and blogs and forced Chen Kaige to withdraw his complaint through their withering criticism. Again, though, the pattern seen in the two examples above is repeated, as Hu Ge's parody remains the only one to emerge in Chinese cyberspace. Nobody else attempted to copy his idea to produce their own parody.

With very few exceptions, Chinese Internet users prefer to remain anonymous, a part of the large group of 400 million Internet users, instead of exposing themselves and their identity to others. As a result, identifiable opinion leaders in online China are usually widely known, but the extent of their influence on others, or their value as indicators of the future of the Internet (or of identity) in China, is hard to gauge.

China's top search engine, Baidu, provides a number of lists of most searched-for terms that is updated daily for different categories of search terms (http://top.baidu.com). One of the lists it provides is a daily list of the most searched-for people in Chinese cyberspace (Baidu, 2010, 6 July).The list demonstrates, though, how rare it is for Chinese Internet users to become sufficiently known to be famous, with only two bloggers in the Top Ten, at numbers five and ten. It is also very telling that the selfless Communist worker and hero Lei Feng has been in the Top 50 for over three years, China's First Emperor has been there for over four years, and Mao Zedong for over seven years, and all three have been dead for quite a while. In general, Chinese people online do not want to stand out, do not want to be identifiable, do not maintain a traceable online identity.

*Human flesh search and the need for anonymity*

Over the past five years, not only the state, but also other netizens have proved to be dangerous for individuals who get noticed (Herold, 2008). The collective of Chinese Internet users has repeatedly demonstrated that they have very firm beliefs about the morality or immorality of specific actions, and that they are willing to pursue and punish individuals who transgress against this moral code. A wife who had an affair with another World of Warcraft player (French, 2006), a foreigner who blogged about his sexual encounters in Shanghai (Soong, 2006, August 28), a husband whose wife committed suicide (Soong, 2008, August 2), a teenager who complained about the national mourning for the victims of the Sichuan earthquake (Messro, 2008), high school students who misbehaved in class (Soong, 2007), a high Party official from Shenzhen who assaulted an 11-year-old girl (Fauna, 2008, November 1), and many others have had to suffer massive attacks on their lives after being noticed and identified by Chinese netizens, using the 'human flesh search engine', also known as RRSS, an acronym for the Chinese pinyin romanization (*ren rou sou suo*). Netizens who notice behaviour that angers them are free to write about their outrage online and to call upon other netizens to help identify and punish the deviants. Netizens will then attempt to identify the deviant using anything that person has 'left behind' on the Internet. Very often, netizens are able to identify the person in question within hours, and then proceed to publish the individual's contact details online with a 'call-to-arms' to all netizens to make use of these details to harass the individual deviant. Such attention can wreck an individual's life, and many of the people who were 'flesh-hunted' in this way had to leave their schools, universities, jobs, etc. and go into hiding (RyanM, 2008).

The biggest and most effective RRSS in China is run by Mop, an Internet portal site with email services, a BBS, blogs, etc. On its RRSS site (http://dzh2.mop.com/) numerous requests for the identification of specific people are posted every day, and Mop users are very aggressive in their harassment of people they regard as deviant. The seriousness of the RRSS, and their importance in China, can additionally be deduced from the existence in China of an RRSS run by Google. Similar to the Scholar, Image, Book, etc. searches provided internationally, in China Google is additionally providing a 'Human Flesh Search' to cater to the demands of the Chinese market (http://www.google.cn/intl/zh-CN/renrou/index.html), something that has so far been unnoticed by Western politicians.

RRSS work through the mobilization of large numbers of people, rather than through accessing existing databases. As a result of the gap between online netizens and offline people, standard search engines do not produce useful results in these cases. Outside China, for example, the email addresses of the authors of this chapter could be entered into the Google search engine(s) and, after some tweaking, substantial amounts of information on the offline life of the authors could be located. By contrast, in the case of the misbehaving high school students mentioned above, some netizens watched their uploaded video and noticed 'English-language words on the blackboard and the Uzbekistan and Chinese national flags', and contacted the embassy of Uzbekistan online to ascertain which school they had visited, which then led to an identification of the students

(Soong, 2007). A mere search online would not have ended in the identification of the students.

## Wuming and the Chinese government

In Chinese cyberspace, the story is *not* about the loss of privacy, but about attempts by the government (and a few others) to establish a link between online and offline individuals.

### *China's expanding surveillance grid*

While it is true that anonymity and privacy have strong and growing salience within modern Chinese culture, this is not to suggest that the Chinese government does not dedicate significant resources to surveilling and keeping records on its population. Much has been written in the past several years about the country's massive surveillance matrix, known as the 'golden shield' project (Bambauer, 2006, Bradsher, 2007; Kalathil & Boas, 2003; Spencer, 2007; Walton, 2001; Wang, 2004). On 28 December, 2005 the Ministry of Public Security promulgated Rules on Internet Security Protection Technology Measures, requiring IPS and Internet Information Services (IISs) to maintain registration and 'Internet movement' data for their customers for a period of 60 days (China Daily, 2006, October 18). China recently upgraded its national ID system with a second-generation national ID card, complete with embedded RFID chip that allows state agents to read identification data without the necessity of physical card presentation. This card is linked to a national population registry that, in addition to providing (highly valued) identity verification services to the general public, appears designed to be a grand repository for a wide range of personal data, from police records to financial, job, education and medical data. Financial and police records are already accessible and many more are to be added in the future. Any piece of personal data that includes a Citizen Identification Number (CIN) is likely to end up within this centralized data system.

It is important to recognize, however, that much Western reporting exaggerates the extent of the current system. While the national electronic dossier system is real and expanding, there remain important institutional sectors where record keeping remains largely paper based, such as the medical sector. And although there is an ongoing and dramatic acceleration in the production of personal financial data and an emergent 'financial identity' for urban Chinese, most business is still transacted with paper currency. Finally, despite recent government pilot projects in Beijing to dramatically reduce or eliminate anonymity via Internet cafés, the vast majority of the country's *wangba*s remain, as of the summer of 2010, bastions of anonymity.

While it is national law that all citizens should carry their national ID cards, many do not. In March 2003 an incident in the city of Guangzhou involving of the death of young migrant worker Sun Zhigang while in police custody sparked a public outcry against police treatment of citizens found out in public without proper documentation. Sun was jailed for not having his 'temporary residence permit' and later died after a brutal beating in police custody. Hard-hitting investigative reporting by the city's *Southern Metropolis Journal* was distributed widely on the Internet and resulted in the case becoming the focus of public attention (China Internet Information Center, 2003). In the wake of the scandal, the central government was forced to transform migrant detention centres like the one where Sun had been mistreated into voluntary service centres, while at the same time abolishing the temporary residence permit requirement that had been present in Chinese law for 20 years. Although the government later reintroduced the permit system, citing the need to manage the migrant worker problem, there continue to be active calls for the abolition of the system, and the topic is considered fair game in the media (Qiang, 2006). There appears to be a growing sense within the Chinese public sphere that state officials cannot simply demand the presentation of ID without cause. Migrant workers and similar marginal populations recognize that carrying the cards at all times (if they possess them) will lead to less friction with police, but for most long-term residents with proper *hukou*s (residential permits), the card is stored in a drawer and only pulled out when needed (such as to open a bank account). This renders the RFID technology largely impotent for now, except for the more marginal, targeted populations who carry the cards in greater number.

### *Fight against real-name initiative*

In private meetings with members of Internet Society of China (ISC), the industry association group which sets policies and standards for online business, officials at the Ministry of Information Industry (MII), requested that the ISC study and develop a policy for the registering of real names for all bloggers. Within days of the meeting, rumours quickly began to circulate on the Internet about the impending policy, leading to a confirmation of the rumours by the *People's Daily* on 23 October. In the article, the *People's Daily* quoted ISC Secretary General Huang Chengching as saying '[w]e suggest, in a recent report submitted to the ministry, that a real-name system be implemented in China's blog industry' (Xinhua, 2006). Huang also noted that much still needed to be worked out about the policy and that this would take time. The article claimed that a recent survey by the ISC showed that half of all Internet users would support such a policy.

Eight days later, one of China's most liberal newspapers, *Southern Weekend*, published a detailed account of the MII's meetings with the ISC and offered a different poll which suggested that both industry leaders and the public were against such a policy in far greater numbers than the *People's Daily* article had suggested:

> The numbers provided by the Internet Society show that half of the netizens support a real-name blogger registration system. In the joint Internet poll conducted by New Cultural Daily and Sohu.com as of November 1, 25% supported and 75% opposed the real-name blogger registration system.
>
> (Zhao, 2006)

The *Southern Weekend* article goes on to quote a key Internet industry figure, Bokee.com president Fang Xingdong, on the logistical difficulties and significant costs that such a programme would entail. With this article, both the netizens at large and private Internet industry publicly voiced their opposition to the government's real-name policy.

In December 2006, the *People's Daily* published an opinion column from an unnamed judicial official in Jiangsu province entitled 'Bloggers should get real in virtual world'. In the article, the author confirmed the planned rolling out of a new real-name policy for certain parts of the Internet, including blogs, and described his support for the policy, pointing out the danger inherent in anonymous communication:

> The authorities believe that requiring bloggers to use their real names will benefit the healthy development of Internet blogs. The free development of blogs in the past few years has led to a chaotic situation. Some have used blogs to disrupt social order and have harmed the interests of the majority. A real-name system will safeguard freedom of speech and also guarantee the sound development of blogs.
>
> In fact as early as 2005 a blog-related lawsuit emerged. Associate professor Chen Tangfa from Nanjing University accused a blog company of having failed to properly deal with insulting comments about him that were spread by an anonymous blogger on the Internet. Chen won his lawsuit in August in what was the first blog infringement case to come into public view. Though the court ordered the company to post a formal apology, it is hard to punish the many anonymous bloggers who wantonly vent their anger while infringing upon others' rights on the Internet. And as slander cases involving blogs emerge in an unending flow, there are increasing calls for the implementation of a real-name system.
>
> In the virtual world of the Internet, it is a thorny issue for infringement victims to preserve evidence. The infringers attack anonymously and it is only possible to track their temporary IP addresses. So there is a clear need to develop identification technology.
>
> (China Daily, 2006, December 13)

Negative reactions from China's Net-using public continued to make their way into mainstream media coverage. In early January 2007, *China Youth Daily* (*CYD*) published a national poll of 1,843 Internet users in which 83.5 per cent were opposed to the plan. A *People's Daily* article citing the *CYD* survey noted that citizens were in support of a similar policy for cell phones, since they understood its role in reducing fraud and cutting down on the scourge of SMS spamming. The article concluded with a clarification of the imminent ISC policy, noting that bloggers would still be free to choose online pseudonyms, and that 'real identities will remain confidential and protected if they do "nothing illegal or harmful to the public"' (Xinhua News Agency, 2007).

An article published in *Liaoning Legal News* argued that the state in fact had no legal authority to compel Internet users to identify themselves and thus could not simply compel real-name registration by way of ISC policy. The argument referred to the text of the 2003 National ID law in which only four specific instances are listed where ID presentation is legally compelled. The fifth instance would require the passage of a national law. As a result, it argued, not only real-name policies for blogs, but also those for online gaming and mobile phones, had no legal basis. In support of the policy's social utility, the article went on to recommend that such laws be passed, since law-abiding citizens should have nothing to fear from exposing their identity to the state (Martinsen, 2007).

The combination of widespread public opposition and carefully reasoned legal arguments exemplified by the *Liaoning Legal News* article appeared to force the government to reconsider. When the government-supported industry association ISC released its 'draft self-discipline code' for bloggers in May 2007, real-name registration was listed as 'encouraged' rather than mandatory (Chen, 2007).

### ShuiMu Tsinghua (SMTH) BBS fight less successful

A few years earlier, however, public protest against a state anonymity-reducing policy did not have as much success. On 16 March 2005, as part of the Communist Party's 'ideological education' campaign, China's most popular university BBS, ShuiMu Tsinghua, stopped permitting access to all but currently matriculating students registered with their real names. A number of other university BBSs across the country were similarly constrained or completely closed around this time (United Press International, 2005). This limited shutdown of ShuiMu Tsinghua ended a tradition of anonymous posting and wide-ranging discussion in which current students, faculty and alumni living all over the world deliberated on topics from the Iraq war to SARS, to controversial issues of Chinese history.

Unlike censorship of websites like the BBC, CNN and Voice of America, seen as a minor nuisance with little impact on most people's lives, the shutdown of the SMTH and other university BBSs affected a large number of students and alumni and was largely viewed with great disdain. In the wake of the BBS crackdown users reacted strongly. The access restrictions caused widespread protests among the users, both online and, more cautiously, offline. Some Tsinghua students wrote essays and poems, expressing their concern and sadness about the shutdown, while board moderators distributed ASCII BBS 'posters' to relay their message of mourning and protest. On 18 March, in a rare instance of offline protest, around a hundred students gathered around a monument on the Tsinghua campus engraved with the logo 'actions are greater than words'. The students covered the monument with origami cranes and other paper figures, traditionally symbols of mourning. Among the more ingenious modes of online protest was the ironic use of quotations by Mao Zedong to criticize the shutdown, such as 'it is right to rebel!' This left BBS moderators with the dilemma of either removing otherwise legitimate quotations of Chairman Mao, or allowing the veiled criticism of the shutdown (O'Kane, 2005).

Despite the outpouring of popular discontent, the policy has remained. One difference, perhaps, was that there was no BBS industry, so to speak, concerned about the 'cost' of the plan. BBS at universities were entirely non-profit ventures.

*IP policy*

The country's lesser-known IP policy, on IP addresses rather than intellectual property, also seeks to eliminate anonymity. There is strong recognition within the state bureaucracy that the new international standard for IP addresses (IPv6) has the capacity to assign every individual one or more unique IP addresses, so that all of an individual's online activity can be tracked and stored and anonymity can be eliminated. During a March 2006 visit to Paris, Hu Qiheng, chair of the ISC, told an *International Herald Tribune* writer, '[t]here is now anonymity for criminals on the Internet in China [...] With the China Next Generation Internet project, we will give everyone a unique identity on the Internet' (Crampton, 2006). Just how significant the role of IPV6 could be in anonymity online is open to some debate. Internet policy discourse about the topic tends to point out that the protocol has considerable room for built-in anonymity, but it depends on specific implementations. Chinese ISPs could conceivably implement the protocol in ways that make it much easier to identify people via their IP addresses.

More recently, according to reports by a CNET columnist, the Chinese government has been working closely with the UN on developing a global strategy for IP identification. The government has proposed technical standards for 'IP Traceback', a technology intended to eliminate the possibility for online anonymity via applications such as the Tor Network. A UN drafting group named Q6/17 met in Geneva in late September of 2008 to discuss the development of this system (McCullagh, 2008). As Bruce Schneier has noted, it is not clear how the UN expects to dictate global Internet policy, but the participation of the US National Security Agency in the IP Traceback drafting group suggests that developments here are worth following (Schneier, 2008).

**Future developments**

The Chinese concept of anonymity is complex and multifaceted. Part of it draws from the traditional Confucian value of collectivism, of the deferment of the individual to the collective interest. However, anonymity now services opposing and more recently ascendant values of libertarianism, privacy and self-determination. It is the more libertarian notions of anonymity that have been evoked in recent public protest against real-name policies, but it may be the collectivist aspect that is more responsible for the broader default tendencies toward nameless (*wuming*) mediated sociality, today epitomized by the ubiquitous QQ number.

This unusual, bipolar salience of anonymity in China is likely to make it an important player in the global evolution of its conceptualization and practice in the coming years. Privacy has grown in importance over the past several decades, along with economic prosperity and increases in residential space, while anonymity has come to be valued more, as compared to other countries such as the US and South Korea. In a recent poll conducted by J. Walter Thompson, Chinese netizens were nearly twice as likely as their American counterparts to agree that it is good to be able to express honest opinions anonymously online (IAC and JWT, 2007). Public debate in Chinese cyberspace is active and engaged, lubricated by the oil of the *Wuming* (nameless) blogger and innovative discursive strategies designed to evade censorship (Esarey and Xiao, 2008). The Chinese public have clearly been less willing to go along with a net-wide real-name policy than have been South Koreans, where a government policy has been in place since late 2008.

We do not want to overstate the value of anonymity to Chinese cultural practices as compared to other values. Under many circumstances, including in Chinese fledgling social networking applications, real names are the default practice. Anonymity does not trump other Chinese values, but may not necessarily conflict with them either. For Chinese ICT users to gain confidence and trust in mediated (e)commerce, however, they needed the means to reliably identify prospective transaction partners. This is why polls in China have shown more widespread public support for real-name requirements in mobile phone numbers, despite being less than enthusiastic for similar policies impacting on online discussions on BBSs and blogs. Cell phones function in this context as portable tools for an economic transaction (ID provides a reliable link to reputation and trust assessment), whereas blogs are part of a non-market production cycle originating from generally fixed locations (home, work or Internet café PCs) in which anonymity affords informational variety and carries less overhead risk.

As is evident with its real-name initiative and IPV6 policy, the Chinese government wishes to reduce or eliminate 'anonymity holes' in cyberspace. As of spring 2010, it has been signalling a renewed effort to institute a real-name policy Internet wide. Already, major portal sites such as Sina and Netease have instituted real-name requirements for news comment posting, but blogs have maintained some anonymity. Knowing how much the Chinese value their anonymity, and what large numbers of people maintain anonymous blogs, it seems unlikely that the public will simply submit to the state's will. The less the Chinese populace trusts its government to meet its basic interests, the more it will demand anonymity in its mediated discussions.

If the government decides to press forward with this policy despite public distaste, we may gain a much deeper appreciation for the social affordances of electronic networked communication technology. China does not share the US tradition of politically neutral NGOs acting in the public interest, and is in fact only a few decades removed from the oppressive excesses and stifling mass surveillance programmes of the Cultural Revolution, but the public today has begun to assert itself in significant ways. While it is easy to talk and write about the Chinese political system as simply authoritarian or totalitarian, there is much more space for the creative negotiation of political interests than China often gets credit for (Akhavan-Majid, 2004; Peerenboom, 2005). Tools for anonymous communication such as the Tor network will likely diffuse at higher rates, while innovations developed within Chinese borders could become popular and circulate globally. Unnoticed nexus points of hardware, applications, networks and social trust will be exploited in ways not yet imagined, continuing the cat-and-mouse game between anonymity and re-identification. Innovations in networking could make it even harder for the government to monitor Chinese cyberspace, masking not only the origins but the content of messages in dark nets beyond the surveillance capacities of the Golden Shield.

In response, the government may begin to promote closed information appliances along the lines of Apple's App Store model, to more effectively keep software and network innovations under control. Given the existence of government corruption at all levels that may be willing to trade anonymity resources for cash, the preponderance of black Internet cafés and other *wuming* spaces is likely to continue, however. As mobile networking and media production begins to take off in China, it will be interesting to see if future cell phone users will attempt to reclaim the kinds of anonymity spaces they have enjoyed within the blogosphere, and how it could impact on mechanisms and social schema for giving and receiving trust.

The potential for anonymity is critical to self-determination and the free exploration of identity. Though it can afford a range of anti-social and even dangerous activities, its relation to self-determination and creativity in the modern world should not be underestimated. Whether or not it is possible for any individual to be truly anonymous when they engage in communication and information retrieval online is one of the 'hard problems' of information science. Nevertheless, among young Chinese, the belief that their activities can be anonymous clearly has an impact on their willingness to engage in certain kinds of behaviour, including the population of the public sphere with fresh ideas. As socio-technical systems around the globe begin to struggle with the right balance between anonymity and accountability, the Chinese experience will play a significant, if not defining, role.

## References

Akdeniz, Y. (2002). Anonymity, democracy, and cyberspace. *Social Research, 69*(11), 223–237.

Akhavan-Majid, R. (2004). Mass media reform in China: Toward a new analytical framework. *Gazette: the International Journal for Communication Studies, 66*(6), 553–565.

Alipay. (2010). Payment methods. Alipay.com. Retrieved March 25, 2010, from http://abc.alipay.com/payment.html

Alonzo, M. (2004). Flaming in electronic communication. *Decision Support Systems, 36*(3), 205.

Anonymouse. (2009). AnonWWW. Anonymouse.org. Retrieved March 25, 2010, from http://anonymouse.org/anonwww.html

Baidu. (2010, July 6). Top personalities of the Chinese Internet. Baidu Lists. Retrieved July 6, 2010, from http://top.baidu.com/buzz/renwu.html

Bambauer, D. (2006). Cool tools for tyrants. *Legal Affairs,* (January–February).

Bradsher, K. (2007, August 12). China enacting high-tech plan to track people. *New York Times,* p. 1.

Chang, J., & Chu, K. (2009, June 3). Anonymity but no place to hide. US–China Today. Retrieved March 25, 2010, from http://uschina.usc.edu/article@usct?anonymity_but_no_place_to_hide_13402.aspx

Chartier, D. (2008, January 9). OpenID and DataPortability.org to gain major support. Ars Technica. Retrieved March 25, 2010, from http://arstechnica.com/software/news/2008/01/openid-and-dataportability-to-gain-major-support.ars

Chen, F. (2007, May 22). China eases off proposal for real-name registration of bloggers. *Xinhuanet.* Retrieved November 17, 2010, from http://news.xinhuanet.com/english/2007-05/22/content_6136185.htm

Chen, J. (2004). Popular political support in urban China. Washington, DC; Stanford, CA: Woodrow Wilson Center Press; Stanford University Press.

China Daily. (2006, October 18). New rules to quash Internet rumours. *China Daily*. Retrieved July 14, 2010, from http://www.chinadaily.com.cn/bizchina/2006–10/18/content_710648.htm

China Daily. (2006, December 13). Bloggers should get real in virtual world. *People's Daily Online*. Retrieved July 14, 2010, from http://english.people.com.cn/200612/13/eng20061213_331956.html

China Daily. (2007, July 6). China city moves to ban anonymous Web postings. *China Daily*. Retrieved July 19, 2010, from http://www.chinadaily.com.cn/china/2007–07/06/content_912280.htm

China Internet Information Center. (2003, July 8). 84 days and nights in Guangzhou. *China.org.cn*. Retrieved July 14, 2010, from http://www.china.org.cn/english/2003/Jul/69295.htm

Crampton, T. (2006, March 19). Innovation may lower Net users' privacy. *New York Times*. Retrieved July 14, 2010, from http://www.nytimes.com/2006/03/19/business/worldbusiness/19iht-chinet20.html?_r=1

Davis, A. (2009, November 30). Twitter, Facebook vs. OpenID: Identity management made easy. Tippingpoint Labs. Retrieved March 25, 2010, from http://blog.tippingpointlabs.com/2009/11/twitter-facebook-vs-openid-identity-management-made-easy/

Dickie, M. (2007, July 8). China city to tighten Internet controls. [Electronic version]. *Financial Times* (London, England). Retrieved March 1, 2008 from http://www.ft.com/cms/s/0/0790fcb6–2d7c-11dc-939b-0000779fd2ac.html?nclick_check=1

Ding, W. (2009). The world of black and white – a case study of Internet practices in an urban village. *Kaifang Shidai* [Open Times], 2009(3), 135–151.

Dormitory Boys. (2008). The Dormitory Boys. The Dormitory Boys. Retrieved July 6, 2010, from http://twochineseboys.blogspot.com/

Dormitory Boys. (2009a). Houshe Nanhair – the Back Dormitory Boys. Sina Education. Retrieved July 6, 2010, from http://edu.sina.com.cn/y/focus/housheboy/index.shtml

Dormitory Boys. (2009b). Housheboy's Channel. YouTube. Retrieved July 6, 2010, from http://www.youtube.com/profile?gl=US&user=housheboy

Dormitory Boys. (2010). Houshe Nansheng Blog. Sina Blogs. Retrieved July 6, 2010, from http://blog.sina.com.cn/housheboy

Esarey, A. & Xiao, Q. (2008). Political expression in the Chinese blogosphere. *Asian Survey, 48*(5), 752–772.

Falanke. (2006, March 3). *Parody of The Promise – The Blood case of the mantou*. YouTube. Retrieved July 6, 2010, from http://www.youtube.com/watch?v=AQZAcT1xaKk

Fauna. (2008, November 1). Government official attacks 11-year-old girl. Chinasmack. Retrieved July 6, 2010, from http://www.chinasmack.com/2008/videos/government-official-attacks-11-year-old-girl.html

Fogie, S. (2008, February 22). OpenID: Single sign-on web identity management. InformIT. Retrieved March 25, 2010, from http://www.informit.com/guides/content.aspx?g=security&seqNum=296

Foucault, M. (1995 [1977]). *Discipline and punish: The birth of the prison*. Trans. by Alan Sheridan (2nd ed.). New York: Vintage Books.

French, H. (2006, June 3). Online throngs impose a stern morality in China. *New York Times*. Retrieved July 6, 2010, from http://www.nytimes.com/2006/06/03/world/asia/03china.html?_r=1

Godula, G., Li, D., & Yu, R. (2009, April 5). Chinese social networks 'virtually' out-earn Facebook and MySpace: A market analysis. TechCrunch. Retrieved March 25, 2010, from http://techcrunch.com/2009/04/05/chinese-social-networks-virtually-out-earn-facebook-and-myspace-a-market-analysis/

Gonsalves, A. (2008, February 7). Major tech companies join OpenID board. Information Week. Retrieved March 25, 2010, from http://www.informationweek.com/news/internet/showArticle.jhtml?articleID=206106080

Herold, D. K. (2008). Development of a civic society online? Internet vigilantism and state control in Chinese Cyberspace. *Asia Journal of Global Studies, 2*(1), 26–37.

Hong, J., and Huang, L. (2005). A split and swaying approach to building information society: The case of Internet cafes in China. *Telematics and Informatics, 22*(4), 377–393.

Hu Ge. (2010). Huge's Blog. Sina Blogs. Retrieved July 6, 2010, from http://blog.sina.com.cn/huge

IAC, & JWT. (2007, November 23). China leads the US in digital self-expression. IAC Media Room. Retrieved July 14, 2010, from http://iac.mediaroom.com/index.php?s=43&item=1455

Kalathil, S., & Boas, T. C. (2003). *Open networks, closed regimes: The impact of the Internet on authoritarian rule*. Washington, DC: Carnegie Endowment for International Peace.

Kong, L. (2007). Online privacy in China: A survey on information practices of Chinese websites. *Chinese Journal of International Law, 6*(1), 157–183.

Li, N., T. Li, & Venkatasubramanian, S. (2007). t-Closeness: Privacy beyond k-Anonymity and l-Diversity. International Conference on Data Engineering (ICDE), pp.106–115.

Liang, B., and Lu, H. (2010). Internet development, censorship, and cyber crimes in China. *Journal of Contemporary Criminal Justice, 26*(1), 103–120.

Liu, F. (2009). It is not merely about life on the screen: Urban Chinese youth and the Internet cafe. *Journal of Youth Studies, 12*(2), 167–184.

Machanavajjhala, A., Kifer, D., Gehrke, J., & Venkitasubramaniam, M. (2007). l-diversity: Privacy beyond k-anonymity. *ACM Transactions on Knowledge Discovery from Data (TKDD), 1*(1), 3.

Martinsen, J. (2007, March 20). Mr. Sun, I'll need to see some ID. Danwei. Retrieved July 14, 2010, from http://www.danwei.org/ip_and_law/mr_sun_ill_need_to_see_some_id.php

McCullagh, D. (2008, September 12). U.N. agency eyes curbs on Internet anonymity. Retrieved October 5, 2009 from http://news.cnet.com/8301–13578_3–10040152-38.html

Messro. (2008). The Liaoning girl curses Sichuan earthquake victims for 4 minutes and 40 seconds. YouTube. Retrieved July 6, 2010, from http://www.youtube.com/watch?v=OkemgmBPZR0

Microsoft. (2009, March 9). Introducing online identity integration. Windows Server TechCenter. Retrieved March 25, 2010, from http://technet.microsoft.com/en-us/library/dd560662(WS.10).aspx

Netease News. (2009, October 29). Waiting for a whole night, just to get one stamped pass. Netease. Retrieved July 6, 2010, from http://news.163.com/09/1029/22/5MR0I8TC0001125G.html

O'Harrow, R. (2006). *No place to hide* (1st Free Press trade pbk. ed.). New York: Free Press.

O'Kane, B. (2005, March 25). University BBS explodes with snark. Danwei. Retrieved July 14, 2010, from http://www.danwei.org/internet/university_bbs_explodes_with_s.php

Ohm, P. (2009). Broken promises of privacy: Responding to the surprising failure of anonymization. University of Colorado Law Legal Studies Research Paper No. 09-12, August 13. Retrieved July 20, 2010, from: http://ssrn.com/abstract=1450006.

Oltsik, J. (2010, March 16). Will Google tip the scale toward OpenID? Network World. Retrieved March 25, 2010, from http://www.networkworld.com/community/node/58614

Open ID Foundation. (2010). What is OpenID? OpenID.net. Retrieved March 25, 2010, from http://openid.net/get-an-openid/what-is-openid/

Peerenboom, R. (2005). Assessing human rights in China: Why the double standard. *Cornell International Law Journal, 38,* 71.

Pennay, P., & Liu, C. (2008, July 23). Video of the week: Furong Jiejie live in Beijing. The Beijinger. Retrieved July 6, 2010, from http://www.thebeijinger.com/blog/2008/07/23/Video-of-the-Week-Furong-Jiejie-Live-in-Beijing

Perez, J. C. (2008, January 17). Yahoo to support OpenID single sign-on. *Washington Post.* Retrieved March 25, 2010, from http://www.washingtonpost.com/wp-dyn/content/article/2008/01/17/AR2008011701175.html

Phillips, D. J. (2004). Privacy policy and PETs – the influence of policy regimes on the development and social implications of privacy enhancing technologies. *New Media & Society, 6*(6), 691–706.

Qiang, G. (2006). 'Temporary residence permit system illegal'. Retrieved November 13, 2007, from http://www.chinadaily.com.cn/china/2006–12/27/content_769202.htm

RyanM. (2008, January 28). Human flesh search engines – crowd-sourcing 'justice'. CNET Asia. Retrieved July 6, 2010, from http://asia.cnet.com/member/RyanM/blog/?v=post&id=63008617

Sapiens Brian. (2005, October 16). Furong Jie Jie's first movie. Latest Hi Tech News & Information. Retrieved July 6, 2010, from http://www.sapiensbryan.com/index.php/furong-jie-jies-first-movie/

Schneier, B. (2007, September 20). Lesson from Tor Hack: Anonymity and privacy aren't the same. *Wired Magazine.* Retrieved July 14, 2010, from http://www.wired.com/print/politics/security/commentary/securitymatters/2007/09/security_matters_0920

Schneier, B. (2008, September 18). The NSA teams up with the Chinese government to limit Internet anonymity. *Schneier on Security.* Retrieved July 14, 2010, from http://www.schneier.com/blog/archives/2008/09/the_nsa_teams_u.html

Sina. (2010a). New blogger signup. Sina. Retrieved July 6, 2010, from http://login.sina.com.cn/signup/signupmail.php?entry=blog

Sina. (2010b). Blog ranking list. Sina. Retrieved July 6, 2010, from http://blog.sina.com.cn/lm/top/rank/

Sister Lotus. (2006). Furong Jiejie. Blogspot. Retrieved July 6, 2010, from http://sister-furongjiejie.blogspot.com/

Solove, D. J. (2004). *The digital person: Technology and privacy in the information age.* New York: New York University Press.

Solove, D. J. (2007). *The future of reputation: Gossip, rumor, and privacy on the Internet.* New Haven: Yale University Press.

Soong, R. (2006, August 28). The immoral foreign blogger. *EastSouthWestNorth.* Retrieved July 6, 2010, from http://www.zonaeuropa.com/20060828_1.htm

Soong, R. (2007). The Haidian 'Teacher Abuse Gate' special. *EastSouthWestNorth.* Retrieved July 6, 2010, from http://www.zonaeuropa.com/2007011_1.htm

Soong, R. (2008, August 2). EastSouthWestNorth: The first 'Human Flesh Search' trial. EastSouthWestNorth. Retrieved July 6, 2010, from http://zonaeuropa.com/20080802_1.htm

Spencer, R. (2007). China likely to become biggest brother. *The Gazette* (Montreal). London: A17.

Sweeney, L. (2002). k-anonymity: A model for protecting privacy. *International Journal of Uncertainty, Fuzziness, and Knowledge-based Systems 10*(5): 557–570.

Tencent. (2010a). QQ request page. QQ. Retrieved July 6, 2010, from http://reg.qq.com/

Tencent. (2010b). Tencent. Tencent. Retrieved July 6, 2010, from http://www.tencent.com/en-us/index.shtml

Tianya. (2010). Blog ranking list. Tianya BBS. Retrieved July 6, 2010, from http://blog.tianya.cn/blogger/Paihang.asp?idwriter=0&key=0

United Press International. (2005, March 18). China tightens rules for online chat rooms. UPI.com. Retrieved July 14, 2010, from http://www.upi.com/Top_News/2005/03/18/China-tightens-rules-for-online-chat-rooms/UPI-18261111147137/

Walton, G. (2001). *China's golden shield: Corporations and the development of surveillance technology in the people's republic of China.* Montréal: International Centre for Human Rights and Democratic Development.

Wang, F. (2004). Reformed migration control and new targeted people: China's hukou system in the 2000s. *The China Quarterly, 177,* 115–132.

Wang, R. R. (2002). Globalizing the heart of the dragon: The impact of technology on Confucian ethical values. *Journal of Chinese Philosophy, 29*(4), 553–569.

Wang, X. (2009, January 12). A mysterious message millionaire. *China Daily.* Retrieved July 6, 2010, from http://www.chinadaily.com.cn/bizchina/2009–01/12/content_7388202.htm

Xinhua New Agency. (2006, October 22). Blog real name system not yet officially decided. *People's Daily.* Retrieved July 19, 2010, from http://news.xinhuanet.com/english/2006–10/23/content_5236067.htm

Xinhua News Agency. (2007, January 9). Real-name online registration system meets opposition in China. *People's Daily Online.* Retrieved July 14, 2010, from http://english.peopledaily.com.cn/200701/09/eng20070109_339327.html

Yao-Huai, L. (2005). Privacy and data privacy issues in contemporary China. *Ethics and Information Technology, 7*(1), 7–15.

Zhao, L. (2006, October 31). The real-name blogger registration system. EastSouthWestNorth (Southern Weekend). Retrieved July 6, 2010, from http://zonaeuropa.com/20061106_1.htm

# 10 Taking urban conservation online

## Chinese civic action groups and the internet

*Nicolai Volland*

Previous studies on the Chinese Internet have tended to focus on the potential of the electronic media to bring about political change, on the Chinese government's efforts to stifle dissent and control the flows of information, and on the methods Chinese netizens have used to breach the technical-bureaucratic regime of Internet control (Chase & Mulvenon, 2002; Harwit & Clark, 2001; Hughes & Wacker, 2003; Kalathil & Boas, 2003; MacKinnon, 2008; OpenNet Initiative, 2005). This focus on the Party-state and on the issue of control and resistance, however, over-looks several crucial questions: who are the people using the Internet, why do they go online, and what do they do there? What are the repercussions of their online activities for their life beyond cyberspace? And, as this chapter asks, what new forms of collective activism and organization has the Internet helped to produce? I argue that the Internet serves not merely as an extension of offline Chinese society, but has come to constitute a hybrid social space in its own right. This space is populated by heterogeneous groups that usually unite around a common agenda, but are otherwise characterized by low degrees of institutionalization and a carnivalistic embrace of voices, ideas, and motivations. These new forms of social activism have remained largely unexplored (exceptions are Yang, 2009; Zhou, 2005; and the articles in Tsui, 2005). In this chapter, I explore the dynamics of agenda setting and the formation of Internet-based civic action groups through an analysis of the website Lao Beijing Wang (http://oldbeijing.org/).

The scope of action for non-governmental organizations (NGOs) in the People's Republic of China (PRC) remains tightly controlled by the Party-state. The Internet, however, has opened up a virtual space for what I call civic groups to bring together like-minded individuals, to promote their particular causes, and to raise awareness of issues underrepresented in the state-controlled public sphere. 'Civic groups', as used in this chapter, refers to coalitions of citizens and non-aligned activists who promote issues of public concern. In contrast to NGOs and what Yang (2009) calls 'citizen activists', these groups are characterized by their informal character, flat or non-existing organizational hierarchies, and their inner diversity and heterogeneity. The people involved with Lao Beijing Wang, for example, come from a variety of backgrounds; what unites them – both online and offline – is their concern for the preservation of Beijing's architectural and cultural heritage in the face of rapid urban change. The formation and work of these groups, I suggest, has been greatly facilitated by the growth of China's online society.

In this chapter I explore the implications of the Internet for two crucial dimensions – the discursive and the organizational – of the work of civic groups in the PRC.

Based on a textual reading of Lao Beijing Wang and on interviews with individuals involved, I examine how they build their arguments and how these arguments have evolved over time. Finally, I ask about the role that the Internet plays in the organization of urban conservationist groups and in the coordination and maintenance of joint activities. I argue that heritage websites like Lao Beijing Wang have allowed non-governmental groups to establish themselves in an alternative virtual public sphere that has, in turn, expanded their access to the otherwise tightly controlled state-managed mass media. The Internet has thus engendered new forms of organization and interaction both within cyberspace and beyond it. Non-aligned civic activists, such as those at Lao Beijing Wang, convene on the Internet, using it both as a space to meet and build coalitions and as a means to raise public awareness of a classic civil society concern, thus creating momentum for a broad-based conservation movement in China. The technical opportunities of the Internet have allowed them to take a flexible approach to pursuing their agenda; instead of merely voicing disapproval of state policies, they self-consciously combine cooperation with resistance and blend interaction with agenda setting. Based on the virtual social space of the Internet, they reach out to actors in the larger social sphere, bridging online and offline activism. The example of urban heritage networks thus shows how non-governmental groups can creatively exploit niches of the Internet to push the boundaries of civic action in the PRC.

This chapter is based on two snapshots of Lao Beijing Wang, from 24 May 2005 and 11 July 2006, that have been downloaded for storage at the Digital Archive of Chinese Studies (DACHS), maintained at the University of Heidelberg (http://www.sino.uni-heidelberg.de/dachs/), and follow-up observations of the website until August 2009. Interviews were conducted during fieldwork in Beijing in March and April 2006.

## Non-governmental organizations, civic action, and the Internet as a social space

Non-governmental organizations in the PRC operate under difficult conditions. While the Chinese Communist Party (CCP) has recognized the need to rely on intermediary organizations as it continues to withdraw from the micromanagement of society, the Party continues to claim the right of 'leading' the nation and all its affairs. This claim puts a theoretical and legal strain on the scope of NGOs and their activities. Moreover, the continuing Party control of the media sector means that non-governmental groups have had limited access to the public sphere where they could openly argue their causes (Volland, 2004).

Organizationally, interest groups in the PRC had to carve out niches for their existence. In some cases, officially sanctioned advisory bodies such as the professional associations that for a long time have served as a transmission line to communicate Party policies downwards, have been converted into organizations that actually lobby for the interests of their members. As they maintain close ties with the local and central state, however, their potential to become bona fide NGOs is limited (Foster, 2002; Unger, 2008). The same is true for the large number of 'government-organized NGOs' created since the 1990s (Hsia & White, 2002: 330; Morton, 2005: 519f; Schwartz, 2004: 42–45; for a more guarded view see Ho, 2001: 914; and Saich, 2000: 125, 139). Self-organized NGOs began to appear in the 1980s and became more numerous in the 1990s. A key event in the growth of China's NGO movement was the UN Women's Conference held in Beijing in 1995, which taught many Chinese civic groups about the patterns of organization and action of international NGOs.

Since 1989, NGOs have been allowed to register with the authorities, which brings some degree of legitimacy, but also closer monitoring and sometimes tutelage (Ho, 2001: 904; Hsia & White, 2002: 337). Alternatively, they can choose to operate outside of the official legal system, as many local groups have done. This course, however, is difficult and dangerous: it invariably results in a high degree of institutional instability and loose organizational patterns; if the activities of such informal groups clash with the interests of the authorities, they may even be accused of illegal association and persecuted (Yang, 2005; Young, 2006). Similarly difficult, for both registered and unofficial Chinese NGOs, is cooperation with foreign NGOs resident in the PRC, which the government regards as suspicious (Hsia and White, 2002; Morton, 2005; Yongding, 2005; see also Wines, 2009, for a recent case). Nonetheless, a large number of activist groups has sprung up in recent years, with varying degrees of institutionalization and different organization, making a detailed definition of Chinese NGOs difficult (Ma, 2002; Saich, 2000).

The Chinese public sphere remains tightly controlled by the Party (Volland, 2004), and media controls have been further tightened under the Hu–Wen administration since 2002. While newspapers and even selected television stations have been able to allocate more space to investigative reporting and socially contentious issues, it was only the spread of the Internet that empowered citizens to participate in the process of news making. Non-governmental groups remain barred from establishing their own publications that would support their particular causes although some of the larger organizations publish unofficial newsletters that are distributed to their members only (Information received with thanks from Yang Guobin). In this context, the Internet is a crucial new tool for NGOs to communicate their issues to the larger public and to coordinate the activities of their members.

The Internet provides easy access to new and fast communication channels outside the state-controlled media. This has been a crucial factor for the growth of activist groups on a broad range of issues (Yang, 2005: 59f). On the one hand, the Internet has made it relatively easy to write and publish on issues that hitherto had rarely or not at all found their way into the official press, or that had been represented exclusively in the modes prescribed by the Party-state. The Internet has allowed for new issues to enter the public sphere, and for alternative perspectives on such issues to compete for the attention of Chinese netizens.

At the same time, the Internet has made it easier for groups of citizens to advertise and coordinate their activities, to communicate among their members, and to attract others with similar interests. This trend has accelerated with the arrival of the 'Web 2.0' and interactive platforms such as blogs, social networking sites, news feeds, and Twitter. The impact of Web 2.0 technologies on the evolution of Internet-based civic action groups, however, is a topic in its own right and is beyond the scope of this chapter.

Both factors in conjunction have aided the rapid growth of civic action groups that try to raise public awareness of issues such as discrimination against homosexuals, the environmental impact of large hydropower projects, and the destruction of China's urban architectural heritage.

## Online activism: urban transformation as a civil society concern

Intervention in the process of rapid urban transformation, such as in the case of Beijing, is a classic example of civic action. The issue of urban conservation began to emerge in the Chinese public consciousness only with accelerating economic growth in the 1980s, when it was discovered by Chinese citizens, together with other new social concerns. Nonetheless, it remained under- and misrepresented in the official public space. Veteran activist Hua Xinmin, for instance, laments the lack of access to the public sphere faced by conservationists (telephone interview, 1 August 2006). Only the Internet allowed individual activists to find other like-minded people, to coordinate their actions, and to push the topic onto a broader public agenda.

The traditional architectural fabric of Beijing dates back to the Ming and Qing dynasties. The city's maze of small alleys (*hutong*) and courtyard homes (*siheyuan*) makes for a unique cityscape that supports a centuries-old urban culture (Naquin, 2000). Both the architecture itself and the culture it hosts, however, are fragile. Yet despite a century of civil wars, occupation, socialist construction, cultural revolution, and earthquakes, the old city of Beijing survived largely intact into the early 1980s (see Hoa, 1981; Lin, 2004; Wang, 2003; but also Wu, 1999; Wu, 2005; and Broudehoux, 2004). It is only rapid economic growth, fuelled by reform policies since 1978, that has brought fast-paced change to Beijing's urban culture since the late 1980s. Large swathes of the old city were razed to make place for high-rise apartment buildings, shopping malls, and infrastructure projects, all with the rationale of 'modernization' (*xiandaihua*). This process has greatly accelerated since 1995, with the influx of foreign capital, a speculative bubble in the property sector, and mounting official corruption.

Selected quarters of the city – such as the Houhai and Qianmen areas – have been rebuilt to cater for a growing tourist industry, especially in anticipation of the 2008 Olympic Games. While this 'facelift' has prevented the destruction of some of the architecturally most precious quarters, their conversion into theme parks has fuelled debates about proper forms of urban redevelopment. Finally, gentrification has become an issue in the remaining *hutong* areas of the city. The transformation of Beijing into a modern city raises a set of complex questions that defy simple answers. Only with the spread of the Internet, however, have these issues entered the broader public sphere.

The Lao Beijing Wang website (http://oldbeijing.org/) has emerged as an important meeting space for activists campaigning for urban conservation (the website was originally hosted at www.oldbeijing.net before shifting to its current address and maintains mirror sites at www.obj.org.cn, www.laobeijing.org, www. oldpeking.org, and www.oldbj.org). The website was set up in January 2001 on the private initiative of Zhang Wei, an amateur then in his 20s who has ever since managed and developed the website. While he is an activist, he has kept a much lower profile than the 'organizational entrepreneurs' discussed by Yang (2005, 60–62).

For Zhang, the website started as a hobby, but it received so much positive feedback that he soon quit his job to devote his time entirely to the cause of Beijing's culture. Since its earliest days, Lao Beijing Wang has grown rapidly: the number of site visitors has risen constantly and the website itself has gone through repeated upgrades; it has moved from basic html encoding to professional ASP (active server pages) based software that has made the site easier to navigate and more user friendly. A milestone was the addition of a multi-channel discussion board in March 2004 that has opened up avenues of multidirectional discussion and exchange and thus attracted more readers and supporters. As of July 2006, the bulletin board counted around 20,000 daily hits (telephone interview, 1 August 2006). Three years later, it boasted 22,551 registered members, up from 6,400 in July 2006 and 2,200 in May 2005 (http://bbs.oldbeijing.org/, accessed 24 August 2009. For the earlier numbers see the archived copies, accessed 18 July 2006, and May 2005 download). The bulletin board hosts 397,000 postings on a total of 28,000 topics, including essays, commentaries, and pictures, making it the largest website in China dedicated to the conservation of Beijing's historical, architectural, and cultural heritage. In what follows, I will attempt a close textual reading of the website, examining the discursive dimension of Internet activism – how the group has built its agenda and its arguments. The next section will take a closer look at the organizational dimension: at the community that has formed around the Lao Beijing Wang website, its patterns of organization and its activities, both online and beyond cyberspace.

Lao Beijing Wang presents itself to its readers with an unobtrusive, text-heavy layout, with a moderate number of images and moving elements, and no commercial advertisements (description as of 18 July 2006). The website is dominated by white and gray tones, presumably a reference to the monochrome colours that dominate Beijing's traditional *hutongs*. The navigational section of the homepage has changed repeatedly, but always maintaining a focus on quick access to the website's main features. As of August 2009, the design highlights recent updates, new postings to the bulletin board, recommended essays, and announcements from the group's photography unit. Taking pride of place in the centre of the homepage's upper section is a panel that provides direct links to five features that represent the core interests of the website: the bulletin board, a documentation of Beijing traditional New Year and temple festivities, the documentation efforts of the photographic unit, the ongoing debate on urban conservation, and selections from two photo exhibitions organized by the group. Columns on the left side contain links to a number of like-minded websites and downloadable features, such as the e-zine produced by the Yandu salon and the collections of the group's photographic unit.

The Lao Beijing Wang website has evolved over time, adapting to technological change and the availability of new network technologies. In 2006, the website relied on a fairly large navigational panel with 49 channels into which content was divided. Further links led to other features, including the bulletin board, the download section, blogs, and an 'English forum'. Some of these remain core elements of the website three years later; others – such as the latter two – have been given up, presumably because of technological difficulties or lack of response. As an active community platform in a larger online society, Lao Beijing Wang continues to grow and change with the needs of the group that populates it.

The centrepiece of Lao Beijing Wang is the featured articles and the discussion board. The interests and the energy of the website's regular and occasional users clearly lie in these two features. In the years since its founding, the site has published thousands of articles related to themes of Beijing's culture and history (as of 24 August 2009, the total count stands at 9,600). The largest number of articles can be found in the category 'Hutongs' (1,668 articles), followed by 'Conservation' (*baohu*, 546 articles). Conservation of the city's traditional architecture is a central concern of the website. Other sections, 'Folk' (*minjian*, 441 articles), 'Food' (*yinshi*, 455 articles), and 'Famous brands' (*laozihao*, 459 articles), however, boast significant numbers of articles as well. The focus of Lao Beijing Wang includes the wide range of Beijing's non-material culture; in the understanding of the website's supporters, urban culture is a living and organic whole that cannot be restricted to architecture alone. Articles on temples and temple fairs, Beijing dialect, Beijing literature, folk arts, local customs, etc. define Lao Beijing Wang as a comprehensive website dedicated to both the material and non-material aspects of Beijing's urban cultural heritage, neither of which can be understood (or preserved) in isolation from the other.

The overwhelming majority of the articles on Lao Beijing Wang are reprinted from other websites, most of them from the online editions of media in the Beijing area, including Xin Jing Bao, Beijing Qingnian Bao, Qianlong Wang, but also Renmin Wang (the website of the *People's Daily*) and Zhongguo Qingnian Bao. Very few articles were written by authors associated with the website itself; these are designated as 'original creations' (*yuanchuang*). This practice is in line with Chinese government regulations that ban online circulation of any items listed as 'news' that haven't been published before by the authorized news media (CNNIC, 2000). However, all articles provide a link at the bottom that leads directly to the discussion board, where opinions are exchanged both on the articles posted and on numerous other themes.

The Lao Beijing Wang discussion board is divided into 34 channels (August 2009, up from 23 in July 2006). The interests of the audience that meet at the website are diverse, as is reflected by the popularity of the various channels. The most active channels – in terms of discussion topics and follow-up postings – are dedicated to entertainment, searching for old neighbours, Beijing's food culture, and amateur photography. Since its earliest days, Lao Beijing Wang has thus grown with the community it has attracted, and has moved beyond its original focus on discussing and documenting the transformation or Beijing's urban culture, which dominated the forums as recently as July 2006. This does not mean, however, that Lao Beijing Wang has given up its initial focus. While they no longer top the list in terms of views and postings, the discussion board sections that are placed most prominently at the top of the page are 'Debate – Old Beijing' (*Zhengming – Lao Beijing*), 'Record – Cultural Inquiry' (*Jilu – Wenhua yanjiu*), and 'Record – Cultural Preservation and Investigation' (*Jilu – Wenwei diaocha*). The last two are designated as the official forum of the photographic unit, where the members publish their pictures and inquiries. 'Debate – Old Beijing', in turn, is the site of an ongoing theoretical reflection on the patterns of urban change in Beijing, or, as the forum itself is described, 'a debate about the contradiction between commercial land development and cultural transmission, in the context of a large-scale movement of urban reconstruction' (http://bbs.oldbeijing.org/). In a reflection on the development of the website, Zhang Wei writes 'In the course of several years, "Debate", "Cultural Inquiry", "Cultural Preservation", and "Professional Photography" have become the centrepieces of Lao Beijing Wang that have attracted numerous netizens to participate in the construction and development of the website' (Zhanggui, 2009, March 12 – Zhanggui, or 'shopowner', a Beijing dialect term, is the pseudonym used by Zhang Wei, the founder of the website). A clear focus on the issues of urban conservation and cultural heritage is thus apparent from the structure of the website and the bulletin board.

This focus is also reflected in the debates on Lao Beijing Wang. The signature thread (and the most long-lived) on the website's discussion board is the debate between the 'conservation faction' (*wenwei pai*) and the 'demolition faction' (*chai pai*). This thread was initiated with a posting on 1 October 2004 by a user with the pseudonym Jams, and was still active almost five years later, having attracted almost 500 responses. The initial posting is brief and to the point, reading: 'Beijing is so old that it presses down upon you, so demolition seems to be a good idea – so how are we gonna tear it down?' (Jams, 2004). When others responded angrily Jams began to elaborate on his position. More people dropped in, and a month later, a heated debate was underway, with the overwhelming majority of postings expressing outrage at the idea of demolition.

In a posting three days after his original comments, Jams explained his standpoint:

No matter Beijing or Nanjing, this problem is not solved by demolition or not demolition. When we talk about demolishing and conserving, we mean in fact preserving something useful or demolishing something useless. From a historical point of view, development is inevitable, conservation is not impossible, but it needs selection. If any dynasty had made no advance over its predecessors, it would have no distinction at all. Culture, uniqueness – these are all matters of individual taste.

When we talk about conservation, what exactly do we want to conserve? If we want to conserve all of it, then I'd rather say tear it all down. Of course, that sounds quite radical. But for what did our ancestors climb down from the trees?

Just talking about demolition doesn't solve the problem, but it isn't so easy with 'conservation' either. Just tell me, what do we want to conserve? Maybe I'm a bit muddle headed, but what exactly should be conserved? Why don't you draw up a list? Don't tell me that all should be preserved, just because it is unique. I ask you, who of the people would, just because of preserving traditions, reject air conditioning, renovations, would use the 'four treasures of the study' to write letters in the form of eight-legged essays; and how many would be willing to read the thirteen classics by the light of an oil lamp, instead of watching TV? Let's find a 'degree' or 'measure,' and then go on discussing!

(Ibid.)

After his clearly provocative opening, Jams now added a lot of nuance to his position and raised a series of complex questions that are indeed at the heart of the debate about urban renewal. The arguments presented by Jams in this posting are well known – modernity, development, rising living standards – and are often cited in the press, by bureaucrats, city planning officials, and property developers. In a follow-up posting, Jams reiterated his point:

Beijing will have to do some demolition, the key questions are: what to demolish and how to do it; what not to demolish, and why. Making these points clear may in fact be more effective than what is going on now. Demolition will always be necessary.

(Ibid.)

Jams' postings are written in a casual tone, yet his arguments are measured, revealing the full complexity of the issue. Jams challenges his interlocutors: he wants them to come up with well-considered and reflected answers, with counterarguments that would produce a serious dialogue between proponents and opponents of the different paths of Beijing's modernization. That is what has eventually happened.

Hundreds of people answered Jams' original posting and his follow-ups. In the course of the discussion, an astonishing range of arguments were presented and contested. Postings grew longer, with lists of arguments in favour of the cause of conservation. An especially active user with the pseudonym Fei Ge, who belongs to the core community of Lao Beijing Wang, wrote two lengthy reprisals under the titles 'Rejecting "Beijing's need for demolition"' and 'Once more rejecting "Beijing's need for demolition"' that received much praise from other users for their systematic treatment of the topic and the refined arguments he presented (Fei Ge, 2004, December 29; 2005, January 20; since registering in November 2004, Fei Ge has published almost 6,000 postings on Lao Beijing Wang and remains active as of August 2009). Others joined in to support his points. Over time, thus, a comprehensive body of balanced and thoughtful arguments emerged that raised the discussions on Lao Beijing Wang to a new level.

Judging from the way Jams formulated his ideas and from the ever new explanations and examples he provided, it seems likely that this was an agent provocateur planted by the owner of the website and his friends. Jams had registered as a user on the very day of his first posting and was active for only a short time – he logged onto Lao Beijing Wang just six times to post his replies (http://bbs.oldbeijing.org/dispuser.asp?Name=jams). He disappeared once the debate started to heat up and involve more people.

There is in fact a time-honoured tradition of employing rhetorical devices such as this to draw attention to emerging debates. At the same time, the agent provocateur can serve as a safety measure when the arguments that are to be scrutinized, attacked, or refuted are in fact those of a person of authority or the government. Probably the most famous instance in modern China was the 'Wang Jingxuan' hoax in 1918, through which the editors of *New Youth* tried to draw attention to their journal and the issues raised in the New Culture Movement (Hill, 2007). In the case of Lao Beijing Wang, the debate between the two 'factions' jump-started a discussion that addressed fundamental questions about the conservation of Beijing's cultural heritage, and that – through collective discourse – produced a systematic argument supporting the conservationist cause of the Lao Beijing Wang community. These arguments, in turn, could be used in larger public debates, beyond those carried on the website itself.

Numerous other threads on Lao Beijing Wang's discussion board address the question of urban renewal and the delicate balance between the need for the new and the preservation of the old. An issue drawing ongoing attention from the conservationist community is the proliferation of new showcase construction projects within the old city. In a 2005 poll, website visitors were asked to cast a vote for the worst 'eyesore' (*'shangfeng baisu' de jianzhu*) in Beijing (Xing Gege, 2005). Of the ten buildings nominated, the new National Centre for the Performing Arts (*Guojia dajuyuan*) received by far the most votes. The Centre, a postmodernist construction designed by the French architect Paul Andreu, is commonly referred as 'the egg,' an allusion to its outer shape, and is located to the west of Tiananmen Square, in the historical centre of the city. Several blocks of ancient *hutongs* were demolished to make place for the construction; the relocation and the debate about the appropriateness of the choice of location had attracted considerable attention in China and abroad (Hawthorne, 2008). The disapproval of the Lao Beijing Wang community was overwhelming – the city's West Railway station, the Millennium Altar, and the Oriental Plaza on Chang'an Avenue came in as distant second, third, and fourth in the poll.

The design of new landmark buildings and their location within the perimeter of the old city has been a constant concern of the virtual community at Lao Beijing Wang. In an effort to draw attention to the issue, Zhang Wei, the website's founder, started a thread in December 2004 (just when the debate between the 'conservation faction' and the 'demolition faction' grew heated) with the title 'Lashing out at the "National Centre for the Performing Arts"' (Zhanggui, 2004, December 21). His posting consisted of just one line, asking visitors 'What do you think about "lashing out at the National Centre for the Performing Arts," everyone tell us their opinion!' Others quickly joined in and gave their opinions, ranging from ironic comments (one contributor called the National Centre [*Guojia dajuyuan*] a 'National brothel' [*Guojia dajiyuan*]) to elaborate and informed architectural discussions. The problem was impressively visualized by a photograph posted by one user, which shows the roofs of the Forbidden City, dwarfed by the National Centre in the background. In the course of the debate, ideas were collected to formulate a coherent argument against the construction of 'eyesores' such as the National Centre. The collective brainstorming that Zhang Wei and his colleagues thus set in motion was very similar to the discursive strategies they invoked in the debate on the dilemma between urban renewal and destruction of traditional *hutong* neighbourhoods.

Groups such as those associated with Lao Beijing Wang emphasize collective discussion and exchange of ideas over top-down communication; in lieu of a formal organizational structure, the discursive moment figures much larger than with NGOs with a higher degree of institutionalization. The group's actions, however, are by no means limited to the discursive level and to cyberspace.

## Patterns of civic action: cyberspace and beyond

I have so far focused on the Lao Beijing Wang website and on the discursive dimension of the group's efforts to promote the conservation of Beijing's cultural heritage. I will now turn to the organizational dimension, trying to take a closer look at the people behind the website, their activities both online and beyond cyberspace, and the modes of organization adopted by Internet-based activists. This discussion will allow us to draw more general conclusions with regard to the changing patterns of organization and institutionalization of non-governmental groups in the virtual social space provided by the Internet. The following section is based on observations and interviews with members of the group, in Beijing in March and April 2006, and on follow-up telephone interviews conducted in August 2009.

The group around the Lao Beijing Wang website is a loosely knit cluster of individuals without any formal organization. They have no member lists, no governing council, and no constitution; they do not convene any meetings apart from those in the course of their spin-off activities. What unites them are (1) their common cause, to raise public awareness of Beijing's traditional culture and promote the conservation of the city's material and non-material heritage; (2) the sustained interaction on the website and especially the bulletin board; and (3) the common activities that have emerged as spin-offs from their website.

As mentioned earlier, the website was registered by an individual activist, Zhang Wei, and run by him and other volunteers, including since 2007 a European 'correspondent' based in Belgium, who turned out to be a Chinese student volunteering for the website's work (telephone interview, 25 August 2009). It is supported exclusively by the owner's savings and by modest donations from registered members and friends. A list of donations can be found at Yi Ming (2005). The highest contribution as of mid-2009 was 4,000 RMB. The group claims not to have received any outside funding, neither from the government nor from any other organizations. Commercial advertisements as a potential source of revenues have been considered but were subsequently rejected by the group. Running advertisements would add a commercial component to the group's cause that would blur its strictly non-profit nature, some of the group fear.

The regular members of the group come from very disparate backgrounds, ranging from students to retirees, from intellectuals to residents of the alleyways. A few of them have a more professional interest in cultural matters: some have published on Beijing and its culture or produced documentary films, and one works in the municipal Cultural Heritage Bureau (*wenwuju*), although he insisted that he participates in the group's activities in his spare time and in a purely private capacity, which was supported by other members of the group. Most of the people associated with the website have come together as a result of their belief in the urgency to take action to protect whatever is left of Beijing's architectural and cultural heritage from further destruction.

The Lao Beijing Wang website has emerged as a platform for other activists with a similar agenda. A good illustration is Hua Xinmin, China's foremost public campaigner for the protection of Beijing's alleys and courtyard houses. Hua, the daughter of Léon Hoa, a French-trained former architect and city planning official, has spearheaded a national and international campaign to protect Beijing's traditional architecture. Thanks to her French passport, she is able to maintain a higher public profile and to speak more critically of the municipal government's approach to urban renewal, e.g. by suing the local government over the demolition of the courtyard home she grew up in, in 2005, a lawsuit that was covered in the international press (Segretin, 2006). While Hua has not volunteered for the administrative work at the website, she keeps in close contact with the Lao Beijing Wang people, occasionally attends their activities (telephone interview, 1 August 2006), and allows her articles to be reprinted on the website (e.g. Hua, 2005). Her case is typical in that it illustrates the mode of loose association and interaction that a website such as Lao Beijing Wang can create to further civic activism in China.

Since the launch of the website in 2001, the nature of the group that has grown around it has changed considerably. The most important step was the crossing over from cyberspace into real-world activism, chiefly through a number of regular activities that have developed as spin-offs from the website. These included weekly performances of *xiangsheng*, a local story-telling tradition from the Beijing area. These events were initially organized by the 'Lao Beijing Wang folk art group' (*Lao Beijing Wang minsu quyi dui*), which took the name Zhiyou club in 2007. The club holds performances, which are open to the public, in a tea house in the old city and has set up its own website (http://www.zhiyouxiangsheng.com), but it retains a close relationship with Lao Beijing Wang and its website, where its activities are advertised. The purpose of these regular performances is to further a popular cultural tradition that has struggled against marginalization by mainstream mass media entertainment.

Another regular activity organized by activists associated with the Lao Beijing Wang website are weekly *hutong* rallies. These rallies are not commercial tours through the most trendy *hutong* areas, but rather regular outings where members bring photographic equipment to visit the remaining *hutong* areas (in particular, areas that have been designated for demolition), and thus to document the historic alleyways and courtyards and the daily life in Beijing's old city before it vanishes. Members of the group have shot tens of thousands of photographs in the first two years of these tours alone, and expressed the hope to set up a comprehensive online archive once the financial, technical, and administrative conditions would allow them to do so (as of July 2009, this has yet to happen. The tours, however, are ongoing and enjoy rising popularity). As with the *xiangsheng* performances, the photo rallies are announced publicly and anyone interested is invited to join (Lao Beijing Wang, 2010). They have received wide public attention and are the most important opportunity for interaction between group members beyond the Internet, a linkage between social spaces online and offline.

Through these spin-offs, the nature of the website and of the group has been transformed. What started as the one-man enterprise of a dedicated amateur has grown in momentum far beyond the original scope: the website has become a platform for like-minded people and activists, allowing them to exchange ideas and information and to coordinate their activities. In the course of the first five years, the original definition of urban culture has broadened as well, including local history, folk customs, and artistic traditions, all beyond the website's earliest focus on Beijing's architectural heritage.

Most importantly, the spin-offs that resulted from their online interaction gave the Lao Beijing Wang group access to those regions of the public sphere that are traditionally off limits to non-aligned groups and alternative opinion in the PRC, the official mainstream media. While groups such as that around Lao Beijing Wang have made best use of new technologies such as streaming video and podcasts (http://www.oldbeijing.tv/index.html), NGOs continue to face great difficulty in attracting attention from Chinese newspapers and TV. It was due to their crossing from cyberspace into the real world and their heightened visibility outside their own online home turf, however, that the activities of the Lao Beijing Wang group and its agenda have received media coverage. The issue of urban conservation has been picked up by the print and broadcast media, both in China and abroad, who have started reporting about the effort to preserve Beijing's architectural heritage. Newspaper journalists and a camera team from CCTV have joined the photo rallies in the *hutong*, and activists such as the website founder, Zhang Wei, have become used to giving interviews. The destruction of the courtyard homes has come to figure regularly in the foreign press, and Chinese papers, too, have adopted a more critical tone when reporting about urban renewal in Beijing. An article in the *China Daily* (Liu, 2006), for example, quotes – probably deliberately – the Lao Beijing Wang website and provides its Internet address. *Zhongguo Qingnian Bao* [China Youth Daily] and *Xin Jing Bao* [New Beijing News] have run long articles on the group and its photo safaris as well; these stories have in turn appeared on the *People's Daily* website (Gao, 2006; Yang & Wen, 2006).

While open criticism of the municipal government is off limits for the media, their sympathetic stance towards the group and its agenda has brought the debate about urban renewal in Beijing to the attention of a broader public. The Lao Beijing Wang group cannot singlehandedly claim credit for increasing public awareness, but its effort shows clearly how Internet-based public action groups can make a significant impact on agenda setting in the Chinese public sphere, and thus in society at large.

## Conclusion: informal civic action in China's online society

In this chapter I have explored the role of the Internet in civic action in the PRC. In a political setting that has tightly restricted both access to the public sphere and the formation of non-state pressure groups, the emergence of an online society has created new avenues for the formulation, expression, and promotion of classic civil society concerns, such as urban conservation. I have argued that the Internet has significantly altered both the ways in which newly emerging ideas (such as urban renewal and the conservation of Beijing's architectural and cultural heritage) are discussed and brought to the attention of the larger public, and the modes of organization and institutionalization of civic non-state groups in the PRC.

With its open structure, wide spread, and ease of access, the Internet has opened up new spaces for the formation of collective ideas. The empowerment of individuals has long been noted as a key breakthrough of the Internet; however, the discussion of the Lao Beijing Wang website shows that the Internet is at least as important as a social space in its own right, where ideas are launched and contested, and systematic and coherent arguments are developed in a discursive manner. At the same time, the Internet has allowed the group around Lao Beijing Wang to disseminate its ideas in the broader public sphere: the spill-over activities linking the online and offline societies have given the activists access to one of the most guarded assets of the Party-state, the mainstream newspapers and TV, where both their ideas and the group itself acquire a new dimension of public legitimacy.

Finally, the Internet has fundamentally changed the prospects for the organization of civic action in the PRC. Most observers of China's fledgling NGO movement have commented on the close interaction of Chinese NGOs with the (central and/or local) state, or on the lack of autonomy of most non-state groups in the PRC. This discussion has raised methodological issues, concerning the proper definition of NGOs in general (summarized by Ma, 2002). The development of an online society in China, however, has led to the growth of a new breed of civic action groups, groups such as that around the Lao Beijing Wang website. As a newly emerging social space with its own modes of networking and communication, the Internet has significantly reduced the needs for institutionalization, allowing for extremely low degrees of formal structures while guaranteeing sufficient internal coherence and concerted action.

These circumstances raise the question whether Internet-based groups of the kind examined here can be called non-governmental organizations at all. In this chapter, I have settled for the alternative term 'civic action group'. With their loose organizational structures, their low degree of institutionalization, and their flat hierarchies, such groups seem indeed to defy the notion of an integrated, purpose-oriented non-official pressure group. However, I would argue that, from a functional perspective, groups such as that around Lao Beijing Wang have come to form a virtual equivalent of traditional NGOs within the context of China's emerging online society. They have singled out an important civil society concern and have autonomously developed their agenda and their arguments. They have gone public with their concerns and have successfully alerted and mobilized a larger public for their cause. In fact, in a polity that places tight restrictions on autonomous organizations and controls access to the mass media and most other channels of communications, any effort of a civic group to form more integrated and stable institutional structures comes with a loss of operating freedom and efficiency to pursue their primary cause.

Members of the Lao Beijing Wang group are conscious of these problems. They admit that a more formal organizational pattern would likely have detrimental effects to their efficacy. Because of the difficult conditions for NGOs in the PRC, they prefer to interact as a spontaneous, loosely knit association of individuals united solely by their common struggle for the conservation of Beijing's cultural heritage. A good example for this guarded approach is an announcement on the website declaring that the weekly *hutong* rallies are entirely spontaneous events, and that none of the participants speaks or is allowed to do so in the name of the Lao Beijing Wang website (Yi Ming, 2006).

It is precisely for these reasons that the Internet as an online social space, with low entry barriers and high participatory potential, has provided the precondition for new patterns of societal communication, interaction, and organization and for the emergence of new forms of civil society groups engaged in civic action in the PRC.

## References

Broudehoux, A. (2004). *The making and selling of post-Mao Beijing.* London: Routledge.

Chase, M. S. & Mulvenon, J. C. (2002). *You've got dissent! Chinese dissident use of the Internet and Beijing's counter-strategies.* Santa Monica, CA: RAND, National Security Research Division Center for Asia Pacific Policy.

CNNIC. (2000, November 7). Hulianwangzhan congshi dengzai xinwen yewu guanli zanxing guiding. *CNNIC.* Retrieved July 16, 2010, from http://www.cnnic.net.cn/html/Dir/2000/11/07/0654.htm

Fei Ge. (2004, December 29). Bo 'Chai, Beijing de xuyao'. *Lao Beijing Wang.* Retrieved July 16, 2010, from http://bbs.oldbeijing.org/dispbbs.asp?boardid=25&Id=994

Fei Ge. (2005, January 20). Zai bo 'Chai, Beijing de xuyao'. *Lao Beijing Wang.* Retrieved July 16, 2010, from http://bbs.oldbeijing.org/dispbbs.asp?boardid=25&Id=1070

Foster, K. W. (2002). Embedded within the bureaucracy: Business associations in Yantai. *The China Journal, 47,* 41–65.

Gao, M. (2006, March 3). Lao Beijing paijidui de hutong 'baoweizhan'. *Renmin Wang.* Retrieved July 16, 2010, from http://culture.people.com.cn/GB/22219/4160870.html

Harwit, E. & Clark, D. (2001). Shaping the Internet in China: Evolution of political control over network infrastructure and content. *Asian Survey, 41*(3), 377–408.

Hawthorne, C. (2008, August 3). Monuments without context. *Los Angeles Times.* Retrieved July 16, 2010, from http://articles.latimes.com/2008/aug/03/entertainment/ca-china-architecture3

Hill, M. G. (2007). *How to make enemies and influence people: New youth and the Wang Jingxuan hoax.* Paper presented at the Association of Asian Studies (AAS) Annual Meeting held 22–25 March in Boston.

Ho, P. (2001). Greening without conflict? Environmentalism, NGOs and civil society in China. *Development and Change, 32*(5), 893–921.

Hoa, L. (1981). *Reconstruire la Chine: trente ans d'urbanisme, 1949–1979.* Paris: Éditions du Moniteur.

Hsia, R. Y. & White III, L. T. (2002). Working amid corporatism and confusion: Foreign NGOs in China. *Nonprofit and Voluntary Sector Quarterly, 31*(3), 329–351.

Hua, X. (2005, February 26). Beijing san tiao hutong de xiaowang. *Lao Beijing Wang.* Retrieved July 16, 2010, from http://www.obj.org.cn/Article/Class81/Class88/7382. html

Hughes, C. R. & Wacker, G. (Eds.). (2003). *China and the Internet: Politics of the digital leap forward.* London: RoutledgeCurzon.

Jams. (2004, October 1). Chai, Beijing de xuyao. *Lao Beijing Wang.* Retrieved July 16, 2010, from http://bbs.oldbeijing.org/dispbbs.asp?boardid=25&Id=891

Kalathil, S. & Boas, T. C. (2003), *Open networks, closed regimes: The impact of the Internet on authoritarian rule.* Washington DC: Carnegie Endowment for International Peace.

Lao Beijing Wang. (2010). Lao Beijing Wang paijidui huodong gonggao zhuanqu. *Lao Beijing Wang.* Retrieved July 16, 2010, from http://bbs.oldbeijing.org/index. asp?boardid=64

Lin, Z. (2004). *Liang Sicheng, Lin Huiyin, yu wo.* Beijing: Qinghua daxue chubanshe.

Liu, W. (2006, July 4). 'Warriors' protect hutong with cameras. *China Daily.* Retrieved July 16, 2010, from http://www.chinadaily.com.cn/home/2006–07/04/content_632197. htm

Ma, Q. (2002). Defining Chinese nongovernmental organizations. *Voluntas, 13*(2), 113–130.

MacKinnon, R. (2008). Flatter world and thicker walls? Blogs, censorship and civic discourse in China. *Public Choice, 134*(1), 31–46.

Morton, K. (2005). The Emergence of NGOs in China and their transnational linkages: Implications for domestic reform. *Australian Journal of International Affairs, 59*(4), 519–532.

Naquin, S. (2000). *Peking: Temples and city life, 1400–1900.* Berkeley: University of California Press.

OpenNet Initiative. (2005). *Internet filtering in China in 2004–2005: A country study.* Toronto, Cambridge, MA: ONI.

Saich, T. (2000). Negotiating the state: The development of social organizations in China. *China Quarterly, 161*, 124–141.

Schwartz, J. (2004). Environmental NGOs in China: Roles and limits. *Pacific Affairs, 77*(1), 28–50.

Segretin, A. (2006, July 11). En vue des JO, Pékin rase gratis. *Liberation.* Retrieved November 15, 2010, from http://www.liberation.fr/ monde/010154679-en-vue-des-jo-pekin-rase-gratis.

Tsui, L. (Ed.). (2005). Special Issue on the Sociopolitical Internet in China. *China Information, 19*(2).

Unger, J. (Ed.). (2008). *Associations and the Chinese state: Contested spaces.* Armonk: M.E. Sharpe.

Volland, N. (2004). *The control of the media in the People's Republic of China.* Ph.D. dissertation. University of Heidelberg.

Wang, J. (2003). *Chengji.* Beijing: Sanlian.

Wines, M. (2009, August 18). Chinese public-interest lawyer charged amid crackdown. *New York Times.* Retrieved July 16, 2010, from http://www.nytimes.com/2009/08/19/ world/asia/19china.html?_r=1

Wu, H. (2005). *Remaking Beijing: Tiananmen Square and the creation of a political space.* Chicago: University of Chicago Press.

Wu, L. (1999). *Rehabilitating the Old City of Beijing: A project in Ju'er Hutong neighbor-hood.* Vancouver: University of British Columbia Press.

Xing Gege. (2005, March 23). Lao Beijing Wang shoujie Bejing shi da 'shangfengbaisu' jianzhu pingxuan timing mingdan. *Lao Beijing Wang.* Retrieved July 16, 2010, from http://bbs.oldbeijing.org/dispbbs.asp?boardid=25&Id=1493

Yang, G. (2005). Environmental NGOs and institutional dynamics in China. *The China Quarterly, 181,* 46–66.

Yang, G. (2009). *The power of the Internet in China: Citizen activism online.* New York: Columbia University Press.

Yang, Y., & Wen, J. (2006, April 3). Lao Beijing paijidui: Wei Beijing shisu shenghuo jian dang'an. *Renmin Wang.* Retrieved July 16, 2010, from http://culture.people.com.cn/GB/40483/40484/4262324.html

Yi Ming. (2005, August 20). Ganxie rexin chuantong wenhua gongyishiye de pengyou wei wangzhan juankuan. *Lao Beijing Wang.* Retrieved July 16, 2010, from http://oldbeijing.org/Article/ShowArticle.asp?ArticleID=8366

Yi Ming. (2006, June 26). Guanyu Lao Beijing Wang paijidui shengming. *Lao Beijing Wang.* Retrieved July 16, 2010, from http://www.oldbeijing.net/Article/Class76/9371.html

Yongding. (2005, November 19). China's color-coded crackdown. *Foreign Policy.* Retrieved July 16, 2010, from http://www.foreignpolicy.com/articles/2005/11/18/china_s_color_coded_crackdown

Young, N. (2006, February 17). Advocacy: NGOs want better communication, not confrontation, with the state. *China Development Brief.* Retrieved July 16, 2010, from http://www.chinadevelopmentbrief.com/node/476

Zhanggui. (2004, December 21). Dui 'Guojia Da Juyuan' de kou zhu bi fa. *Lao Beijing Wang.* Retrieved July 16, 2010, from http://bbs.oldbeijing.org/dispbbs.asp?boardid=25&Id=976&page=2

Zhanggui. (2009, March 12). Guanyu tiaozheng, guifan 'jilu-wenhua yanjiu ban' tiezi de tongzhi. *Lao Beijing Wang.* Retrieved July 16, 2010, from http://bbs.oldbeijing.org/dispbbs.asp?boardid=9&Id=44049

Zhou, Y. (2005). Living on the cyber border: 'Minjian' political writers in Chinese cyberspace. *Current Anthropology, 46*(5), 779–803.

# Conclusion

## Netizens and citizens, cyberspace and modern China

*David Kurt Herold*

The Chinese Internet is a wild place, enabling Chinese Internet users to engage in an endless variety of activities, including a number that are not permissible in offline China. It can be interpreted as an online form of the Bakhtinian carnival that serves as a pressure valve for the people, but also as an arena in which to laugh at and challenge government authority, while interacting freely with many similar-minded netizens in the familiarity and anonymity of the Internet.

As the different chapters in this volume have demonstrated, this online carnival is very connected to offline China, despite being 'separate'. Online interactions and activities often influence offline events, and online information is beginning to change people's (self-)perceptions, identities, and relationships offline. In contrast to the Internet users in other countries, though, Chinese netizens are less connected to the World Wide Web, and therefore less influenced by 'global' Internet trends. Instead, Chinese Internet users have developed their own forms and sites of interaction, communication, e-commerce, politics, etc. and their own, *Chinese* Internet culture.

The main reason for the development of this Internet 'with Chinese characteristics' is the strong involvement of the Chinese government in online China. Government officials issue regulations, censor information, limit the expression of online opinion, make it difficult for Chinese netizens to engage with the non-Chinese Internet, attempt to influence online opinion, etc. The state is far more (openly) involved in online China than governments in America or Europe are with the non-Chinese Internet.

The future of online China, and maybe – given the sheer weight of numbers of Chinese Internet users – the future of the Internet in general, will depend to some extent on the Chinese government's plans for the Internet. Its approach to the Internet so far has been very different from the approaches of American and European countries, and with the numbers of Internet users shifting ever more in China's favour, this approach might become the model of the Internet in general that other countries follow, rather than emulating the previously dominant United States.

In the past, it has been hard to pin down the general attitude of the Chinese government to the Internet, beyond guessing at it from numerous statements about aspects of the Internet made by government officials at different levels and in various contexts. In early June 2010, though, the Information Office of the State

Council, i.e. the Chinese central government, published its first ever Internet White Paper to outline the official views of the Chinese government on the current status and the future of the Internet in China (Information Office of the State Council of the People's Republic of China, 2010). This White Paper has caused a stir among observers of the Chinese Internet because of the Chinese government's stated intention to keep regulating, censoring, and controlling the part of the Internet that can be accessed from within China's borders. In online comments, ranging from short statements to more in-depth discussions, China has been accused of 'Doubletalking' (Slaten, 2010), or of 'networked authoritarianism' (MacKinnon, 2010), which is 'antithetical to the U.S. position', as the United States stands for 'international freedom of expression' (Price, 2010) and should therefore continue to pressure the international community not to follow China's example.

While some of the discussions raise valid points and some of the sites offer very good summaries of the White Paper (e.g. MacKinnon or Price), most suffer from a very peculiar form of selective blindness or memory loss regarding the attitude of the United States towards the Internet, which invalidates the main thrust of their arguments against the White Paper. Without getting involved in the details of their arguments, two examples can serve to illustrate a more realistic evaluation of the position of the US government towards the Internet and Internet 'freedom'.

In 2000, a French judge ordered the American company Yahoo! to conform to French laws and to make it impossible for French Internet users to access pages on its auction site that advertised and sold Nazi memorabilia, which are illegal in France (Enos, 2000). A US judge 'overturned' this ruling a year later on the grounds that having to follow the French judge's ruling would breach Yahoo!'s constitutional right to 'freedom of expression' (Lawson, 2001). Three years later, though, the French judge's verdict was upheld on appeal in the United States with the explanation that a US court could not interfere with the rulings of a foreign court (Pinsent Masons, 2004). For the Internet and the American position on online 'freedom' this produced the legal situation that, according to the laws of the United States, the Internet is *not* a free, international space, but subject to the local jurisdictions of the countries from which users *access* the Internet. This raises the interesting question: if this ruling is valid for France, shouldn't it be valid for China as well even if 'we' do not agree with the content of Chinese laws? Put differently, if France is 'allowed' to block its citizens from viewing certain online content based on French laws, then why should China not be 'allowed' to block Chinese netizens from accessing content that contravenes Chinese laws and regulations?

In 2006 (McCarthy, 2006) and in 2008 (Kearney, 2008), US law enforcement arrested people offering sports betting online, although the owners of the sites were not US citizens and the servers were not located in the United States. The European Union was pressured into agreeing with the prosecution of Europeans and European betting sites, despite previous agreements to the contrary (Kearney, 2008). Ultimately, this had the effect that non-US citizens and their websites have to comply with US laws, or face the threat of extradition to answer to US authorities. If the United States is 'allowed' to enforce its own *national* laws on the *world-wide* Internet, why shouldn't China be 'allowed' to do so?

The White Paper published in June 2010 presents the views of the Chinese government on the Internet, and is very informative on its perspective on the set-up of the Internet in China and its wishes for the future development of the Internet worldwide. The White Paper is based around two main ideas about the Internet and their consequences for online China. The first asserts that 'within Chinese territory the Internet is under the jurisdiction of Chinese sovereignty. The Internet sovereignty of China should be respected and protected', while the second describes a trio of stakeholders in the Chinese Internet, consisting of the Chinese state, the economy, and the people, and emphasizes the need to balance their needs and requirements for the Internet in China (Information Office of the State Council of the People's Republic of China, 2010).

The *Internet sovereignty* that the Chinese government claims is a concise summary of the state ownership of and the many regulations for the Internet that limit online China and, as such, not very surprising. The term 'sovereignty', however, carries international connotations that demonstrate that the Internet set-up in China is not an accidental by-product of China's development, but the expression of a fundamentally different approach to the World Wide Web than has emerged in Europe and America, where competing private enterprises provide the physical infrastructure of the Internet. The Chinese government does not merely want to 'protect' its own citizens from the influences of the global Internet. It is advocating a new global structure for the Internet based on the sovereignty of nation-states, which should include their sovereignty over the Internet as it is accessed from within their borders.

> National situations and cultural traditions differ among countries, and so concern about Internet security also differs. Concerns about Internet security of different countries should be fully respected. [...] Though connected, the Internet of various countries belongs to different sovereignties.
>
> (Ibid.)

Instead of a *global* Internet, the Chinese government is arguing for a *zoning* of international networks, so as to create *national intranets* whose connections with each other are protected and regulated through international cooperation agreements between nation-states and supervised by the United Nations, instead of being under the control of the private, non-profit Internet Corporation for Assigned Names and Numbers (ICANN). The Internet, which has so far been allowed to grow based solely on technological inventions and the decisions of private investors, should be redesigned to mimic the development of nation-states from the vague definition of boundaries under the control of largely localized powers, in the political history of the world, with the United Nations functioning as an international arbiter between individual nations and their 'Internet'.

> China holds that the role of the UN should be given full scope in international Internet administration. China supports the establishment of an authoritative and just international Internet administration organization under the UN system through democratic procedures on a worldwide scale.
>
> (Ibid.)

This nation-state centred structure for the Internet is based on the Chinese government's 'concern about Internet security', which it defines broadly as 'an indispensable requirement for protecting state security and the public interest' because 'the Internet is an important infrastructure facility for the nation' (ibid.). The Internet is not merely a place for individuals to entertain themselves, or for companies to engage in business activities, but has instead grown to become an indispensable part of the well-being of the entire country. As a result, threats to the Internet in a country are becoming threats to the country as a whole, and are therefore to be evaluated as threats to the national security of a country, which means – in the opinion of the Chinese government – that the government of the country should take control of and administer 'their own' Internet.

As mentioned before, within each nation-state the Chinese government sees three stakeholders whose interests, needs, and concerns have to be balanced out to achieve a 'harmonious Internet environment, and build an Internet that is more reliable, useful and conducive to economic and social development' (ibid.). To reach this state of a 'harmonious' online China, the Internet in China has to meet the requirements of all three stakeholders, that is, help with 'development of the national economy', 'meet people's increasing demands for information', and allow for the creation of an 'e-government while enhancing the capability of governance' (ibid.).

The model of the Internet presented by the White Paper should not be under-stood as the desperate attempt by a 'Communist' regime to control the uncontrol-lable, but rather as an expression of the worldview of a government increasingly run along Confucian lines and ever more steeped in Chinese culture and tradi-tions. The social and cultural background to this model of the Internet is not the US constitution's phrase 'life, liberty and the pursuit of happiness', but rather a Chinese version of it, which, following Confucianism and its current interpreta-tion, could be paraphrased as 'life, harmony, and the pursuit of wealth' (see Chu and Cheng in this volume).

The economic impact of the Internet is described as vital to China's develop-ment, underlining the Chinese government's view that the Internet has become an important part of a nation's well-being and is therefore to be regarded as important to a nation's security. The Internet has an 'irreplaceable role in accelerating the development of the national economy' (ibid.), especially as the Chinese govern-ment hopes to overtake America and Europe's economies with its help. The White Paper describes the Internet as 'an engine promoting the economic development of China', which leads the Chinese government to actively promote the use of the Internet by Chinese people. The stated goal for the future of the Internet in China is the adoption of the Internet by 45% of the population of China by 2015, i.e. a growth of the population of online China to just under 800 million netizens, which means almost doubling the number of Internet users in China, as compared to July 2010 (Catacchio, 2010).

> The Internet in China has been developing along with the country's reform
> and opening-up. It conforms to the requirements and promotes the progress
> of China's reform and opening-up. As China's economy and society continue

to make swift progress, and people's demands for cultural products keep increasing, the Internet will reach more people, who in turn will make higher demands on it. The Chinese government is determined to further promote Internet development and application, and raise its accessibility to 45% of the population in the coming five years, so that more people can benefit from the Internet.

>                    (Information Office of the State Council of the People's Republic
>                                                                     of China, 2010)

The people in China have 'increasing demands for information', which have to be met by 'government at all levels', with the Internet playing an increasing role 'in satisfying people's right to know' (ibid.). Beyond the mere access to information, though, Chinese people are described as living out their lives online, which means the Internet now has to 'effectively satisfy the varied spiritual and cultural needs of the people', as a result of which 'cyber culture has become an important component of the Chinese culture industry' (ibid.).

> In China more and more people are collecting information, enriching their knowledge, establishing businesses and realizing their aspirations, and communicating to know each other better through the Internet. Soon after earthquakes hit Wenchuan in Sichuan Province and Yushu in Qinghai Province, and a severe drought plagued southwest China, netizens used the Internet to spread disaster relief information, initiate rescue efforts and express sympathy and concern, fully demonstrating the irreplaceable role of the Internet. The Internet has revolutionized our way of work and lifestyle.
>
>                                                                          (Ibid.)

The White Paper also focuses on the obtaining and sharing of information on the Internet, regarding it as one of the key benefits of the Internet for the people in China, as 'the Internet has become an important channel for people to obtain news' and to share this news with others while 'fully enjoy[ing] the freedom of speech on the Internet' (ibid.). More than the Internet in non-Chinese countries, the Chinese Internet is built around the exchange of information and opinions, and websites in online China reflect this communication focus in their emphasis on the inclusion of feedback mechanisms, and of general, and usually anonymous, internet forums, which the government supports, as 'the protection of online privacy is closely connected with the people's sense of security and confidence in the Internet' (ibid.).

> Vigorous online ideas exchange is a major characteristic of China's Internet development, and the huge quantity of BBS posts and blog articles is far beyond that of any other country. China's websites attach great importance to providing netizens with opinion expression services, with over 80% of them providing electronic bulletin service.
>
>                                                                          (Ibid.)

The right to privacy and the freedom of expression online are not absolutes, though, but also subject to the need for a balance between the economy, the people, and the state, 'in accordance with the law'. While such limits are 'obvious' for European and American democratic countries, any such statements by the Chinese government are usually treated with scorn and suspicion, and interpreted as 'doubletalking' (see above), which is probably due more to 'Western' disagreements with the content of laws in China than to objections against the limitation of 'absolute' freedom online. While the Chinese legal situation in general is highly unsatisfactory, as, for example, MacKinnon points out, quoting Hu Yong (MacKinnon, 2010), the issue at stake in the White Paper is not the legal system of the People's Republic of China, but rather the 'obvious' truth that the freedom of an individual 'ends' where the freedom of the next individual 'begins'.

> The citizens' freedom and privacy of correspondence is protected by law, which stipulates at the same time that while exercising such freedom and rights, citizens are not allowed to infringe upon state, social and collective interests or the legitimate freedom and rights of other citizens. No organization or individual may utilize telecommunication networks to engage in activities that jeopardize state security, the public interest or the legitimate rights and interests of other people.
> (Information Office of the State Council of the People's Republic of China, 2010)

The Chinese state will employ its power and its ownership of the infrastructure of the Internet 'to create a healthy and harmonious Internet environment [...] conducive to economic and social development' (ibid.). The power of the state over the Internet in China is considerable, and as mentioned in the Introduction to this volume, any freedom or power that Chinese netizens have is granted to them by the state and its officials. Despite this imbalance of power, the Chinese state declares in the White Paper that state organs and officials have to hold themselves accountable to Chinese netizens to an extent that is astonishing compared to *offline* China.

According to the White Paper, the Chinese state commits itself to require 'governments at all levels to [...] give prompt explanations to issues of public concern', so that 'the Internet's role in supervision is given full play' (ibid.). As the chapter by David Kurt Herold in this volume shows, this statement is not just pretence, but a reflection of what is happening in China – not always to the extent that netizens might wish, but still with noticeable effects. The central government appears to be serious in its stated intention to allow Chinese netizens (but not 'normal', offline citizens) to supervise and to criticize government officials and institutions, which, ironically, is far more than any 'democratic' government in Europe or America will allow its Internet-using citizens.

> The Chinese government has actively created conditions for the people to supervise the government, and attaches great importance to the Internet's role in supervision. Governments at all levels are required to investigate and

resolve in a timely manner all problems reported to the government by the
public via the Internet, and to inform the public of the results.

(Ibid.)

This supervision of the government by the people, or the communication
between government and the people, is not perfect, nor is it the solution to all
of China's problems, or even a solution to the casual and frequent abuse of
laws and regulations by government officials against individuals or groups in
China. MacKinnon (2010) is certainly right in her assertion that 'the regime
actually uses the Internet not only to extend its control but also to enhance its
legitimacy', instead of attempting to directly solve some of the problems caused
by its chaotic administrative and legal system. The question remains, however,
whether the Chinese approach is inherently bad or not – the answer to which
depends on one's beliefs about the relative merits of the political philosophies,
ideologies, cultures, and traditions underlying the US-style republican system,
the social-welfare state democratic systems in Europe, or the attempts by the
Chinese state to define a new form of democracy 'with Chinese characteristics'.
The assertions of the White Paper should not be taken at face value, but neither
should they be ignored as mere attempts to sugar-coat the oppressive power of
the Chinese state over its people. Chinese government authorities have increasingly listened to Chinese netizens over the past few years, and they have opened
channels of direct, *online* communication, ranging from occasional online chats
between officials and netizens to the creation of websites that allow netizens to
register complaints. Many of the complaints have caused the authorities to act
to address problems, or to dismiss and arrest corrupt officials, or to reprimand
individual officials who were taking advantage of their power – but not all of the
complaints are followed up, and some officials appear to be too important to be
punished, in which case, it is the netizens and their postings who get 'dismissed',
silenced, and, to use a popular phrase on the Chinese Internet, 'harmonized'.
That China's (central) government admits to the necessity of opening up direct
channels of communication *online* to its own citizens is evidence already that
the Chinese state in its current form is *not* working, and that the systems of
control and oversight over different levels of government are not able to guarantee the proper functioning of the Chinese system of governance. The seat of
China's central government at Zhongnanhai in Beijing might not be heaven, nor
Hu Jintao the emperor, but they are still far away from ordinary citizens, and
seem to feel the need for feedback outside the state hierarchy's established lines
of communication.

The authorities attach great importance to [...] public opinion as reflected
on the Internet, which has become a bridge facilitating direct communication between the government and the public. [...] The opinions expressed
by the public online are receiving unprecedented attention. The leaders of
China frequently log onto the Internet to get to know the public's wishes,
and sometimes have direct online communication with netizens to discuss
state affairs and answer their questions. It has become a common practice

for governments at all levels to consult the public via the Internet before formulating policies of particular importance. The public's opinions have been sought through the Internet during the annual sessions of the NPC and CPPCC. For each of the past three years, as many as several million items of advice and suggestions have been received through the Internet, providing valuable reference for the government to improve its work.

(Information Office of the State Council of the People's Republic of China, 2010)

The White Paper concludes with the proviso that the Internet is still expanding and changing rapidly, 'with new situations and problems emerging constantly', and while it offers fascinating insights into the perspective of the Chinese government on the Internet in China, there is a lot more to discover, as the chapters in this volume show and hint at.

The Bakhtinian carnival that is China's cyberspace seems to be a solution to some of the problems *offline* China and its government have, while also answering some of the desires of *offline* Chinese citizens, who are invited and encouraged to become *online* Chinese netizens. Ultimately, though, it is even more than that. It is also a challenge to the non-Chinese world, as the Chinese government attempts to avoid following the models provided by European and American countries and their systems of government, in pursuit of its own path to national development. In marked difference to other countries, the path chosen by the Chinese government includes the online carnival of Chinese cyberspace as a vital component for the development of China, and as an officially accepted source of corrective impulses for offline China – which might support its claims to legitimacy, but might also undermine its stability and power.

The provocative, mirthful inversion of prevailing institutions and their hierarchy as staged in the carnival offers a permanent alternative to official culture – even if it ultimately leaves everything as it was before. It is this irrepressible, unsilenceable energy issuing from the carnival's alternative appeal – and not so much the particular manifestations of folk cultural practice – that disrupts official, institutionalized culture.

(Lachmann, Eshelman, & Davis, 1988: 125)

## References

Catacchio, C. (2010, July 15). China now has 420 million Internet users, 277 million access by mobile phones. *The Next Web*. Retrieved August 5, 2010, from http://thenextweb.com/asia/2010/07/15/china-now-has-420-million-internet-users-277-million-access-by-mobile-phones/

Enos, L. (2000, May 23). Yahoo! forced to bar French from Nazi auctions. *Ecommerce Times*. Retrieved August 4, 2010, from http://www.ecommercetimes.com/story/3387.html?wlc=1280907310

Information Office of the State Council of the People's Republic of China. (2010, June 8). The Internet in China. *China.org.cn*. Retrieved August 4, 2010, from http://www.china.org.cn/government/whitepaper/node_7093508.htm

Kearney, C. (2008, January 7). U.S. arrests 8 in online sports betting operation. *Reuters*. Retrieved August 4, 2010, from http://www.reuters.com/article/idUSN0742137820080107

Lachmann, R., Eshelman, R., & Davis, M. (1988). Bakhtin and carnival: Culture as counter-culture. *Cultural Critique* (11), 115–152.

Lawson, S. (2001, November 9). Judge dismisses French case against Yahoo. *PC World*. Retrieved August 4, 2010, from http://www.pcworld.com/article/70323/judge_dismisses_french_case_against_yahoo.html

MacKinnon, R. (2010, June 15). China's Internet White Paper: networked authoritarianism in action. *RConversation*. Retrieved August 4, 2010, from http://rconversation.blogs.com/rconversation/2010/06/chinas-internet-white-paper-networked-authoritarianism.html

McCarthy, M. (2006, July 19). U.S. cracking down on offshore betting industry. *USA Today*. Retrieved August 4, 2010, from http://www.usatoday.com/sports/2006–07–18-online-gaming_x.htm

Pinsent Masons. (2004, August 25). Yahoo! loses US appeal over French ruling on Nazi auctions. *Out-Law.com*. Retrieved August 4, 2010, from http://www.out-law.com/page-4833

Price, M. E. (2010, August 3). The battle over Internet regulatory paradigms: An intensifying area for public diplomacy. *Newswire*. Retrieved August 4, 2010, from http://uscpublicdiplomacy.org/index.php/newswire/cpdblog_detail/the_battle_over_internet_regulatory_paradigms_an_intensifying_area_for/

Slaten, K. (2010, June 10). China's doubletalking Internet White Paper. *china/divide*. Retrieved August 4, 2010, from http://chinadivide.com/2010/chinese-state-council-internet-white-paper-doubletalk.html

# Index

'Great Firewall of China' (GFW)  2–3,
   54, 84
Green Dam Youth Escort Online Filtering
   Software affair  23, 30–7, 81
Greenberg, J.  163
*Guangming Daily*  75
*guishugan* (belonging)  100

Habermas, Jürgen  10–11, 60
hackers  154
Han Han  82
Han, Q.  35
Hanser, Amy  93
Hao Mingjin  136–7
harmonious society  36, 78, 98, 103, 127
Hars, A.,  152
Hays, J.  2
He Bing  165
He Xie  78–9
Hecaitou  74
hegemony: and resistance  71–3
Henderson, S. J.  154
hierarchy: FOSS  156–7
Hiner, J.  149
Hoa, Léon  194
homophones  78–80, 81–2, 84
homosexual marriage: MMOGs  110
Hsu, Francis  28
Hu Ge  73–5, 76–7, 83, 171
Hu Jintao  56, 128
Hu Qiheng  177
Hu-Wen administration  186
Hu Yong  205
Hua Xinmin  187, 194
Huang Chengching  174
Hudong.com  82
Hudson, W.  10
'Human Flesh Search Engines' (*Renrou
   Sousuo*, RRSS) *see* RRSS
'human quality'  26
human rights issues  54
*hutong* rallies  194–5

Iannini, Michael  157, 161
ICTs: development of  24–6
ID cards  173–4
ID law  176
identity: anonymity and  166–9; and the
   Chinese government  173–7
identity politics  103
'immanent transcendence'  27
in-game marriage: aftermath  116–20;
   cultural uniqueness  109; *dajia*
   objections  111; feminine types of avatar
   115–16; gender bias  109–11; legal

disputes  118–19; and mass media  118;
   *renyao*  111–12, 113–15; same sex  110;
   study methodology  107–8
independence movements  54
industrialization  25
information sharing  204–5
interaction and organization discourses  6
interconnecting networks  42
interest groups  185–6
Internet: as carnival  10–13, 83, 128,
   200, 207; development  1, 24–6, 40,
   89; future  200–1; and NGOs  186–7;
   portrayal of by mass media  56; as space
   10–11; structure  1; as tool of resistance
   5–6
'Internet addiction'  8
Internet cafés  3, 45–6, 50, 89, 91–2, 93–4,
   95, 103
Internet forums: responses to Green Dam
   software and The Declaration  33–5
Internet freedom: Freedom House
   assessment  85; and US government
   201
'Internet Games'  95–6
Internet police  110  46
Internet police force: cartoon mascots  49,
   55; formation  40–2; legal basis  42;
   mechanisms used  47–9; scope of work
   42–7
Internet-related crimes  46–7, 50
Internet Service Providers  2
Internet Society of China (ISC)  174
Internet sovereignty  202
Internet users: demographic of  4; number
   of  24, 30, 40; survey  56–7
interpersonal relationships  29
IP policy  177
IP Traceback  177
Iron Lady  113
ISC (Internet Society of China)  174
Ito, M.  102

Jackson, L. A.  4
Jams  190–2
Jenkins, H.  102
Jiang Zemin  79
'Jingjing'  49, 55
*Journey to the West*  73

Kaixinwang  170
KDS  169
KDS Life forum  99–100
Keane, Michael  61–2
keyword blocking  2, 3, 54
Killer Game clubs  92, 94, 95, 96–7

# eupdates

Taylor & Francis Group

Want to stay one step ahead of your colleagues?

Sign up today to receive free up-to-date information on books, journals, conferences and other news within your chosen subject areas.

Visit
**www.tandf.co.uk/eupdates**
and register your email address, indicating your subject areas of interest.

You will be able to amend your details or unsubscribe at any time. We respect your privacy and will not disclose, sell or rent your email address to any outside company. If you have questions or concerns with any aspect of the eUpdates service, please email eupdates@tandf.co.uk or write to: eUpdates, Routledge, 2/4 Park Square, Milton Park, Abingdon, Oxfordshire OX14 4RN, UK.

For Product Safety Concerns and Information please contact our EU
representative GPSR@taylorandfrancis.com
Taylor & Francis Verlag GmbH, Kaufingerstraße 24, 80331 München, Germany

www.ingramcontent.com/pod-product-compliance
Lightning Source LLC
Chambersburg PA
CBHW071420050326
40689CB00010B/1919